COMMUNITY CARE AND THE FUTURE OF MENTAL HEALTH SERVICE PROVISION

Second Edition

Community Care and the Future of Mental Health Service Provision

Second Edition

SIMON GOODWIN

Department of Applied Community Studies
The Manchester Metropolitan University

Avebury

Aldershot · Brookfield USA · Hong Kong · Singapore · Sydney

Published by
Avebury
Ashgate Publishing Limited
Gower House
Croft Road
Aldershot
Hants GU11 3HR
England

Ashgate Publishing Limited
Old Post Road
Brookfield
Vermont 05036
USA

British Library Cataloguing in Publication Data
Goodwin, Simon
Community Care and the Future of Mental
Health Service Provision. - 2 Rev. ed. -
(Avebury Studies of Care in the Community)
I. Title II. Series
362.20941

ISBN 1 85628 479 4

Printed and Bound in Great Britain by
Athenaeum Press Ltd, Newcastle upon Tyne.

Contents

List of tables

Acknowledgements

While writing this book I have had the good fortune of meeting a number of people who, while not necessarily agreeing with all of my views, have helped sustain for me the knowledge that its subject matter is of critical importance for many people. Their support and advice have proven invaluable. In this regard I would like to thank all those I have met at the Ashwood Day Centre in Leeds and Lawton Tonge House in Sheffield. In particular I would like to thank Paula Melville, Rick Hennelly, Teresa Hagan, Lorraine Knights and Alan Walker. Special thanks go to Gail Norman.

Introduction

The crises of the bourgeois order are continuous... (they) are due to its intrinsic contradictions... These crises frequently heighten in all their dimensions...not only in their economic but also in their political and civil dimensions...When this occurs, the social tapestry that is sustained and made cohesive by the bourgeois hegemonic ideology starts unravelling and all components are touched upon...It is in these periods of crises when the relationship between the parts and the whole appears most clearly.

(A.Gramsci, L'ordine nuovo, Vol. IX, 1919-1920, 1954. Trans. V.Navarro 1978,p.179.)

The lot of a Secretary of State and his junior ministers cannot be an easy one.

(Royal Commission on the National Health Service, 1979, para. 19.12.)

Between the mid-19th century and mid-20th century the number and size of mental hospitals in England and Wales increased considerably, and it was generally recognised that they were appropriate and beneficial places for mentally distressed people to receive care and treatment. In the second half of the 20th century however this emphasis upon an institutional service has

1

been reversed. The mental hospital in-patient population peaked in 1954 and has since declined, the numbers held at any one time being reduced by two-thirds within 40 years. Today, the decline in the size of the in-patient population continues, and the government has made clear its intention of closing the majority of mental hospitals.

This reduction in the scale of institutional provision has generally been perceived as part of a process of reform rather than neglect, for in the post-war period institutional provision for mentally distressed people has been subject to much criticism. It has been argued that mental hospitals are less beneficial than once thought as places of therapeutic intervention, and that people experiencing mental distress benefit from being supported in their normal environments. What has emerged, since the late 1950s, is a policy of community care. This emphasises the importance of building up local support structures that will enable people to carry on their normal lives without recourse to long-stay mental hospital admission: 'The social aim of the community-care movement is one that advocates that the environments of handicapped people should, as far as possible, reflect normal community life, and that forms of institutional care that segregate them from society are unacceptable.' (Bennett and Morris, 1983,p.13).

Over the last thirty years the state has accepted, indeed advocated, that the community care policy provides the most appropriate means for dealing with mentally distressed people. Thus, commeasurate with the process of de-institutionalisation, efforts have been made to increase the availability of care and treatment within the community. This has involved a multitude of initiatives, including the development of psychiatric units in district general hospitals, increased emphasis upon providing psychiatric services in primary care settings, the creation of community psychiatric nurses, the provision of domiciliary services and the development of residential and day care facilities, and an increased emphasis on the role of voluntary groups, friends, relatives and neighbours in the provision of care for mentally distressed members of their community.

The community care policy remains central to the state's strategy for dealing with mentally distressed people. It is generally accepted that this will be so for the forseeable future, and no alternative method of organising services is currently anywhere near the centre of the political agenda. The policy retains general support, in principle at least, from both academics and practitioners of varied political persuasions (House of Commons, 1985a; Ramon, 1988).

This, however, does not preclude the fact that the policy has been

2

subject to a range of serious criticisms. While the scale of institutional care has declined substantially, it is argued that insufficient community based facilities have been developed (Walker, 1982). This is compounded by the fact that the policy simply assumes that some form of social network exists 'out there', in the community, that will provide the social support required by mentally distressed people. The results of this, for many discharged mental patients, have been little short of disastrous (Jones, 1983a; Davis, 1988).

Moreover, the community care policy has been characterised by a lack of clear definition (Abrams, 1977,p.125). While it clearly envisages that mentally distressed people should receive care and treatment within community settings, the notion of 'community' remains confused. This reflects in the lack of clear objectives in the development of mental health policies. It is suggested for example that residential care in the community can be as isolating and institutionalising as the old mental hospitals. Equally, mental hospitals can provide in-patients with a community in which to live - witnessed for example by the 'therapeutic community' movement. This lack of conceptual clarity appears intrinsic to the notion of community care; '...the exact meaning of community care is, to say the least, confused' (Walker, 1986,p.5).

The starting point for this study, then, is as follows. Given the abject failure of the community care policy to provide anything like adequate services for mentally distressed people the question that arises is why, after 30 years of the policy, should it continue to retain our allegiance? In short, two questions are of immediate and central importance; is the community care policy desirable - does it really plan for the best way in which to resolve the problems of mentally distressed people? And secondly, is the policy feasible - within current socio-economic conditions is it likely that the policy will ever be fully implemented?

Now it is as this point that a serious impasse is reached, for insufficient analysis has been conducted that allows us to consider these questions adequately. In place of critical discussion about the nature of the policy; of the range of interests and needs served or hindered, or of the reasons why it found favour at a particular time in a particular place, there tends to be almost platitudinous assumptions made about the 'goodness' of community care. Given that the policy represents a reform the problem tends to be conceived only in administrative terms of how to most successfully implement it. A vast literature has arisen, prescribing various solutions for the problems faced; in one form or another we are told that '...if community care is to be successful, it needs to be carefully

3

planned, and adequate resources have to be devoted to it.' (Johnson, 1987, p.68). Given the serious and continued failings of the policy, this alone is not adequate. It is time to be more critical. What is required is an analysis of the purposes of the community care policy, that does not simply assume that it is intended to meet the needs of mentally distressed people.

The concern of this book is precisely with the need to develop a more adequate analytical understanding of the community care policy. For without such an understanding of the nature of the community care policy, of how and why it arose, it is difficult to meaningfully develop a set of views on its value, or on how likely it is that it will ever be implemented. To develop this analysis we first review existing explanatory models of the origins and development of community care for mentally distressed people. The strengths and weaknesses of these are identified, and used as a basis on which to develop a new model. This is then used to provide an account of how and why the community care policy evolved. Two key periods, 1948 to 1963 and 1975 to the present day, are identified in which it is argued that the major policy developments occurred. In developing this analysis an account is presented which helps more adequately explain the nature and development of the policy than currently exists.

The conclusion reached is already known by many, that the community care policy lacks coherence as a strategy for treating and caring for mentally distressed people. What is explained, however, is the nature of that incoherence; how it was implicit in the origins and formation of the policy, and why the policy remains central to state mental health services despite the problems that have arisen.

1 Existing explanatory models: The Social Democratic and the Marxist accounts

The last 25 years has witnessed rising academic interest in studying the nature and development of welfare provision in advanced capitalist societies. Using a variety of disciplines, and from a variety of perspectives, a large number of accounts have been generated about the purposes welfare serves, and the problems that such provision can cause (see Taylor-Gooby,1985). This increased activity has resulted in greater attention being paid to mental health services (see Sedgwick, 1982a). Regarding our particular concerns however, of explaining how and why community care for mentally distressed people developed in England and Wales, there is still little work. Essentially there are just two explanatory models, Social Democratic and Marxist, that specifically attempt to deal with these questions. In this Chapter we will review the adequacy of each of these.

The social democratic model

This model provides the conventional, and dominant, understanding of the development of the community care policy. Room (1979) argues that it can provide a macro-sociological account of social policy comparable to the Marxist model and, drawing principally upon the work of Marshall and Titmuss, attempts to develop this. First, Room draws upon Marshall's distinction between civil and social rights. Civil rights concern individual rights to '...dispose freely of ones's property and labour power in the market place.' (Room, 1979, p.58). Social rights, in contrast, concern '...publicly

5

defined and guaranteed claims to certain life chance outcomes: notably those distributed through the contemporary social services.' (Room, 1979, p.58). Thus, while civil rights refer to individual claims to be free of constraints over conduct in the market place, social rights in contrast refer to outcomes where people - by virtue of being part of a group - might expect to receive certain benefits.

Further to this, Room argues that '...it is a central theme of the Social Democratic approach to social policy that its formulation involves real value choices...' (Room, 1979, p.60). That is to say, the future is contingent, and depends in part upon what policy decisions are made. Historical determinism is decisively rejected. Also, he argues that social policy has the capacity to generate common moral commitment to the social order of Western societies. This, Room argues, provides a critique of the Marxist conception of necessary and fundamental class antagonisms within capitalist societies by providing a common interest, and therefore a basis for social integration. It is, he claims, '...the principal thesis of the Social Democrats that the collective experience of universal social rights will evoke the moral commitment and disregard of pure interest that realization of the collectively chosen future requires and entails.' (Room, 1979, p.252).

A further important theme to draw out, although not elaborated by Room, is the reliance the Social Democratic model places upon a pluralist conception of the political process. The principal feature of this model is that it concentrates attention upon the democratic form of government, its procedures and rules, rather than the functions of the state and interests held within it. Attention is focussed upon the will, and decisions of leaders, as well as the various pressure groups and interest groups that seek to have influence within the political process. It is held that power within society is widely diffused (Lukes, 1979). As a result no one group dominates the political process, but rather decisions are made that reflect the balance of forces as they exist at a particular moment in time. Power within society is then defined in terms of which group most successfully influences the decision making process. Within this process the government is viewed as a neutral arbiter of conflicts, without bias towards any particular interest or power bloc.

These themes are central to the Social Democratic analysis of community care. The emphasis tends to be upon the importance of social action rather than social structure, and the contingency rather than determinacy of historical development. Emphasis is placed upon the plurality of reasons for the development of community

6

care; 'Deinstitutionalization is a fact in Great Britain...The fact, however, is less the expression of a single process and a coherent philosophy than the outcome of a number of trends that have different objectives, emphases, and intellectual foundations.' (Bennett and Morris, 1983, p.5). Brill for example argues that the origins of community care lie in the increased sensitivity to social issues and increased intervention in social affairs by government that arose during the Second World War (Brill, 1980). Bennett maintains that the egalitarian philosophy associated with the emergent welfare state, together with changes in psychiatry towards recognising the importance of social factors in the creation of mental distress, were the major impetuses behind the community care policy (Bennett, 1978). However the most authoritative Social Democratic account of the development of mental health services has been provided by Jones, whose work we might most usefully examine more thoroughly.

On reviewing her own arguments, Jones concludes that it is almost impossible to produce general theorems about the development of mental health services:

> If history has a shape and purpose, they are so unimaginable in scope that the small fragment recorded here is no more than a dot in the corner of a vast Persian carpet; as to the future, if there is any lesson to be learned from the past, it must be a sense of the surprisingness of change...the multiplication of quite unpredictable variables. (Jones, 1972, p.xiii).

Yet, despite such a view, she argues that the origins of community care can be identified within 'three revolutions' that occurred in the 1950s; the pharmacological revolution, the administrative revolution, and the legislative revolution. While Jones makes no claim regarding exactly what the influence of each was, she nevertheless argues that between them they caused the development of a more community based system of treatment and care for mentally distressed people (Jones, 1972, p.291).

The pharmacological revolution

In the early 1950s a range of psychotropic drugs were developed, that were utilised by psychiatrists in mental hospitals from the mid-1950s. Jones leaves little doubt as to the importance of this development in prompting the change from institutional to community forms of care. The newly available drugs, she claims,

7

enabled psychiatrists to control the more florid behaviour patterns, thus inducing sufficient calm within patients to allow for therapeutic intervention:

> ...it meant that patients could go home sooner: once a condition was stabilized, there might be no need for further hospitalization provided that the patient had home support, and the doctor could be sure he would take his pills. It also meant that some patients did not need to come into hospital at all, because their symptoms could be controlled and the illness treated while they remained at home. Imperceptibly the emphasis began to shift from talk of 'after-care' to talk of 'alternative care. (Jones, 1972, p.292).

While Jones does acknowledge that the therapeutic value of the new 'wonder drugs' was initially overstated, and that they only help ameliorate rather than actually cure mental distress, the claim nevertheless is that the use of these newly discovered drugs was a causal factor in the development of community care (Jones, 1979, p.561).

The administrative revolution

During the 1950s a series of administrative changes were made in the way services for mentally ill people were provided. The 'open door policy' was widely introduced in mental hospitals, with many locked wards opened and emphasis put on reducing the length of stay of in-patients. The number of people seen at out-patient clinics rapidly increased and varied new systems were experimented with such as the therapeutic community, day hospitals, social clubs, and psychiatric units in general hospitals. Within these changes Jones contends that the move from an institutional to a community based service can be detected; '...common themes can be discerned: the move from traditional patterns to new and flexible ones; from stereotypes to fresh and illuminating discoveries; from clinical models to social ones.' (Jones,1972, p.303).

The legislative revolution

The final leg of Jones' account concerns the response of the state to the changes in mental health provision that were going on around it. She refers to the Royal Commission on Mental Illness and Mental Deficiency which sat from 1954 to 1957, which '...summarized the main problems and the main trends of public opinion, and provided a blue-print for a comprehensive mental health service.' (Jones, 1972, p.304). The report was largely accepted by the Government and provided the central planks of the Mental Health Act, 1959. The main themes of this were that treatment should be provided on a voluntary and informal basis where possible, a new system of safeguards for the patient where compulsion continued to be used was introduced, and a change in emphasis towards community based services was encouraged. In comparison to the analysis of the origins of the community care policy, the explanation given within the Social Democratic model for what has gone on since is less well developed. As early as 1961, in a speech delivered at the Annual Conference of the National Association for Mental Health, Titmuss noted the lack of money being spent on community provision for mentally ill people. In the financial year 1959/60 just £3.5 million was spent on such facilities which, as he scathingly pointed out, compared unfavourably with the £4.9 million spent on compensation and expenses in dealing with fowl pest in the same year (Titmuss, 1963, pp.223-224).

Since then a large literature bemoaning the failure of political will to provide sufficient resources to develop care in the community facilities has appeared. Noting the lack of services in the early 1970s, Ennals questioned whether community care was a 'myth or reality' (Ennals, 1973, p.67). Reviewing developments in community care services for dependent people, Parker argues that '...while the levels of community-based services did increase...(they) were rarely large enough to meet all the identified needs for those services.' (Parker, 1985, p.5). Jones also now argues that the community care policy has failed to provide adequate services for mentally distressed people:

> We have stopped providing asylum...'Treatment' has been reduced to the provision of medication...We have almost ceased to care... (Jones, 1981, p.20).

In order to consider the value of the Social Democratic model we will consider three areas; its analytical framework, the application of the model to some particular issues, and finally the concept of mental distress employed.

Some of the assumptions within the analytical model are called into question by the way in which mental health services have developed in the post-war period. The divergence between the rhetoric and the reality of the policy, where governments have consistently failed to match policy statements with sufficient funding to create community based facilities, suggests that in fact rather than see increasing importance being attached to the social rights of mentally distressed people, they have in fact been largely ignored. Similarly, the lack of development of community care facilities tends to undermine the pluralist conception of the government that is utilised. The analysis offered seems unable to explain why, when political pressure exists for a policy to be implemented, within a democratic system in which it is assumed that power is widely dispersed, it fails to occur. The assumption that government is a neutral arbiter of conflicts would at least suggest that greater response to the demands made for better services would have been forthcoming.   Yet, as Offe notes, academics using such a perspective have been disappointed; '...they habitually overestimate their capacity to induce at least some unease among those political and administrative actors to whom proof of the discrepancies between 'ought' and 'is' is presented...' (Offe, 1984, p.91).

In recent years, Social Democratic writers have been left with little to say on these issues. Reflecting this state of affairs, Jones provides no explanation of why, when all agree that community care services are insufficiently developed, government has repeatedly failed to provide more adequate funding. Without a explanatory framework in   which to analyse this pattern of development we are simply left with a moral plea for greater efforts to be made on behalf of mentally distressed people: 'Ultimately it depends on your priorities. It depends on whether you really want a microchip society with nuclear warheads, or whether you think civilization depends on preserving compassion and human caring.' (Jones, 1981, p.23).

In addition to these problems with the analytical framework a further set of problems can be identified in the way the Social Democratic model is applied. Jones' presentation of the 'three revolutions' to explain the origins of community care in the 1950s provides an important example of this. In particular, there has been increasing criticism of the importance attached to the 'pharmacological revolution'.

The association posited between the use of a new range of drugs in the 1950s and a reduction in the mental hospital population has proven difficult to maintain. Sedgwick notes that 'In certain progressive hospitals in Britain, active attention to rehabilitation and resettlement and the unlocking of closed wards had led to a swift and drastic reduction in the number of inpatients...considerably in advance of the introduction of the phenothiazine drugs.' (Sedgwick, 1982a, p.198). And such time discrepancies are even greater in other European countries. In France, where the first psychotropic drugs were developed in December 1950, the residential population peaked some twenty years later in 1970. In Italy the number of mental hospital beds actually increased between 1961 and 1971, and in Spain the numbers held in mental hospitals as a percentage of the population more than doubled between 1960 and 1975.

With psychotropic drugs being widely available for some thirty years, Sedgwick concludes that their use in the treatment of mentally distressed people gives rise to no particular trends in service provision (Sedgwick, 1982, pp.199-200). Furthermore, he argues that to assume the palliative effects of the new drugs would have a particular effect upon mental health policy is unwarranted. Emphasis upon the physical effects of drugs obscures the social context in which they are used, and when taking this context into account he suggests no simple relationship can be established:

> In Britain today, for example, it is noticeable that the function of a particular medication, such as largactil or modecate, varies from that of an out-patient prescription with a specific anti-psychotic action to that of a general purpose bromide, doled out in massive frequency to long-term prison inmates or chronic mental patients as a convenient chemical straightjacket or liquid cosh (Sedgwick, 1982, p.200).

Further evidence of the limited effects the introduction of psychotropic drugs had on the organisation of mental health services can be gained by examining their impact upon the perceptions of psychiatrists in the 1950s. As Table 1.1 demonstrates, between 1948 and 1957 the rate of recovery of mentally distressed patients as reported by psychiatrists almost halved, the rate of relieving symptoms increased by almost half, while the numbers not improved was little changed. These statistics do not suggest any great optimism about the efficacy of psychotropic drug treatments. Moreover the years after their introduction in 1954 demonstrate similar trends to those before, suggesting that no sea-change in the perceptions of psychiatrists occurred in terms of being able to so effectively curtail florid behaviour that in-patient treatment and care for many patients was no longer required.

11

Table 1.1
Trends in reasons for discharge and departures from mental hospitals and other institutions (%)

Year	Relieved	Recovered	Not Improved
1948	46.5	41.3	12.3
1949	50.0	37.0	12.7
1950	53.3	33.2	13.5
1951	54.4	32.1	13.6
1952	55.3	31.5	13.1
1953	57.5	29.9	12.6
1954	57.7	30.3	11.9
1955	60.2	28.4	11.4
1956	62.7	26.6	10.7
1957	65.5	23.8	10.7

Source: percentages derived from figures given in the Annual Reports of the Ministry of Health.

These statistics, indicating the therapeutic caution of psychiatrists in the 1950s, are reflected in the initial assessments made of the newly available drug treatments. Following the introduction of chlorpromazine (marketed as 'largactil') in 1954, clinical tests tended to conclude that it provided a useful addition to the existing battery of physical treatments (such as electro-convulsive therapy and psycho-surgery), with particular value for controlling psychotic excitement (e.g. Anton-Stephens,1954; Charatan,1954). In a review of psychotropic drug tests, Hoch concluded in 1958 that 'As far as we know the drugs do not influence a disease or disorder; they eliminate or alleviate symptoms only...' (Hoch, 1958). Hordern and Hamilton come to a similar conclusion. They argue that psychotropic drug treatments demonstrate no particular efficacy over and above the already existing methods of treatment, and indeed suggest that the results obtained were no better than had been achieved through the introduction of 'moral treatment' more than a century earlier (Hordern and Hamilton,1963).

The Annual Reports of the Chief Medical Officer also tend to acknowledge the limited efficacy of psychotropic drugs, and their value as additions to existing physical treatments rather than revolutionising psychiatric therapies. It is noted that '...the curative effects originally claimed have not been substantiated.'

(Chief Medical Officer, 1954, p.109), and more specifically, reflecting the perception of psychotropic drugs as being simply an additional weapon to the existing arsenal of physical treatments, chlorpromazine is noted to have an effect comparable to a frontal lobotomy (Chief Medical Officer, 1954, p.108). In 1954 the Chief Medical Officer considers it too early to yet assess how these drugs will be used, or to what effect. Moreover in 1957 he acknowledges that the nature of mental distress is as yet little understood, and notes an urgent need for more research. In this context the new newly available drug treatments are seen as one further step in psychiatric treatment, rather than representing any decisive advance in the management of mentally distressed people.

The role ascribed to psychotropic drugs within the Social Democratic model, as a major factor in the development of community care is exaggerated. The statistical evidence available in the 1950s gives no indication that the introduction of psychotropic drugs provoked any great change in the pattern of care and treatment being given by psychiatrists; rather they seem to have helped maintain a pattern already established. Moreover, with such drugs only having just been introduced, their value and the implications of their use were only just beginning to be assessed. Thus, as Scull concludes;

> ...the introduction of psychotropic drugs may have facilitated the policy of early discharge by reducing the incidence of florid symptoms among at least some of the disturbed...But that their arrival can be held primarily responsible for the change (in policy) is clearly highly implausible. (Scull, 1984, p.89).

Yet despite the development of this critique, writers within the Social Democratic tradition still tend to accept the importance of the new drugs. In a recent analysis of the development of mental health services Martin argues that '...it is highly improbable that the discharge of established long-stay patients could have been maintained or the length of stay of newly-admitted patients could have ben brought down and kept down, had it not been for the efflorescence of psychotropic drugs...' (Martin, 1984, p.2). Equally, Jones in her more recent publications still holds to her original arguments;

> Probably the most important single factor was the development of the psychotropic drugs which made possible the control of

mood-swings and hence the suppression of symptoms...It has made possible a massive reduction in mental hospital beds by enabling many patients to be treated by their general practitioner, or in out-patient clinics, and others to stay for much shorter periods. It enabled mental hospitals to open the doors of most wards, and to give patients a much greater freedom of movement. (Jones, 1983, p.226).

Such a statement as this seems to pay insufficient regard to the recently developed critique of the importance of the development of new drugs treatments in the 1950s.

In addition to this argument over the importance of the pharmacological revolution, we can also question the pertinence of the administrative and legislative revolutions within Jones' account of the development of community care. As we saw earlier, the administrative revolution is presented as an explanation for a range of changes made in how mentally distressed people are provided for. Her claim is that it provides one of the three parts of an explanation for why the changes in service provision occurred, even if '...it (is) impossible to trace cause and effect with any confidence.' (Jones, 1972, p.291). But even with this qualification it is difficult to follow the logic of the argument, for the administrative change described is the very phenomenon requiring explanation. That is to say, there is no differentiation made between explanation and description in the presentation of material.

Similarly, concerning the legislative revolution, it must be asked how this strand of analysis helps explain the origin or evolution of the community care policy. Questions such as why the state should interest itself in providing for the mentally distressed? why the issue should enter the political agenda quite so forcefully in the 1950s? and why community care should prove to be the favoured system after a century and more of support for an institutional system? are not addressed by this style of analysis. As such, while providing vivid detail of changes within mental health service provision, the Social Democratic model leaves us none the wiser as to why the change in policy happened in a particular way at a particular time.

The final area we need to examine in the Social Democratic model is the conception of mental distress employed. In her earlier work Jones does not provide an explicit definition of mental distress. She does however imply it is a condition of pain and suffering that is subject to variable definition; that '...the way in

14

which the mentally ill...are defined and cared for is primarily a social response to a very basic set of problems.' (Jones, 1972). But since writing this the issue of what constitutes mental distress has become more widely discussed and its importance in informing understanding of methods of treating mentally distressed people has become more generally appreciated (Clare, 1980; Sedgwick, 1982a; Kennedy, 1983). Recognising the importance of this debate, Jones has since attempted to offer a more sophisticated conception of mental distress. It is, she argues, '...the condition of people who are suffering from lasting and disabling stress for no ascertainable or sufficient cause, or whose behaviour is so bizarre or so unacceptable that it is causing considerable stress to those around them.' (Jones, 1983a, pp.218-219). Moreover such a definition, she claims, '...is not intended to imply either acceptance or rejection of the medical model, or any particular ideological stance. It is used simply because it is more precise than 'deviance', which includes many people whose behaviour may be anti-social, but is explicable in other terms, and it is less pejorative than 'madness'.' (Jones, 1983a, p.219).

Although Jones argues that this definition of mental distress is objective, or value free, it is difficult to maintain such a claim. The two reasons given for designating somebody mentally ill; lasting and disabling stress without ascertainable or reasonable cause, and bizarre or otherwise unacceptable behaviour, are both dependant for their meaning upon a social and value based context. Taking the first of these, it must be asked how it is possible to assess what constitutes ascertainable or sufficient cause without making reference to an ideological stance of some sort? For the notion being tested here is capacity for rational action, and the base line for such a test would seem to be the dominant conception of rationality within a society. While such an approach may not subscribe to any particular model of mental distress, its overall ideological stance is clearly one in support of the status quo. Equally, the criterion of bizarre or unacceptable behaviour is open to similar criticism, where the values used to judge such behaviour are likely to be based on dominant conceptions of normal or acceptable behaviour. The model assumes that a consensus exists that can be appealed to in order to justify the designation of people as mentally ill. Any apparent absence of ideology within the diagnostic procedure, rather than be taken to imply a value free judgement being made, could instead be taken to imply the presence of a hegemonic value system. This possibility, however, is not considered.

Moreover, within the concept of mental distress presented, there is an important ambiguity. In 1972 Jones wrote that '...the real needs of patients (are)...in three main groups: problems of childhood, associated with birth and growth: problems of early adult life, associated with the wear and tear of a working life: and problems of middle and later life, associated with the degenerative process.' (Jones, 1972, p.300). Now this suggests that mentally distressed people are indeed victims, in that they have proven unable to deal with life's stresses and have fallen by the wayside. Yet when we examine the more recent definition, quite the opposite position is presented. For Jones is arguing here that mental distress cannot be considered a rational or reasonable response to either social or physical conditions. As such, rather than constituting a victim status, mental distress is better understood as unintelligibility where, literally, the condition does not make sense to the (mentally 'healthy') majority of the population (Ingleby, 1982).

An important aspect of the definition of mental distress given by Jones is that features specific to that condition alone define the condition; the mad and the bad can not simply be considered under the general heading of deviancy. By recognising this she provides a basis upon which to consider how mentally distressed people themselves have had an impact on the development of mental health services, in terms of examining what problems, demands or threats they pose; it provides a basis for examining just why the state should be involved in providing mental health services at all (Ingleby, 1983). This however is not followed up in the subsequent analysis. The account presented is of the development of services by social reformers seeking to provide help, and not a response to any pressures being exerted by mentally distressed people themselves. It is an account that assumes an evolutionary view of society, where increasing levels of benevolence are exhibited towards disabled groups. Yet, while typical of the Social Democratic approach to the study of social service provision (Baker,1979), such an approach fails to adequately consider the potential importance of other, possibly less benign, motivations for the state provision of social services for mentally distressed people.

The Social Democratic account of the origins and development of community care for mentally distressed people is clearly subject to a number of problems. The account is unable to provide an analysis of why the state has failed to provide more adequately developed services in the community. The 'three revolutions' emphasised by Jones do not adequately explain why the state undertook such a drastic alteration in its mental health policy, from an institutional to a community based system. Overall, it displays a tendency to empiricism which, although results in a detailed account of how the policy developed, tells us little about why it arose.

It is, on reviewing the Social Democratic model, difficult to accept that such views can be presented simply as assumptions over how and why community care for the mentally distressed arose. It is the inertia of dominant viewpoints, rather than coherence of argument, that allows such a model to continue to be presented without amendment. Despite this, the model retains its place as the most widely accepted explanation for the development of community care for mentally distressed people. Writers within the Social Democratic tradition continue to repeat similar arguments to those presented by Jones without due regard to their accuracy:

> It became possible to control, if not cure, the symptoms of many psychiatric disorders by the use of drugs, and therefore it was possible to discharge patients after fairly short stays in hospital, continuing the drug therapy, in many cases, as out-patients. This made possible an open door policy in the hospitals, both in the sense that patients were out quickly and that within the hospital a more relaxed atmosphere could be achieved... (Brown, 1985, pp.246-247).

More generally, many of the assumptions within the Social Democratic model continue to be repeated without due regard to the problems associated with the analysis made. In a review of the recent development of mental health services for example, Martin, in his opening remarks, comments that:

> The promotion of 'care in the community' as the preferred objective of government policy for the mentally ill flowed from the convergence in the late 1950s of several different trends and developments. Clinical innovations, administrative and legal changes, advances in professional and in public attitudes played parts which are separately identifiable, even though it may be impossible to assign a precise weighting to the influence of any one of them. (Martin, 1984, p.1).

The continuing dominance of the Social Democratic model,

despite problems with it, reflects in the current debate about how community care services should be further developed. In an important report on mental health services by the House of Commons Social Services Committee, it states:

> In the 1950s, primarily for mental illness services, the pace of reform gathered, as a result of the introduction of new drugs, such as Reserpine and Chlorpromazine, and social treatments, and the Royal Commission on Mental Illness and Mental Deficiency of 1954-57, culminating in the 1959 Mental Health Act. (House of Commons, 1985, para.13).

Equal support for this position is offered by the 'Caring for People' White Paper (DoH, 1989):

> This policy became possible as research and clinical experience showed that treatment was equally or more effective when less reliance was placed on long term in-patient care...additionally, more effective drug treatments, such as the major tranquillisers which were introduced in the 1950s, transformed the prognosis of the most serious mental illnesses. (DoH, 1989, para 7.4).

These reports have been central to recent discussion about what further changes are required within mental health services. It is, however, difficult to propose changes that are both desirable and feasible, when such an account of how and why the policy evolved is retained (Goodwin, 1989).

The Marxist model

The Marxist explanatory model has been developed largely in response to the problems with the Social Democratic account. The main representative of this approach is Scull (1984). He contends that an adequate account must be historically grounded, and informed by the structure of the prevailing social formation; 'A proper grasp of the sources of this change will be shown to rest on an understanding of the internal dynamics of the development of capitalist societies.' (Scull, 1984, p.134).

The central question identified within this analysis is why the mental hospital population should be decanted? - a process he refers to as 'decarceration'. Two reasons are posed. Firstly, only in the 20th century has it become feasible; '...with the advent of a wide range of welfare programs providing...support, the opportunity cost of neglecting community care in favour of asylum treatment - inevitably far more costly than the most generous scheme of welfare payments - rose sharply.' (Scull, 1984, p.135). Given this, Scull then adopts an argument presented by O'Connor (1973b) about just what the state in late capitalism can afford to do; 'Simultaneously, the increasing socialization of production costs by the state, something which has been taking place at an increasing pace during and since the Second World War...produced a growing fiscal crisis, as state expenditures continuously threatened to outrun available revenues.' (Scull, 1984, p.135). Thus it is Scull's thesis that the development of welfare systems has made 'decarceration' feasible, and the relative cheapness of this policy compared to institutional care makes it - for the state - desirable. Finally, the 'fiscal crisis of the state' has been the driving force behind 'decarceration', indeed making the policy change necessary.

With this thesis Scull claims to provide a method of understanding the nature and development of community care for mentally distressed people. The resulting policies are explained in terms of this framework, where the state's enthusiasm for decanting mentally distressed people from mental hospitals is matched by its recalcitrance when developing community services; 'Once the drive for control of soaring costs is seen as the primary factor underlying the move towards decarceration, both these and a number of other aspects of this change which formerly appeared either fortuitous or inexplicable become readily comprehensible.' (Scull, 1984, p.140).

For Scull, the community care policy represents a dereliction of statutory responsibilities made necessary by the financial pressures experienced by the state. For mentally distressed people the result is in many cases the experience of being dumped into poor ghetto areas, or small, badly run and unregulated private homes, where the community is found to have a hostile face, and where no recourse can be found in the previously available asylum of the mental hospital; '...for many...ex-inmates and potential inmates, the alternative to the institution has been to be herded into emerging 'deviant ghettoes', sewers of human misery...' (Scull, 1984, p.153).

The moral condemnation of post-war policies for mentally distressed people is all too apparent in Scull's work. Yet the thesis is presented primarily as an explanatory account of why services have developed as they have; '...in the absence of any theoretical understanding of the decarceration process taken as a whole...

critics have generally been unable to grasp the full significance of their own observations...It is precisely this broader organising framework that this book has sought to provide.' (Scull, 1984, p.152). It is on this basis that we will consider his analysis. As with the Social Democratic model we shall examine three aspects; the analytical framework, the application of the model, and finally the concept of mental distress.

The methodology adopted by Scull is avowedly Marxist. In concluding his argument he comments; 'Placing the decarceration movement in historical context, I have argued that this shift in social control styles and practices must be viewed as dependant upon and a reflection of more extensive and deep-seated changes in the social organisation of advanced capitalist societies. In particular, it reflects the structural pressures to curtail sharply the costly system of segregative control...'(Scull, 1984, p.152). The emphasis is therefore mainly, almost wholly, on a single determining factor; the requirements for continued capital accumulation.

Yet in developing this argument Scull is less than clear about what exactly constitutes the requirements of capital accumulation. He draws upon the work of O'Conner (1973b) and Gough (1975) without consideration of the status of his sources other than that they are both 'Marxist' writers. But while O'Conner bases his analysis of capitalist economic crisis tendencies upon the 'underconsumptionist' theory of Baran and Sweezy, Gough's analysis is based on the 'distributional struggle' between capital and labour. These two schools make competing claims over how to understand the mechanisms of capitalist development that lead to crisis. The first tends to concentrate on 'laws of motion' of capitalist production, including '...an intrinsic contradiction between the conditions of production of surplus value and the conditions of the realization of surplus value.' (Wright, 1975, p.20). The second tends to concentrate on analyzing endemic class conflict, the result of which is to erode the capacity to generate surplus value within the process of capitalist production. Such views are not easily reconciled; the role of class struggle in the first is outside of the central mechanism of crisis, and in the second it is directly implicated as the cause of crisis. In view of the importance attached by Scull to these issues, we might expect him to be a little clearer about his own analysis of what constitutes the process by which capitalism tends to crisis.

A problem with many Marxist accounts of the development of welfare services in capitalist societies is a tendency towards

20

'fundamentalism' (Lee and Raban, 1988). This concerns a '...marked theoretical emphasis on the role that welfare policies play in continuing to sustain capitalist social relations. Such arguments...are all too often pursued crudely and mechanically.' (Lee and Raban, 1988, p.109). This is a problem that appears in Scull's explanatory model. In developing a Marxist analysis he attempts to employ the historical materialist method, by emphasising the importance of the economic 'base' in relation to the political and ideological 'superstructure'. But in pursuing this he reveals a considerable tendency to reductionism, where almost everything can be explained in terms of the 'needs' of capital accumulation. In this there is little room for class struggle, or even to allow for variable outcomes as the 'contradictions of capitalism' work themselves out. Now there has of course been considerable debate around the issue of just how the relationship between 'base' and 'superstructure' should be theorized, and within the range of views that have been developed some support for reductionist positions has been made (Cohen, 1984). But the manner in which Scull assumes that the needs of capital will necessarily prevail in state policy formulation, loses any sense of the dialectical method that most Marxist writers attempt to employ (Coates, 1984; Miliband, 1977).

This tendency towards fundamentalism tends to generate two types of problem in Marxist analyses; economism and functionalism. We find both of these arise in Scull's explanatory model. The first of these, referring to an unwarranted priority being given to the economic as opposed to the political and ideological levels of society, appears in the manner in which Scull appropriates O'Conner's theoretical model. Firstly, Scull fails to adequately differentiate the 'fiscal crisis of the state' and the crisis tendencies of the capitalist mode of production. The former is simply taken to be the inevitable result of the latter. Using O'Conner's work, Scull claims that the state must attempt to solve its financial crisis, and that the shedding of expenditure on institutional services for the mentally distressed is part of this. But this tends towards a too dogmatic reading of O'Conner's work, for he was only attempting to identify the more general nature of the crisis to which the state in advanced capitalism is prone, and not any specific strategies that the state would be forced to adopt. As O'Conner states:

> This study is at root an interpretation of the economic development and crisis tendencies of this period. It should not be read

as a comprehensive study of state budgetary planning and policy, nor as a source or reference book in the field of state finance. (O'Conner, 1973a, p.79).

As a result, there is a lack of regard given to the role of the state as a 'relatively autonomous' agency, capable of making a variety of decisions some of which may not necessarily be in the interests of capital. As one Marxist writer notes, '...the state cannot, and must not be taken, as perfectly functioning to reproduce capitalist relations.' (Urry, 1981, p.6).

Secondly, Scull concentrates almost entirely upon the emphasis given by O'Conner to the requirement that the state acknowledges the requirements of capital accumulation - this being reflected in his emphasis on the necessity to reduce the costs of mental health service provision. But this tends to ignore the equally important emphasis given by O'Conner to the requirement that the state acknowledges the requirements of legitimation. For O'Conner, the problems facing the state evolve out of contradictory demands emanating from both of these. Yet Scull does not consider adequately the extent of pressure exerted on the state for the provision of 'legitimate' mental health services. His emphasis upon the needs of capital accumulation results in a total lack of consideration of the 'contradictory' nature of the state's position within capitalist societies. As Held notes, '...while the state is dependant on the process of capital accumulation, the multiplicity of economic and electoral constraints on policy mean that the state is not an unambiguous agent of capitalist reproduction.' (Held, 1984, p.357). At best, then, we can describe Scull's theoretical model as incomplete.

When applying the theoretical model, Scull tends towards a functionalist style of analysis. This concerns the process of explaining social processes in terms of what functions they perform; in this case what functions they perform to aid continued capital accumulation. He does attempt to avoid this by acknowledging the 'contradictory' nature of state welfare policies, whose origin lies in meeting working class demands as well as seeking to maintain the capitalist social formation (Scull, 1984, p.136). This however does not reflect in the use made of the model, and a result of this tendency to functionalism is a lack of sensitivity to the evidence available on the form that policies for the mentally distressed have taken. He tends to ride roughshod over much of the data, imposing a theoretical structure without sufficient regard to the complexity of the processes involved. This can be demonstrated by examining some of the propositions he makes in relation to what has actually occurred.

A key proposition within Scull's analysis is that community care is cheaper than institutional care. He recognises that the fixed costs of mental hospitals remain relatively stable despite the falling residential population, but maintains that the state has been able to avoid costly rebuilding programmes of old Victorian buildings by arguing that their use is only short term. Furthermore he accepts that these savings in capital costs are partly offset by the resulting expenditures on community care provision, but because of the paucity of the latter the net savings are still considerable (Scull, 1984, p.174). Hence he still maintains that '...decarceration provides a direct and immediate source of relief to the state's fiscal crisis whose importance is obvious, even while its dimensions are extraordinarily difficult to estimate with any precision.'(Scull, 1984, p.144).

A weakness of functionalist arguments is their circularity, and this argument over relative costs demonstrates this elegantly. For Scull first assumes that in changing from an institutional to community based system of care the state sought cost savings, and hence because that change has been implemented cost savings must have arisen. With such an argument, it is pointless demonstrating, as some have done, the fact that community based systems of care can be expensive (Kaplan, 1978; Jones, 1983), because Scull's argument assumes that the cheapest feasible policy will be implemented. The very existence of community care proves its cheapness in relation to institutional care. In later Chapters we discuss more fully just what costs have been involved in the development of community care, and what importance the state attaches to this factor. And, as we shall demonstrate, the concern with the cost of mental health service provision has played a major part in influencing the development of services. This however is not to imply a functional necessity. If it were so, it would for example be difficult to explain why the mental hospital population in Japan has soared since the end of the Second World War (Hafner,1985), and why the cost of mental hospital provision in England has continued to rise during the post-war period (Goodwin, 1989)

Problems with this functionalist style of analysis also arise when considering the timing of events in Sculls account. He argues that the principal spur to decarceration was 'fiscal crisis', yet the mental hospital population peaked in 1954 and then began to decline, many years prior to any 'fiscal crisis' (Sedgwick,1982a).

This raises a serious question mark over the entire thesis, for the structural features of the analysis upon which Scull puts such weight cannot be used quite as simply as he attempts.

Recognising the serious of this point, Scull has attempted to answer it (Scull,1984, pp.172-173). First, he shifts the onset of fiscal crisis from the 1950s to the 'mid- to late-1960s' without explanation (Scull, 1984, p.172). Next, he presents a further explanation for the changes. He notes that admission rates were rising and hence '...an extraordinary expansion of the mental hospital system would have been required to house this influx.' Further, the existing hospital stock was in '...a terminal state of decay and dilapidation.', and would need an enormous influx of resources that were not available, while the running costs of existing hospitals were rapidly increasing; 'The subsequent fiscal crisis merely added to these pressures and made them far more intense and urgent ' (Scull, 1984, p.173).

This revision raises more problems than it solves. The problem we are left with is what, if anything, is left of the original thesis. By subordinating the importance of the fiscal crisis, and by referring to a series of more contingent events in this way, the original importance attached to the nature of the capitalist social formation is lost. Moreover the importance attached to these more specific causes can also be questioned. The reference made to rising admission rates fails to take into account that this was a long standing trend; admission rates had begun to rise sharply in the 1930s (Bott,1976). By the early 1950s over crowding was recognised as a serious problem, but the response of the Department of Health (discussed in more detail in Chapter 4) at the time was to plan new hospitals. Only later in the decade did deinstitutionalisation appear a feasible solution to the problem of over-crowding. Thus Scull's reference to rising admission rates clearly does not constitute an explanatory factor in the simple way he presents it.

Similarly, his reference to the rising costs of the hospital service is insufficiently detailed. While it is true that the building stock was quite inadequate, we find that through the 1950s considerable effort was made to find capital expenditure to improve that stock. Both in real terms, and as a percentage of total capital expenditure on hospitals, mental hospitals received a rising share of resources throughout the 1950s. Equally, there was much concern about the shortages of nursing staff. To attract more staff, psychiatric nurses were paid an additional allowance on top of the normal nursing salary. An extensive advertising campaign was undertaken, and an arrangement even made for National Service to be deferred for the period of training of male psychiatric nurses, together with a promise that when called up they would be employed in that capacity.

The final area of Scull's model we need to examine is the concept of mental distress utilised. At the psychological or individual level, the question 'what is mental distress'? is not addressed. He does not consider it relevant to examine the nature of such a condition as it is individually experienced when considering the development of mental health services. Rather, it is at the sociological or group level that he develops the notion of mental distress, whereby he aims to elucidate its nature as characterising a certain group of people within capitalism.

When identifying mentally distressed people, Scull is relatively free in his use of terminology. They are referred to variously as 'mad', 'mentally ill', a 'problem population', and a 'subgroup' of the 'dangerous classes'. However the principal characteristic of such people is deviancy; the mentally distressed are, Scull claims, a living threat to bourgeois rationality (Scull, 1984, pp.26-30). As such these people are necessarily subject to a process of social control; a process analyzed as part of the overall project of class domination, where the states's labelling of certain deviants as mentally ill constitutes the mystification of an essentially oppressive relationship by transmuting antagonistic class relationships into individual psychiatric problems of the proletariat (Scull, 1984, p.29).

Similarly to Jones' analysis, this conception of mental distress is ambiguous. Most frequently mentally distressed people are defined as deviants because they do not work, and live outside of market relationships, but sometimes are also considered to be victims of social control measures brought to bear on them. The notion of deviance implies that mental distress lacks any substantive status, being merely a socially constructed category reflecting oppressive class relationships within capitalism. Yet reference to mentally distressed people as victims implies the reverse; that a real disablement has occurred. While it may be that these disparate positions might be synthesised, Scull does not do so.

Furthermore the analysis of mental distress as being a threat to continued capital accumulation, is poorly supported. The only argument offered is that the mentally distressed are unable to participate in wage-labour and consequently represent a threat to capitalism. Yet just why this should pose a threat is never made clear, for continued capital accumulation does not depend upon every able bodied proletarian being involved in wage labour.

25

Moreover, continued capital accumulation is not simply dependant upon this one dimension of the economic productiveness of the proletariat, but also involves cultural reproduction. Yet how the definition and application of the category of mental distress is affected by this is not considered.

Scull's work is an important contribution to the debate about the origins and development of mental heath services, and has received considerable attention. It provides an analysis that usefully identifies some important issues concerning how we should understand the nature and development of the community care policy. Principally, these concern the need to locate an analysis within the prevailing socio-economic conditions, and the need to challenge the state's presentation of social policy as simply a process of reform intended for the common good. But while Scull may have identified a series of problems and issues that are relevant to understanding community care there are, as the above review indicates, serious problems with the analysis. It tends towards 'globalism' (Matthews, 1987) where the specific characteristics of a society at a particular time, and characteristics of particular groups being considered, tend to be subsumed under the weight of over-reaching theoretical ideas that, on examination, do not offer detailed propositions about how and why policies develop in certain ways. Moreover, the process of generalization from specific examples is not proven appropriate. The assumption that decarceration reflects imperatives of capitalism ignores the fact that the policy has not been applied to all groups held in institutions (Hudson,1983). Reflecting this style of analysis, the account developed is overly deterministic. It tends towards a unilinear analysis of policy development, as social control, and ignores contradictory imperatives within capitalism that might allow for some truly benevolent content within state welfare policies. In addition, at a more prosaic level, such an analysis tends to ignore the considerable problems the state has in achieving coherence of any sort in the development of policies. In total, many useful insights are offered, but they do not add up to the analysis promised of an account of the development of the policy linked closely to the nature of the capitalist social formation.

Conclusion

The Social Democratic and Marxist accounts of the origins and evolution of the community care policy provide us with competing models of explanation. Emphasis is placed on either the subjective or objective context, the importance of either 'micro' or 'macro' inputs to the analysis, and the role of welfare as either care or control. The Social Democratic model is strongest in its explication of how the policy evolved, but has little to say about why. Conversely the Marxist account concentrates on the question of why the policy evolved, but provides little detail of how it arose. While both models provide a variety of insights into what has occurred, neither has been able to present a sufficiently coherent and comprehensive explanatory understanding of the various aspects of the community care policy.

But perhaps what emerges most clearly is that the faults we have identified in each account are in many ways complementary. In Scull's account we have seen an almost total disregard of the role of actors and ideas within the policy making process. In Jones' account, we have seen an almost total disregard for imperatives emanating from the nature of the capitalist social formation within the policy making process. The result in both accounts is a tendency to ignore social forces, within either the sphere of social structure or social action, that (as we shall demonstrate in subsequent Chapters) are nevertheless of considerable importance to developing an explanatory understanding of mental health service provision.

This observation is of course only part of a larger debate about how to theorise the welfare state. Mishra, in a review of approaches to its study, notes that the 'social administration' framework - we might take Jones work as a good example - tends to be empirical and pragmatic. Welfare policies are studied with the intention of changing them. The concern therefore tends to be with the here and now, what the effects of policy are and what reforms should be made (Mishra 1983). Such an approach Taylor-Gooby and Dale refer to somewhat disparagingly as 'abstracted empiricism', where the study of welfare remains separate from other features of the society in which it is located (Taylor-Gooby and Dale, 1981, p.9). And currently, with the welfare state under political and economic attack, the result of this Mishra contends is that 'Social administration thus increasingly finds itself servicing a welfare state whose very rationale is in question, but about which it has very little to say.' (Mishra, 1983, p.799).

The opposite side of the coin is represented by Marxist approaches to welfare. In 'The Fiscal Crisis of the State' O'Connor (1973b) argues that state welfare expenditure is largely undertaken to legitimate the capitalist economic order. Yet, as he now accepts, the

27

relationship between social structure and social action is not quite so straightforward, or functional; '...social integration may be possible on the basis of new social and political symbols, or the manipulation of old symbols by cultural leaders, politicians, etc.' (O'Connor, 1981, p.45). Equally Gough's analysis of the driving force of class conflict between proletariat and bourgeoisie, in pushing capitalist societies towards social and economic crisis (Gough,1979), has proven difficult to sustain. With the proletariat 'failing' to rally to the socialist cause as unemployment rose in the late 1970s and early 1980s, he now concedes that '...the predictions of a legitimation crisis have not been realized' (Gough, 1983, p.474). Moreover, '...the original argument remains too deterministic, deriving political outcomes too directly from an analysis of the objective contradictions of the welfare state without giving sufficient weight to their political and ideological mediations.' (Gough, 1983, p.474). Whether or not Marxist writers can overcome these difficulties is still perhaps an open question. However, as Mishra notes, it remains the case that '...a major weakness of the Marxist approach seems to be its ambivalence about the status of the political as an explanatory category.' (Mishra, 1983, p.805).

These kind of weaknesses have been recognised in many social policy analyses, and frequently the argument pursued is that a synthetic position incorporating the strengths of each approach should be developed. Hall et. al. propose the notion of 'bounded pluralism' as a means of analyzing the development of welfare services. With this notion, they argue that the importance of structural constraints can be acknowledged, while also recognising that within these boundaries various conflicts and compromises might arise. (Hall et. al., 1975, p.151). Ham identifies three existing approaches, marxism, pluralism and structuralism, all of which he argues have strengths that might be drawn from. By doing this, he claims that an analysis can be conducted that recognises both macro and micro levels, both objective and subjective forces, in the policy making and policy implementation process (Ham 1982, Chap. 7). Mishra too now acknowledges the failure of any one approach to provide an adequate method, and argues for '...a sociology of the welfare state that incorporates some of the methods and approaches of Marxist as well as Liberal political economy.' (Mishra, 1983, p.806). Similarly, Lee and Raban acknowledge the failure of many Marxist and Fabian analyses to provide an adequate method, and argue for '...a fusion of the critical elements of Fabianism with a realistic version of Marxism.' (Lee and Raban, 1988, p.2).

28

The problem here, however, is what we mean by synthesis. The simple juxtaposition of apparently useful features of different perspectives into some kind of eclectic analytical model can give rise to greater difficulties than its solves. Let us take 'bounded pluralism' as an example. Its claim is to provide adequate recognition and understanding of the variety of forces that affect the development of state welfare. Yet, left unstated within such a model is just exactly what constraints a capitalist socio-economic structure places upon policy makers, and to what extent those policy makers are able to affect that structure. Moreover the consciousness of the policy makers themselves is not considered, in terms of to what extent they are free-thinking and 'objective', socially determined, or simply see their own interests to lie with sustaining capitalism.

The underlying problem with this sort of approach is that the initial premise, that different approaches offer particular strengths that can be excised and incorporated in a new model, is incorrect. Many Marxist analyses do attempt to recognise the importance of the political level within the capitalist social formation, but fail to provide a sufficient account of it because of assumptions within the overall model concerning for example the origins and development of consciousness (based on the process of production), and a tendency to over-emphasise the degree of restraint placed on the political process by the needs of capital accumulation. Equally, Social Democratic accounts recognise the dependency of the policy making process upon economic success, but argue that people are in greater control of their own destinies in terms of consciousness being more autonomous, and the ability of the political level to determine the pattern of development of the economic level (Banting, 1979; Room, 1979). In effect we can all accept, from whatever position we occupy, the notion of 'bounded pluralism'; it is a metaphysical term that alludes to what we can all see occurs, but offers little in terms of explanatory understanding. Such models are simply re-statements of old problems, principally concerning issues around the relationship between social structure and social agency.

This, however, is not to suggest that the shift towards developing synthetic positions is inappropriate. Rather, it points to the fact that such models need to be more sophisticated than simply incorporating the stronger aspects of various perspectives. It suggests that the use of a synthetic position to explain the development of state welfare must be located upon a firm theoretical base that is clear in its analysis of these key sociological questions. Given this, it might then be possible to incorporate the strengths of different perspectives within a synthetic position without simply disappearing into a blind alley, the end wall being composed of the contradictory propositions of the various perspectives utilised. This is the starting point for the next Chapter, where we will attempt to develop a new explanatory model which might provide a more adequate understanding of how and why community care for mentally distressed people evolved.

2 The sociology of mental health service provision

Existing explanatory models of the origins and development of the community care policy for mentally distressed people are, as we have seen in Chapter 1, subject to a number of serious methodological criticisms. A key problem we have identified concerns the relationship between social structure - the prevailing socio-economic organisation of a society, and social action - the behaviour of individuals and groups within that social structure (Lee and Raban,1988, pp.135-137). This problem is one of the central issues addressed by Critical Theory. This reflects in the work of Habermas, the current doyen of this perspective. The arguments he develops are long and complicated, and we cannot attempt here to examine them in any depth. Nevertheless there are a number of features of his work that will inform our subsequent analysis, which we should elucidate.

Habermas argues that labour and language constitute two analytically distinct dimensions of evolution which are both essential to the organisation and reproduction of human life. The first of these concerns the development of the forces of production, while the second concerns the development of normative structures of interaction. These two dimensions of human evolution result in the development of two different types of knowledge. The technical interest develops as a result of the labour process, and refers to an interest in developing knowledge with which to achieve mastery over nature. The extent of development of this interest circumscribes the possible development of the forces of production. Secondly, the practical interest develops as a result of the use of language, and concerns an interest in the interpretation of the way in which societies are organised. The development of practical learning circumscribes the range of possible structures of social integration.

Further to this, Habermas maintains that the practical interest in interpreting the world gives rise to a third interest, an emancipatory interest. This refers to the development of an interest in overcoming relations of domination; what Habermas refers to as distorted communication. His claim is that through the very use of language there is a tendency towards developing greater communicative competence, involving the growth in desire and ability to perceive and overcome oppressive power relationships. The aim is the achievement of an ideal speech situation, where the use of language is rational and clear. Achievement of this would involve overcoming relations of domination pertaining within a society.

The emphasis of the analysis is, therefore, upon the development of learning within the technical, practical and emancipatory spheres of human interest. Based on these arguments, Habermas suggests the notion of organisation principle as a means of analyzing the development of societies:

> By principle of organisation I understand those innovations which become possible through learning processes that can be reconstructed in a developmental logic, and which institutionalise a new societal level of learning. The organisation principle of a society circumscribes ranges of possibility; in particular, it determines within which structures changes in the system of institutions are possible; to what extent the available productive capacities can be socially utilized or the development of new productive forces can be stimulated; and thereby also to what degrees system complexity and steering performances can be heightened (Quoted in McCarthy, 1978, p.272).

In presenting the notion of an organisation principle, Habermas is attempting to reveal the logic of historical development within a framework that places greater emphasis upon the relations of production than Marx gave. There is, he claims, a developmental logic, based on the learning mechanisms within individuals. Rather than the development of the forces of production, it is the development of normative structures based upon practical-moral learning that constitutes the 'pace-maker of social evolution'. The development of technical knowledge and the implementation of new productive forces, rather than being of primary importance as in Marx's model, largely follows and is controlled by this process. As

32

such, this represents a major modification to Marx's own work, although Habermas contends that it retains a materialist premise because problems of sustaining production and reproduction still constitute the source of threats to a society's existence.

Habermas does not however argue that this developmental process is inevitable. While the evolution of the species must go through various stages if development is to occur, this process is neither a necessary nor uninterrupted one. Habermas emphasises the fact that the state has open to it a number of 'steering mechanisms' with which to contain and subvert dissent. It is only if and when such steering mechanisms fail that an 'evolutionary thrust' occurs, with the levels of learning in practical and technical knowledge being incorporated into a new and 'higher' organisation principle.

Now the reason for outlining this theory here has not been simply to present an ideal model with which to analyse mental health services. Critics have pointed to a variety of problems with the theory, which Habermas has not always effectively countered (Thompson and Held, 1982). A major concern has been with the validity of the distinction he draws between work and language as dual formative processes in social evolution. Similarly, the theory of communicative competence, which underlies the emphasis placed upon the development of critical thought and the subsequent questioning of social organisation within capitalist societies, has been subject to considerable criticism (Keat, 1981). At a lower level of abstraction, the reconstruction of a legitimate state project by the Conservative party in Britain in the late 1970s raises doubts about the potency of the development of an emancipatory interest.

For our purposes however, this theoretical model provides us with a basis on which to overcome many of the problems identified in the Marxist and Social Democratic accounts of mental health service provision. It provides us with a relatively sophisticated model of societal change and development that places emphasis upon both social structure and social action, and on the relationship between the two. It incorporates the strengths of the Marxist perspective, historicism and materialism, while overcoming its tendency to ignore human perception, subjective experience and social action. Thus, while remaining aware of the criticisms that have been levelled at the model, we might nevertheless employ it to help develop a more adequate account of the evolution the community care policy for mentally distressed people.

In Chapter 1 we found that both the Marxist and Social Democratic accounts fail to develop adequately sophisticated arguments on a number of themes. Three major issues arose; the nature of late capitalism, the role of the state, and the concept of mental distress. Utilising the Critical Theory perspective, we first present a number of arguments with the aim of improving our analysis in each of these areas. An attempt is then made to employ this discussion in developing a new model with which to develop an explanatory understanding of mental health services.

Legitimation crisis

In his 'Legitimation Crisis', Habermas (1976) attempts to provide a schematic framework with which to analyse the nature and development of the late capitalist social formation. He starts by defining the notion of crisis. Central to this is the dual nature of any societal crisis, where problems of system integration (the social structure) combine with problems of social integration (social action) to generate a threat to the continued viability of a society as presently constituted. Only when such threats occur to both areas simultaneously is there a possibility of a societal crisis occurring. The organisation principle upon which a society is based contains, as we noted above, a certain range of adaptations that it can make to counter or suppress such problems, but if such steering mechanisms are not sufficient to meet existing threats to the social order crisis, involving a rupture in the organizational principle of a society, will ensue.

A systems model is used to characterise and analyse modern capitalism. Three sub-systems are identified; the economic, the political-administrative, and the socio-cultural. Within each of these sub-systems Habermas argues there are certain potential crisis tendencies which may afflict them.

Point of origin	Systems crisis	Identity crisis
(Sub-systems)		
Economic	Economic crisis	
Political	Rationality crisis	Legitimation crisis
Socio-cultural		Motivation crisis

Source: Habermas, 1976, p.45.

The argument pursued is that in one or more sub-systems there is

34

a tendency for the 'requisite quantity' of systems products to fail to be generated. Consequently there will be a tendency towards crisis in the particular domain of that sub-system. Such change will be resisted by the implementation of steering mechanisms in an attempt to maintain the identity of the capitalist system. Just what this involves is detailed below, but first we should emphasise that Habermas notes the unpredictability of the outcome of such management strategies. Their success or otherwise is determined by the level of resistance and conflict that develops, but just what crises - if any - develop cannot be determined simply by theorising.

The possibility of economic crisis is based on the Marxian analysis of the contradiction between the socialization of production and its private appropriation. However, with developments in capitalist relations of production in the 20th century, Habermas argues that crisis tendencies this engenders concerning increasing conflict between bourgeois and proletarian classes have been ameliorated. Because the state has increasingly organised the production of 'collective commodities', such as education and scientific progress, labour is used increasingly efficiently; in Marxist terms thereby allowing a rise over time of relative surplus value. As a result the Marxian analysis of a necessary tendency to economic crisis based on immutable contradictory processes within the production process is replaced by '...an empirical question whether the new form of production of surplus value...can work against economic crisis.' (Habermas, 1976, p.57). Secondly, with the growth of a private monopolistic sector, the price of labour power becomes increasingly determined by quasi-political negotiation rather than market forces, because the increased costs of production can be passed on by companies holding monopoly positions. The result, Habermas contends, is that '...it has been possible-above all in the capital and growth-intensive sectors of the economy-to mitigate the opposition between wage labor and capital and to bring about a partial class compromise.' (Habermas, 1976, p.57).

With these changes in the organisation of production Habermas maintains that the possibility of economic crisis has been much reduced. However, the suspension of economic crisis relies upon increasing intervention by the state in the production process. By becoming evermore involved in regulating the social relations of production, the state increasingly becomes the focus of demands from a variety of competing groups within society. Socialization of the costs of production creates ever growing demands upon its ability to raise adequate levels of taxation. The result, it is argued, is that crisis tendencies in the economic sub-system are displaced into the political-administrative sub-system. Hence the possibility of a 'rationality crisis' within the political-administrative system arises as the political system, facing rising demands, tends towards failure in its attempts to devise adequate steering mechanisms to cope with the varied demands made up on it. While the displacement of economic crises creates problems for the political system, Habermas does not argue that they will necessarily create insurmountable problems for the steering mechanisms employed. While some policies may fail, there are no clear criteria for judging at what point these reach an unacceptable level. Further, the state can make clear the contradictory demands that are being made upon it and so open the decision making process to compromise between the various competing parties. In total, the social systems problems faced within capitalist societies will not necessarily attain crisis proportions. However, when combining this analysis with threats to social integration, Habermas goes on to argue that there are greater possibilities for change that the available steering mechanisms may not be able to manage.

The capitalist state, Habermas contends, is legitimated by claims to abide by the principles of equality, justice and freedom. But these claims become increasingly difficult to sustain because, as the state becomes more involved in maintaining capital accumulation, there is a tendency for an increasing number of political issues to become thematised. What was once assigned to the private sphere becomes subject to state control and therefore open to questions of choice, planning and control. Thus in areas such as heath, education, and transportation the state becomes increasingly vulnerable to disputes over policy formation. It must recognise the constraints of continued capital accumulation yet also retain legitimacy.

But as with the possibility of economic and rationality crises, Habermas acknowledges that legitimation crisis tendencies are not insoluble. The state is, potentially, able to avoid the development of a legitimation crisis as a result of the separation of 'form' and 'content' within the political-administrative sub-system (Offe,1984). The form of the state is democratic, in as much as the political leaders are elected by the mass of the population, and who claim to represent their interests. However, the content of state policy must recognise the constraints imposed by the needs for continued capital accumulation such that the political concerns of the elected representatives are only of secondary consideration. This helps avoid the thematization of the antagonism between capital accumulation and the legitimacy of capitalist societies.

Moreover, Habermas argues that there has been an expansion of

36

'instrumental reason' from the economic to the political-administrative sub-system. This concerns the 'scientization' of politics whereby technocratic solutions to normative problems are devised and applied. Political issues, concerning moral problems, tend increasingly to be held open to organizational solution, with the sole issue being to devise the most efficient means to attain given ends. This provides the state with additional legitimacy, as the arena of debate over the variety of possible policy options is constrained by the emphasis on expert judgement on how to achieve given ends.

To this point, Habermas does little in his argument to rescue the Critical Theory tradition from its pessimistic conclusions over the likelihood of capitalism being overthrown. The problems arising within the economic and political-administrative sub-systems can, he suggests, be effectively countered by steering mechanisms. However, the argument is taken further by introducing the notion of a 'motivation crisis' within the socio-cultural system, and it is in this that he argues the central and most important threats to the capitalist system occur:

> A legitimation crisis must be based on a motivation crisis - that is, a discrepancy between the need for motives declared by the state, the educational and occupational systems on the one hand, and the motivation supplied by the socio-cultural system on the other (quoted in McCarthy, 1978, p.371).

Habermas argues there are two main patterns of motivation within advanced capitalist societies. 'Civil privatism' refers to a low level of participation and interest in the political sub-system, with voting being the only real involvement. 'Familial-vocational privatism' refers to an orientation towards family life, leisure, consumption, and towards interest in career advancement. Now the problem here, Habermas contends, is that while these patterns of motivation are necessary to sustain the organizational principle of capitalist societies, because they tend to reduce interest in the state's activities which are becoming less legitimate, they are nevertheless being undermined by developments within such societies.

The argument developed is that civil and familial privatism are sustained by pre-bourgeois and bourgeois traditions. The first of these concerns traditional world views such as that contained within religions. Such views are being progressively undermined by the growth of rationality in modes of explaining the world; Darwinism for example. The bourgeois traditions derive from the ideology of liberal capitalism, and state activity is tending to undermine these. Thus, for example the ideology of possessive individualism is being eroded by the increasing socialization of the costs of production by the state, such that individual use of and choice over material goods is reduced. Also, the orientation towards exchange value within the labour market is being eroded by the increasing numbers of people living and working outside of market relations, as the state tends to enlarge its own workforce and programmes of maintenance for various segments of the population.

Thus the key argument in Habermas' theory of crisis tendencies in late capitalism is that existing patterns of motivation are being undermined while state intervention and the growth of more rational modes of thinking have opened up areas of living to argumentation, such that previously held assumptions over the naturalness of existing social arrangements are no longer uncritically accepted. 'Discursive will formation' has at least in some small parts of society become operational and has 'motive forming power'. The legitimation crisis therefore, concerns the conflict between the needs of the political system that has had displaced upon it the economic contradictions of the capitalist system of production, and demands emanating from the socio-cultural system for political participation and the rational justification of state policies. The needs and demands facing the state become increasingly difficult to reconcile, as it attempts to maintain the conditions for capital accumulation while retaining legitimacy for its own actions.

The state

Consideration of the nature of the state is clearly an important area when examining social policy. Assumptions about its nature, as we have seen in Chapter 1, underlie perceptions of the aims of state social policy. We also saw in Chapter 1 that existing explanations of mental health service provision utilise inadequate conceptions of the state. The Marxist conception, as employed by Scull, is of a state acting wholly in the economic interests of capital, without reference to other competing interests - the most obvious omission being the interests of labour. The Social Democratic model, as we saw, conceives the state as a neutral arbiter between competing interest groups, yet has had to acknowledge some interests have been completely disregarded in the development of community care for mentally distressed people. Thus if we are to improve upon existing analyses of mental health services, we need a more adequate model of the state within capitalism. Again we will turn to a writer within the Critical Theory tradition - Offe - to provide this.

Interest in the state amongst writers on the Left has increased considerably in the last two decades (McLennan et al.,1983). This was initiated by the debate between Miliband and Poulantzas over the role that it took in capitalist societies. Miliband tended to adopt an instrumentalist position, arguing that the penetration of the state by representatives of capital was a crucial area of analysis in determining the role the state took in defending the class interests of the bourgeoisie (Miliband,1972). In contrast Poulantzas argued that this emphasis upon agents was quite irrelevant, because the state was locked into a structural relationship of dependence with capital, and therefore necessarily acted in its interests; this being something it would do irrespective of the class backgrounds of state personnel (Poulantzas, 1972).

Offe entered this debate in the 1970s, presenting a theory of state action intended to bridge the gap between these two positions (Offe, 1984). A key point in his work is that rather than attempt to analyse the capitalist state as Marxist accounts tend to, his focus is upon analyzing the state in capitalism. Instead of asking how capital takes over or controls the state, he argues that the state exists as an independent entity, that nevertheless finds itself progressively more enmeshed in attempting to reconcile contradictory tendencies within capitalism. He argues that two principal forces acting on the state can be identified, the need to sustain capital accumulation and the need to present that process to the general population as a legitimate one. Thus Offe's conception of the state is of an institution with its own interests and concerns, whose problem is how to survive within the increasingly hostile environment of the capitalist social formation.

Because of its institutional separation from the economy, Offe argues that the state is dependant upon the flow of revenue through taxation on private capital. The state lacks the power to take control of the organisation of the production process, and so has little option but to attempt to maintain the conditions for private capital accumulation in order to safeguard its own revenues. Thus the argument presented is that there are structural pressures on state personnel to sustain to the best of their ability the capitalist economic system:

> Since state power depends on a process of accumulation which is beyond its power to organize, every occupant of state power

is basically interested in promoting those political conditions most conducive to private accumulation. This interest does not result from an alliance of a particular government with particular classes or social strata also interested in accumulation; nor does it necessarily result from the privileged access of the members of the capitalist class to centres of state decision-making, a privilege which in turn makes it possible for that class to 'put pressure' on the incumbents of state power to pursue their class interest. Rather the institutional self-interest of the state in accumulation is conditioned by the fact that the state is denied the power to control the flow of those resources which are nevertheless indispensable for the exercise of state power (Offe, 1984, p.120).

The analysis implies neither a conspiracy nor a simple functional relationship between the state and capital. Rather, the state is interested in sustaining capital accumulation for its own survival. At the same time however, it must retain legitimacy with the general public in terms of appearing representative of all interests, and responsive to democratic pressure.

The concept of mental distress

In our discussion of the Marxist and Social Democratic accounts we argued that the models of mental distress employed are somewhat confused. We need therefore to utilise a more adequate concept of mental distress upon which to base our understanding of the nature of mental health service provision.

To start, we might consider just what areas of social life we are investigating, for the very notion of 'mental distress' as generally used and applied covers an enormous range of conditions. For example, to group Alzheimer's disease, schizophrenia, manic-depression, endogenous depression and psychopathy together is obfuscating. The former, associated with ageing, may well be properly dealt with in a medical context involving the treatment of an 'illness', but such a model is far more difficult to apply to these other conditions. The first point, then, is that it is impossible to generalise about the nature of mental distress as understood within psychiatric taxonomies. This reflects in the fact that such taxonomies change over time, an important change for example being the decision by the American Psychiatric Association in 1973 that homosexuality should no longer be considered a mental illness.

40

Any concept of mental distress must make reference, implicitly or explicitly, to some conception of humankind. We saw earlier that the existing Social Democratic and Marxist models tend to accept a static or passive conception of humanity, without interests and subject to mental distress when swayed by adverse forces. However an alternative - indeed Marxist - conception of humanity holds that people are creative and productive. Their consciousness of the world and of themselves is shaped through the social relations of the production process. As such people are active participants in their own development - a product of historical struggle as much as a product of nature (Ollman, 1971).

There are two implications this has for our concept of mental distress. Firstly, it is historically bound. That is to say, if people are creative beings then this implies that any mental distress they suffer can only be understood in terms of their interaction with the environment. Secondly, and following from this, mental distress should be understood not as socially created, but socially constructed (Ingleby,1981). This is the key distinction between concepts of mental distress used in existing accounts, and what will be used here. For the concern is not simply with adverse conditions, but with how they are appropriated by people in historically specific circumstances. The implication of this analysis is that mental distress should be understood as a socially constructed phenomenon deriving from struggle between a person's interests and actions, and the particular environment in which they find themselves.

To illustrate this we might consider the example of a depressed housewife. Continued capital accumulation depends in part upon the exploitation and oppression of women (Barrett, 1980). Their domestic work provides an unpaid labour force to capital. Yet for many women this position as isolated labourers within the home in unsatisfactory. For example, it has been found that mothers of young children, and who do not work outside of the house, experience a high level of 'clinical depression' (Brown and Harris,1978). Similarly Klerman and Weissman found, in a study of the effects of marriage, that women's creative needs tend to be suppressed:

> Being married 'protects' men against mental illness; for the women, however, marriage produces difficulties which promote mental illness. The married women's role is usually more stressful since it involves only one major source of gratification, the home life. The role of the housewife is unstructured and

41

invisible, with self imposed rather than objective standards of performance...Rather than attaining clearcut goals, women spend more time adjusting to external contingencies (Klerman and Weissman, 1980, p.82).

Thus, if we understand such women as creative and productive human beings, then the 'mental illnesses' they suffer might be understood as the product of the tension between their needs and interests and the debilitating conditions in which they find themselves. Mental distress constitutes the socially constructed reality of their environment, where the disparity between their needs and an oppressive environment results in mental distress. The resulting depression is not simply a product of adverse conditions, but reflects the tension between human needs and the position women find themselves in, and the lack of resources to resolve it.

This argument can be generalised to cover a large range of conditions diagnosed as mental distress. On two major dimensions of power, class and gender, people located at the powerless ends (that is women, and working class) tend to experience high levels of mental distress. Surveys have found that semi-skilled and unskilled manual workers tend to report over 50% more psychological symptoms than non-manual workers (Cochrane, 1983, p.25), overall '...it is clear that in whichever way the evidence is gathered, and whatever index of psychological ill health is used, the findings are consistent that lower social status is associated with a higher risk of psychological problems' (Cochrane, 1983, p.25). Similarly, women tend to report far higher levels of mental distress than men. They outnumber men at all points of psychiatric referral and experience higher rates of admission to mental hospital. For depressive psychotic and psychoneurotic conditions the rate of hospital admission for women is twice that of men (Cochrane, 1983).

'Mental distress', in many (though perhaps not all) of its manifestations, represents a socially constructed phenomenon that is intrinsically related to the nature and development of societies; in this case British capitalism. It is a category that allows for the setting of limits about what constitutes acceptable behaviour, and also allows for the legitimate management of people who 'fail' to perform certain roles. As Cockburn notes:

If capitalism is to survive, each succeeding generation of workers must stay in an appropriate relationship to capital: the relationships of production must be reproduced. Workers must not step outside the relation of the wage, the relation of property, the relation of authority. So reproducing capitalist relations means reproducing the class, ownership, above all reproducing a frame of mind (Cockburn, 1977, p.56).

A comparison of this view with a more conventional position of what constitutes mental distress will help draw out the implications of the analysis being made. Clare (1980) presents perhaps the most sophisticated defence of pyschiatry's conceptualization of mental distress. In an effort to distinguish between mental distress and deviance, he considers the case of the housewife:

> The housewife who is unwilling to leave her house is not necessarily mentally ill. She may have decided that shopping for her husband and family is a slavish and degrading activity, that her role as a housewife is no more than ritualized prostitution, and that as a protest against the persistent devaluation of women in contemporary capitalist society she has decided to withdraw her labour. Such behaviour might well be dubbed deviant. It cannot be termed mental illness. However, if she is unwilling to leave her house not because of such reasons (or not primarily so) but because she is unable to do so without being overwhelmed by terror and panic, then her condition is viewed as a mental disturbance. The psychological part-function which is disturbed in this case is the housewife's affect or mood state. The 'deviant, maladapted, non-conformist behaviour' of refusing to shop is psychiatrically pathological only if it is accompanied by the manifest disturbance of some such psychological function (Clare, 1976, p.30).

What we have analyzed above as an experience of confusion and misery characteristic of a state of powerlessness and suppression of human interests, Clare considers a mood disorder suitable for treatment. Women who are able to resolve the problems they individually face within a patriarchal society, by for example rejecting conventional sex-roles, are not suitable for treatment. But for those, typically working class women, who remain locked into this confused state, then a course of tranquilizers is generally deemed the most appropriate response to their suffering. In this context the role of the psychiatric profession as an agency of social control becomes clear; its remit is to negotiate and manage the 'social construction of reality' of people who 'fail' to successfully perform roles required within society.

The use of theory: explaining the development of community care

We have now identified a number of areas that are of importance when considering the development of mental health service provision. This analysis provides the theoretical backdrop necessary to develop an adequate explanatory understanding of mental health service provision in post-war England and Wales. An important point that has emerged in this discussion concerns the nature of the capitalist social formation, and the exigencies that generates for the state. These exigencies lie within two categories, threats to system integration and threats to social integration. Ultimately these threats, we have argued, must be addressed by the state if only to ensure its own survival. Now bringing our focus specifically upon mental health service provision we might attempt to define more precisely the nature of those threats.

To do this we shall first employ the analysis presented by O'Connor in 'The Fiscal Crisis of the State', in which he attempts to expose contradictory pressures acting on the state that the exigencies deriving from capital accumulation and legitimation create (O'Connor, 1973b). As discussed in Chapter 1, he now accepts that the presentation of the contradiction between accumulation and legitimation was too simplistic. However this is not to suggest that the idea of antagonistic forces acting on the state that it must attempt to manage is redundant. Rather, the implication is that more regard needs to be given to the complexity of forces, and to the element of uncertainty involved in any prediction about how such forces interact.

O'Conner argues that state expenditures serve one or more of two functions.

1. Social Capital: This term refers to '...expenditures that are required for profitable private accumulation and that are indirectly productive.' (O'Conner, 1973a, p.80).

This category is then divided into two sub-sections:

A. Social investment, which '...consists of projects and services that increase the productivity of a given amount of labour-power.' (O'Conner, 1973a, p.80).

B. Social consumption, which '...consists of projects and services that lower the reproduction costs of labour from the stand point of private capital.' (O'Conner, 1973a, p.80).

44

These two categories are derived from Marx, and represent in O'connor's analysis 'social constant capital' and 'social variable capital' respectively. State expenditure on each of these will aid capital accumulation by tending to raise the rate of profit of private capital.

2. Social Expenses: These '...consist of projects and services which are not even indirectly productive, but rather which are required to maintain social harmony, to fulfil the 'legitimization' function of the state. The best example is the welfare system, which is designed chiefly to keep the peace among unemployed workers.' (O'Conner, 1973a, p.80).

Hence this category has quite the opposite characteristics to that of social capital. It is a burden upon private capital, in the sense that it is a drain upon the available pool of surplus value, and the higher it rises the more serious that burden becomes.

Within this analysis O'Conner argues that welfare expenditure is largely a social expense; a burden upon private capital accumulation, necessary to maintain the legitimacy of the capitalist social formation. But as Wright warns the causes, and impact, of state expenditure are varied and can not simply be established theoretically:

> ...the crucial thing to analyse becomes not merely the forces which produce a general expansion of state activity, but also the extent to which those forces selectively expand the unproductive or indirectly productive activities of the state, and the extent to which either surplus-expanding or surplus-absorbing taxation tends to grow more rapidly (Wright, 1975, p.27).

What this implies is that greater attention is required to the detail of just what pressures exist for welfare expenditure, and the particular effect or impact that expenditure has upon the social formation.

For Scull, as we saw in Chapter 1, mental health services are provided in order to deal with deviants; people who refuse to or are unable to participate in wage labour. The services provided constitute surplus-absorbing expenditure, having no benefits for the process of capital accumulation, and as such must be minimised. For O'Conner, as noted above, welfare expenditure also primarily constitutes surplus-absorbing expenditure; or in his own terms, a social expense. These assumptions however are unwarranted. To

45

demonstrate this we shall here simply consider the varied impact that expenditure can, potentially at least, have upon the capitalist social formation, and the potential variety of imperatives generating the need for state expenditures on mental health services. In subsequent Chapters we will investigate these issues more thoroughly with particular regard to the development of the community care policy.

Firstly, and most importantly, state expenditure upon mental health services has, potentially at least, considerable significance for the maintenance of profitable private accumulation; the category of social capital. In our discussion of the concept of mental distress we noted that its definition is related to the current requirements of the capitalist social formation for 'adequately' socialised proletarians. The role of mental health services in this respect is to provide a system with which to deal with those who are unable or unwilling to maintain such behaviour patterns. This role can be understood in terms of lowering 'the reproduction costs of labour from the standpoint of private capital'; the category of social consumption. If we return to our example of the housewife, it is likely to be far cheaper from the point of view of private capital to provide her with psychiatric treatment, thereby allowing her to continue her role as a domestic labourer, than simply allowing her to break down, possibly involving children being taken into care, marriage break-down and so on. Yet at the same time, we have also noted that the experience of mental distress constitutes a condition of extreme misery. It is perhaps obvious to state that many people are concerned with this, desiring that social services are provided to alleviate the problem. Thus mental health services also have a role in securing the legitimacy of the state; in O'Conner's terms, a social expense.

Theoretically at least, there is no reason to assume that mental health services simply constitute a burden upon the process of capital accumulation; expenditure might prove to be surplus-expanding or surplus-absorbing depending upon the particular requirements of capital accumulation and of legitimation at any one time. In addition, any analysis undertaken to examine the impact of mental health service provision upon the capitalist social formation is further complicated by the fact that the state is by no means a passive actor, simply responding to the competing imperatives of accumulation and legitimation. The state actively seeks to influence the environment in which it exists. A key example in this, as we shall examine more closely in Chapter 4, concerns the role the state has taken in actively promoting a view of mental distress as an

46

illness - a view which if accepted, and utilised as an organizational premise for the delivery of mental health services, has substantial implications for the particular impact of mental health services upon the capitalist social formation.

Furthermore, there is no reason to assume that demands for legitimate mental health services will be unilinear. It is now generally accepted, by both Marxist and other writers, that there is no homogeneous working class movement, with clearly thought out lines of analysis about what constitutes oppression and what constitutes emancipation (Mann, 1970; Held, 1983; Coates, 1984; Offe, 1984). This implies that demands for 'legitimate' mental health services may be varied and indeed contradictory. As we shall examine further in Chapter 3 and Chapter 6, groups of workers express varying views over how mental health services should be provided. Pressure groups may or may not accept that mental distress is an illness requiring medical intervention; MIND and the National Schizophrenia Fellowship for example currently disagree strongly on this issue. This suggests therefore, that any consideration of the importance of demands for legitimate service provision must take into account the particular constellation of interests and views at any one time, and most certainly not make any assumption that demands made will necessarily conflict with the needs of profitable capital accumulation.

These points all indicate the importance of empirical research; it is impossible, as the Marxist model attempts, to simply theorise the processes by which the community care policy has developed. Nevertheless, as the Social Democratic model reveals, empirical research without adequate theoretical underpinning is equally flawed. In what follows we attempt to tread this middle ground, between abstract theory and 'abstracted empiricism'. Firstly, we can identify three general factors which the state must acknowledge when developing its mental health policy; cost, control and legitimation.

Cost

If, as we have argued, the state depends upon capital accumulation for its own resources, then clearly the availability of funds to it are limited by the prevailing economic conditions. Further, the state is directed in what projects it can undertake; foremost it must address problems within the accumulation process but of course is only able to extract a certain level of funds before it tends to burden the accumulation process to such a degree that it in any case falters, or

47

indeed collapses. With the massive expansion of capital accumulation that has occurred in the 20th century we might expect to find an increase in the scope for state projects. But with the crises associated with the cycle of boom and slump that has characterised the development of capitalism we might also expect to find the level of available funding for state projects, and the scale of activities required to maintain capital accumulation, might vary considerably. It is this that constitutes the notion of cost, where the state must attempt to survive within the parameters set by the accumulation process pertaining at any one time.

Control

Although the literature on social control is extensive, the particular meaning of the term frequently evades precise definition. On reviewing the relationship between deviance, social control and mental illness, Busfield notes that:

> ...Social control is a loose term that labels some aspect of social interaction as undesirable and suggests there is a manipulation of one individual by another (the more powerful) or one individual by some institutional arrangement or practice. In the case of psychiatry we need, for example, to distinguish the 'social control' that stems from denial of the value-laden nature of notions of mental health and illness from the social control involved in treating problems as individual rather than social in character (Busfield, 1986, pp.110-111).

Furthermore an important question rarely addressed is why control at all? (Mathews, 1987). People, or institutions, do not (generally) 'control' for the fun of it, but because they feel threatened to the point where they consider response is necessary. If we are going to make any sense of the idea of social control we need to examine specific periods and elucidate just what threats there are that require control, if threats to system and social integration are to be avoided. It is in this sense that we need to be clear about the content of the notion of control, before any concern might be had with the form of processes by which such threats are dealt with.

Utilising Habermas' work we have identified four crisis tendencies to which late capitalist societies are prone. The more precise nature and strength of these in post-war England and Wales will be investigated later, but first we need to detail the general link between mental illness and these types of crisis tendency. The key notion with which to do this is proletarianization. That is to say, proletarian status within late capitalist society constitutes the 'appropriate' patterns of attitudes and behaviour necessary within the mass of the population necessary for the continued reproduction of the social formation. This does not just involve turning up for work at the correct time, and providing a designated amount of labour power, but also concerns cultural norms concerning for example gender roles, attitudes to consumption, leisure, the family and so on.

Using the definition of mental distress presented earlier, we can establish links between such a condition and threats to both system and social integration. Taking the example of the housewife presented earlier, a variety of threats can be seen to occur. If she fails to provide unpaid domestic labour, to raise children as a new proletarian generation, and to service her husband's sexual and emotional needs, then threats to economic and cultural reproduction arise. Just which of the four crises tendencies might most be exacerbated is an open question, for the state - as we have seen - has some scope for manoeuver between playing one of against the other. But such room for manoeuver is constrained the more present 'mental illness' is amongst the proletariat, and the attempt to remove those constraints constitutes the content of control processes.

Legitimation

Since the early 1970s the concept of legitimation has been frequently appealed to in order to support a range of propositions about what the state can and cannot do. It is frequently held, within a range of perspectives, that 'The Limits of Legitimacy' (Wolfe, 1977) set parameters to state action that it ignores at its peril; the loss of legitimacy being something that gives rise to threats to social integration (Mishra, 1984, pp.221-250). The importance attached to the concept of legitimacy reached its zenith in the late 1970s, as the post-war consensus broke down. However, with the reconstruction of a state project, based around the ideas of the New Right, there has been some criticism voiced over the deterministic assumptions made about the dire consequences likely to arise if legitimacy was lost. In a review of this, Taylor-Gooby notes:

> Earlier writers who discussed the crisis in the interventionist state, emphasised the inability of capitalist governments to resolve the balance of pressures on them, turn which way they might. The central point of the new approach is that specific

49

policies, attacking state welfare, enable governments to satisfy the demands of ideology and capitalism and to maintain stability. The reversal of public opinion puts the state back in command (Taylor-Gooby, 1985, pp.19-20).

This is not to suggest that the notion of legitimacy is entirely misplaced, but rather that the assumptions made about its pertinence have tended to be too deterministic. With the ready appeal to national symbols such as the Royal Family, and national enterprises such as the Falklands war, the legitimacy of the state is clearly not dependant solely upon on pursuing economic and social policies that meet mass demands. Certainly there are points of potential tension between the need for legitimacy and certain activities of the state, but whether or not such tensions become pertinent has proven difficult to theorise. This suggests that the question over what the 'limits of legitimacy' are remains, at least in part, an empirical one.

These three factors, cost, control and legitimation, represent three exigencies bearing on the state that it must attempt to deal with when developing its mental health policy. Their exact content and importance is a matter for empirical investigation - something pursued in subsequent Chapters - but we can at this point at least posit the possibility that certain antagonistic tendencies will exist amongst them. This can be detailed as follows.

Cost and control

In our discussion of cost we argued that the state is constrained by the accumulation process, in terms of the funds it has available with which to make and implement policies. We also argued that those policies must be directed at maintaining the accumulation process. At the same time however the need to maintain control places a burden upon state expenditures. The state is compelled by its own interests to provide mental health services, but must do so within the constraints imposed by the cost criterion.

At a theoretical level this is not necessarily a contradictory process, in terms of cost and control imposing wholly antagonistic requirements upon the state. It may be for example that sufficient tax revenues are derived from capital accumulation such that expenditure on mental health services can be accommodated. Moreover the impact of mental health services may have a beneficial impact on capital accumulation by improving the efficiency of the proletariat. The simple point however is that both must be addressed, and that at certain times there may be problems in doing so. If state finances are severely constrained by the cost criterion, then this will generate considerable problems for maintaining control.

Cost and legitimation

The requirement placed on the state that its policies should at least appear legitimate has cost implications. For mental health policy to appear legitimate it must be adequately funded, such that the claims about the benevolent intent of psychiatric intervention has some credibility. Without such legitimation, criticism of the state itself might be expected to develop, and hence irrespective of whether the state can afford to fund legitimate mental health services, it will be strongly impelled to do so.

Again we need to be careful about the importance attached to this theoretical proposition. There is no reason to assume the state will be faced with any major problem in finding sufficient revenue to fund legitimate mental health services. Equally, it may be that changing the way in which mental health services are organised and delivered could result in costs being reduced while retaining legitimacy. Thus once more we face primarily an empirical question concerning whether this antagonism ever becomes of consequence to the state.

Control and legitimation

The exercise of control, through the provision of mental health services, conflicts with the claims of the state to represent all interests within society. For the exigencies compelling the state to exercise control, as we have seen, are basically in the interests of capital. Thus the democratic, and legitimate, form of the state conflicts with the content of its policies. It is precisely for this reason that control is exercised indirectly, through the social construction of mental illness and its subsequent 'treatment'. While it is an empirical question as to what effect a loss of legitimacy would have on the state if the benevolent veneer of mental health services broke down, it is nevertheless the case that control and legitimation exist as opposing exigencies on the state in relation to mental health service provision.

Our concern now is with how this can be applied to the specific problem of developing an explanatory understanding of mental health policy in post-war England and Wales. The contention to be developed here is that a model of social policy development presented by Offe (1984) improves upon the models we reviewed in Chapter 1, and provides a basis upon which to proceed to a more adequate analysis. First, then, we need to briefly examine the argument he makes.

We saw earlier that Offe develops an analysis of the state in which he argues it must support continued capital accumulation, if only to ensure its own survival. Taking this further, he argues that state social policy is concerned with addressing two sets of problems:

> ...we seek to defend the thesis that the explanation of social policy must indeed take into account as causal factors both 'demands' and 'systemic requirements', that is, problems of 'social integration' and 'system integration' (Lockwood), the political processing of both class conflict and the crises of the accumulation process (Offe, 1984, p.103).

The maintenance of system and social integration is problematic because of the contradictions within and between these spheres of the capitalist social formation. It is this that Offe refers to as the 'meta-problem':

> ...the 'meta-problem'...may be summed up by this question: how can strategies of social policy be developed and existing institutions modernized so that there can be satisfaction of both the political demands 'licensed' in the context of the prevailing political rights of the working class and the foreseeable exigencies and labour and budgetary prerequisites of the accumulation process? (Offe, 1984, p.104).

The meta-problem, then, refers to environmental exigencies to which the state is subject. Taking this a stage further, Offe argues that the state must attempt to make these pressures compatible, if only to avoid threats to its own survival. But of course this process of reconciliation is a difficult one because of the potentially contradictory nature of the exigencies to which the state is subject. The problem for the state in its policy making process is how to achieve 'internal rationalization'. That is, how to develop policies that successfully make compatible antagonistic aspects of the meta-problem.

For the state, the issue is not so much about how to solve problems within its environment as such, but rather 'The problem to which state policy development in the social policy domain reacts is that of the precarious compatibility of its own institutions and performances.' (Offe,1984, p.104). This point marks an important distinction between Offe's analysis and the Marxist model we reviewed earlier. For we are not concerned here with a capitalist state reacting to the problem of the working class, but rather a state in capitalism that attempts to constitute the working class for its own interests-a process we referred to earlier as proletarianization.

The final leg of this model concerns the impact of policy initiatives. This may for example concern the allocation of rewards through the taxation system, or it might less directly set the terms of conflicts by empowering some social groups and/or disempowering others. Consideration of this area is required in order to establish the eventual impact of policy developments; something that may be very different from what was wanted or intended. The results of policy initiatives, successful or otherwise, will then be a significant factor over time in establishing the policy making environment that the state must constantly seek to deal with.

To summarize, then, we can analyze the policy making process in the following terms. First, the state is faced with a set of problems that it must make compatible (these being based on the conflicting needs and demands that we have analyzed in terms of cost, control and legitimation). Second it must devise policies to achieve this and implement them. Third, these policies will have an impact (anticipated or otherwise) that will alter the balance of the meta problem being faced (either for better or worse). We are then back to the first stage of a set of problems facing the state. While we might conceive the process in this way, all three stages are of course occurring simultaneously, with a constant interplay between state and society. In terms of analysis however this method of identifying various stages allows us to examine systematically the process by which mental health services evolve. Thus we now need to establish how to apply this analytical model to specific historical periods. Again we will utilise Offe's work here. He posits three processes of analysis when examining social policy, which we can utilise here in a discussion more specifically of mental health policy.

Firstly, '...it must be shown that, when the modalities of the generation, financing and distribution of social policy activities are altered, the actors in the state apparatus actually find themselves in the dilemma of reconciling 'licensed' demands or recognized needs, on the one hand, with the perceived 'exigencies' or tolerance of the capitalist economy for 'unproductive' social policy expenditure, on the other hand'. (Offe, 1984, p.107). What this means for an analysis of mental health services is that the criteria of cost, control and legitimation must be shown to be of significance to the state, and that as their significance changes over time the state is compelled to address the newly arising problems of incompatibility.

If indeed it can be established that state social policy innovations can be linked with threats of social and system disintegration, then Offe argues '...the second step is to identify the solution strategies that-aside from the specific themes and tactics of political self-representation that tend to accompany such innovations-are applied within the administration itself to the consistency problem - a problem that is usually not designated as such.' (Offe, 1984, p.107). This task, then, concerns identifying the processes of administrative rationalisation that the state undertakes in an attempt to regain compatibility of the contradictory aspects of the meta-problem. As Offe notes, this may well be conducted at an ideological level that mystifies the 'real' processes of conflict that are occurring. Finally, '...there must be an uncovering of the 'external effects' of such solution strategies, there more or less latent benefits and burdens, the consequent increases and decreases of power, together with the pattern of conflict that strategically guides the process of socially implementing social policy innovation.' (Offe, 1984, p.107). What this means, is that the policy impact - rather than the policy output - needs to be examined and assessed with regard to how successfully the 'meta-problem' has been addressed. In the case of mental health services, it concerns assessing how successfully cost, control and legitimation have been made compatible in comparison to what might have been the case without policy innovations being made.

In the following Chapters, these three tasks will be undertaken with regard to mental health services in England and Wales since 1948. In particular two periods, 1948 to 1963 and 1975 to the present day, will be examined and it will be argued that key developments and changes can be identified in these periods. Overall, the argument to be developed is that the explanatory model developed in this Chapter provides an adequate basis on which to explain how and why the community care policy arose.

3 The socio-economic context of mental health services, 1948–1963

To examine the context of mental health policy making in the immediate post-war period we shall, following the model presented in Chapter 2, consider the twin areas of the 'meta-problem' and the 'compatibility problem'. The meta-problem refers to the environment in which the state operates, and which determines the demands made upon it, and the resources available to deal with those demands. In our discussion of Habermas' 'Legitimation Crisis' we noted four crisis tendencies, two in the domain of system integration and two in the domain of social integration. We will now utilise these to organise a discussion of the meta-problem facing the state in the 1948 to 1963 period. Taking system integration first, we start by examining the possibility of an economic crisis within the economic sub-system, and a rationality crisis in the political-administrative sub-system. Following this we examine the possibility of a legitimation crisis, and a motivation crisis, within the domain of social integration. Having considered the importance of these, we examine the extent to which the state is faced with a problem of making the three criteria of cost, control and legitimation compatible.

Economic crisis tendencies

We begin our account just three years after the end of the Second World War, in which Britain's world dominance had been brought to a sudden end (Gamble, 1981, p.103). Moreover, a serious economic downturn in the winter of 1947 had briefly lifted unemployment to over two million, and war time austerity measures such as rationing and controls over industry were still much in evidence. However, despite these difficulties the reconstruction of British industry was in fact successfully underway. The new industries, such as electrical engineering,cars and chemicals, had all been firmly established by 1950, and Britain still held one quarter of world trade.

This improvement in the performance of the British economy continued, and was in fact to represent the start of the 'long boom' when 'For twenty-five years after 1948 the capitalist section of the world economy experienced a quite unprecedented and unbroken period of economic growth.' (Coates, 1984, p.26). The British economy grew at a faster rate in the 1950s than at any time previously in the 20th century, averaging 3.5% per annum for 1950 to 1955, and 2.3% per annum for the remainder of the decade (Coates, 1984, p.27). Moreover this growth was accompanied by very low levels of unemployment, remaining between 1.2% and 2.3%. Inflation was also low, staying at or below 5% other than for a brief period in the early 1950s when it reached 9% (Madgwick, 1982, pp.82-83). The main economic difficulty experienced by successive post-war governments was occasional balance of payments problems. These resulted in a series of financial crises, in 1949, 1951, 1955, 1957 and 1961. However, even these were of relatively small proportion, with the balance of payments gap rarely exceeding 5%; an amount easily made up by the surplus on invisible trade (Gamble, 1981, p.114).

If the story of Britain's absolute economic performance in this period is one of some success, it is nevertheless the case that its relative condition (when compared to other core capitalist countries) continued to decline. While Britain experienced a booming economy, others did even better.

Table 3.1
Economic growth 1950-1965 (annual percentage rate)

	1950-55	1955-60	1960-65
OECD	5.7	3.9	5.9
USA	5.0	2.4	5.8
EEC	8.2	6.7	5.6
JAPAN	18.0	16.0	11.6
GB	3.5	2.3	3.2

Source: Coates 1984, p.27.

Britain experienced a lower rate of economic growth than all its main competitors. Between 1950 and 1976 productivity in Britain grew at an annual average rate of 2.8%, while France experienced a growth rate of 4.9%, Germany a growth rate of 5.8%, and Italy a growth rate of 5.3% (Gamble, 1981, p.20). These trends are reflected in the percentage share of world trade that Britain managed to hold over the immediate post-war period. In 1950 Britain still held 25.5% of world trade, but by 1960 this had fallen to 16.5%, and by 1970 to 10.8% (Gamble, 1981, p.21).

Between 1948 and 1963 Britain's economic condition appears extremely favourable, with the major targets of full employment, sustained growth, low inflation and a positive balance of payments all being achieved. Yet underlying this, Britain's relative economic position was in decline. Increases in productivity and economic growth in Britain were relatively low. This relative decline of British industry suggests that future economic problems may increase, but in the immediate post-war period this decline had little real effect. As such, it would seem that the structural space available to the British state in which to develop policy in this period was expanding, in as much as economic growth provided a basis for the state to raise larger revenues, and so increase its policy options.

Rationality crisis tendencies

A rationale for state action must never be assumed to exist, particularly within capitalist societies where the competing interests of capital and labour presents antagonistic demands and needs. Indeed this point is well illustrated by the history of Britain immediately prior to the period we are considering here. Between the First and Second World Wars the British state was uncertain how to manage the social reproduction of a capitalist society experiencing its worst ever depression. The dominant neo-classical economic ideas of the day derived from a past era, and were found totally inappropriate to conditions of slump. When demand was less than supply, and social dislocation was massively apparent, the rationale for reducing state expenditure was a difficult proposition for governments to accept, yet no other course of action seemed feasible. Perhaps the most famous expression of this came in 1931, when the besieged minority Labour government fell apart as it failed to agree on a course of action; reducing public expenditure on benefits appeared the only available path, yet it was unacceptable.

Coming closer to 1948, however, we find that a new rationale for state action develops rapidly. A major impetus to this was the experience of total war between 1939 and 1945. Firstly, in war, particularly a total war of the scale faced, the state is faced with increasing pressures to organise on a massive scale to deal with the crisis situation. Action, which previously may not have been acceptable, is now perceived as necessary. As Marshall notes:

> ...total war obliges governments to assume new and heavier responsibilities for the welfare of their people, especially by controlling the production and distribution of scarce necessities, like food and fuel, and by looking after those who have been made homeless by invasion, evacuation, or aerial bombardment. The experience of total war is bound to have an effect on both the principles of social policy and the methods of social administration (Marshall, 1967, p.75).

Secondly, the British state was compelled during the Second World War to acknowledge the interests and demands of labour, in an effort to incorporate the mass of the population into the war effort. Gamble goes so far as to argue that 'The war established social democracy in Britain. The patient strategy of containment of the Labour movement finally broke down as German tanks poured into France...The working class now exerted more pressure on government.' (Gamble, 1981, pp.103-105). The threats posed by war, then, provided the basis for a new post-war settlement that was less autocratic than previously existed.

With changing pressures came changing ideas about the role and capabilities of the state. Most notably, Keynes and Beveridge are associated with this. Keynes' economic ideas were not new. He had in the inter-war period demonstrated in his 'The General Theory of Employment, Interest and Money' the fragility of Say's law - that supply creates its own demand - and presented policy prescriptions on how governments should manage the economy (Keynes, 1936). He argued that the state should actively manage demand, reducing or increasing public expenditure in inverse proportion to the level of demand within the economy. But it was only with the experience of total war that these ideas were actively taken up. Especially as post-war reconstruction came on to the agenda, where the promise of reform was paramount, Keynes took an active role in formulating government economic policy. The White Paper on Full Employment (1944) embodied this new thinking, reflecting the general acceptance of an extended role for government in managing the economy with the aim of maintaining full employment and economic growth.

The ideas underlying the 'social' component of the post-war settlement were largely contained in the Beveridge Report (1942). It presented a comprehensive package of reforms providing insurance against the hazards of a market economy; 'Universality of population coverage, comprehensiveness of risks covered, adequacy of benefits and the citizenship notion of the social services (provided as of right to all and not as a form of charity to the few) were the hallmarks of this approach.'(Mishra, 1984, p.7). The proposed reforms were presented in detail, and made explicit the need for government intervention to make such proposals a reality.

Clearly, the 'economic' and 'social' aspects of this package did not exist in isolation. Rather, economic management would provide the basis for provision of improved welfare benefits, and in turn the new Welfare State would help manage the mass of the population, which in turn would benefit economic production. It was this complementarity which provided the strength of a new rationale for the state, that contrasts so strongly with what had gone before.

This reformulation of the state's rationale had a considerable impact upon the conduct of political parties in the immediate post-war period. The two parties of government, Labour and Conservative, tended to converge over issues of how to govern the country. The consensus was based upon a general satisfaction with the performance of the economy, with both the Labour and Conservative parties advocating the use of Keynesian demand management techniques. Despite the radical nature of the Labour governments of 1945-51, when the major institutions of the Welfare State were created and many of the basic industries nationalized, the three Conservative administrations that followed had little difficulty accepting these changes. Indeed so strong was this convergence of thinking that the term 'Butskellism' came to be used to describe government economic management of this period (after the Conservative Chancellor, Butler, and his Labour predecessor, Gaitskell).

It is perhaps worth noting some dissension existed. On the Right, Friedman and Hayek both deplored the new consensus, arguing that it would lead to 'serfdom' and economic ruin (Mishra, 1984, p.1). Moreover, in the mid-1950s as austerity gave way to an 'age of affluence', some criticism developed that collective provision was no longer needed and that people should be free to spend on whatever services they desired. Influential writers such as Galbraith argued that poverty was now a marginal problem, this providing the basis for such critiques.

But these ideas were not in keeping with their time. Towards the end of the 1950s a new generation of social researchers were beginning to have impact. In Britain Titmuss and Townsend highlighted the relative poverty of large numbers of people for whom the welfare state had not proven the panacea it was intended to be. Thus the consensus based around the ideas of Keynes and Beveridge reasserted itself. Writing in the mid-1960s, Marshall reflects this; '...the issues at stake in the sixties turned out to be less concerned with social ideology than with social engineering.'(Marshall, 1967, p.97). So firmly established is the new rationale of the state, that Marshall feels confident enough to argue that critical discussion of it lies beyond reasonable argument.

This review of economic and rationality crisis tendencies indicates that few serious threats to system integration existed in the immediate post-war period. The threats that did exist could be ameliorated within the available 'structural space', and with available management techniques. Dissension was peripheral to the more fundamental reality of the successful reconstruction of a state project based around the central pillars of Keynes and Beveridge. This is not to suggest that the state's position had been entirely stabilised, as Taylor-Gooby notes, '...if there was a substantial measure of political consensus on the foundation of the welfare state, consensus was something that contained real political conflicts.' (Taylor-Gooby, 1985, p.59). The point however is that these conflicts were in the main latent, and hence exerted little immediate influence on the state.

Legitimation crisis tendencies

The post-war settlement based on the proposals of Keynes and Beveridge was, as we have seen, viable for the state to implement. This appears to have provided the state considerable legitimacy. In the late 1950s and 1960s several political commentators developed the argument that a consensus existed concerning the basic organisation of society; the so called 'end of ideology' thesis. Representing this position, Lipset argued that '...the fundamental political problems of the industrial revolution have been solved: the workers have achieved industrial and political citizenship; the conservatives have accepted the welfare state; the democratic left has recognised that an increase in overall state power carries with it more dangers to freedom than solutions for economic problems'

(Lipset, 1963, pp.442-443). Butler and Stokes reach similar conclusions. They argue that the importance of class conflict in British society diminished substantially as a result of economic prosperity and developments in welfare provision (Butler and Stokes, 1974). Developing a less sanguine analysis, Marcuse argued that the absence of conflict is based upon the development of coercion within society, rather than normative agreement (Marcuse, 1964). However the results - increased stability of the political system - are the same.

This view of Britain as a society characterised by a political consensus was strongly supported by Almond and Verba in their 'The Civic Culture', the first nationwide survey of political attitudes undertaken by academics (Almond and Verba, 1963). They found that British people generally accepted the legitimacy of the state's authority, and supported the system of government. The study provided empirical evidence to substantiate claims about the stability and consensual nature of the British political system in the immediate post-war period. It revealed that the British political system enjoyed a high level of support. On being questioned about what features of Britain they were most proud of, almost a half of respondents mentioned - without prompting - the system of government and political institutions.

The legitimacy afforded the political system reflected in the experiences of the main political parties. The Conservative Party, which held office between 1951 and 1964, sustained considerable political support with its 'one nation' style of conservatism. It presided over a period of sustained economic growth, while at the same time witnessing an unprecedented rise in the consumption of material goods by the mass of the population. This growth was based upon rising real wages. Between 1949 and 1963 manual workers weekly wages rose on average almost 5% per annum, while the general index of retail prices rose on average by some 4% (Madgwick, 1982, pp.82-83). Thus, after winning consecutive elections in 1951 and 1955 the Conservative Prime Minister, Harold Macmillan, was able in 1959 to declare to the nation that they had 'never had it so good', and win a third successive term in office in that year.

For the Labour Party, as now, such Tory success resulted in deep divisions and argument. In an effort to find new electoral popularity a strong 'revisionist' element emerged, which sought to acknowledge the changes being wrought in society, and bring the Labour Party up to date. For their main representative, Anthony Crosland, this meant a wholesale revision of the socialist position. He argued

61

that the combination of Keynes and Beveridge had brought about a fundamental change to the capitalist social order, such that no necessary relations of exploitation existed:

> ...today traditional capitalism has been reformed and modified almost out of existence, and it is with a quite different form of society that socialists must now concern themselves. Pre-war anti-capitalism will give us very little help (Crosland, 1956, p.97).

The manner in which the Labour Party sought to embrace the supposedly new dawn reflects the considerable legitimacy of the state's position, for it appeared to many within the Party that substantial social reform was possible and indeed actually occurring. An examination of patterns of voting helps explain the legitimacy of this 'middle ground' of political life. Although the Conservatives were in government for some 13 years, the Labour Party maintained substantial support. Its electoral standing remained relatively high, receiving not less than 34.5% of the vote and some 258 seats in parliament in each of the three general elections held in the 1950s. (Madgwick, 1982, pp.4-5). Moreover, the Labour and Conservative parties shared a substantial majority of the overall vote. In the February 1950 election, they shared 77.5% of the 86.5% of the electorate who voted, and in 1959 they shared 73.3% of the 78.3% who voted. This dominance reflected in their share of seats in parliament, with their being no more than 9 MPs sitting for other parties between 1950 and 1964 (Madgwick, 1982, pp.4-5).

This legitimacy was also aided by the decline of threats to the state. With an apparent decline in the importance of class as a dimension of conflict, the old labour/capital divide was argued to no longer represent a major dimension of conflict. This was perhaps overly stressed by some writers at the time. Kerr (1962) argued that industrial development across the whole world were bringing about the convergence of diverse societies. The result would be the development of 'pluralistic industrialism', where the occupational status of groups replaced class as the basis of conflict. But while being overstated, it does reflect a perceived decline in the importance of class conflict. Secondly, the conception of a better alternative had evaporated. In the 1930s with Britain in economic depression, the Soviet Union powering ahead in economic and social reform had in contrast appeared relatively attractive. But in the post-war period conditions in Britain appeared massively improved, while the Soviet example of actual socialism had been heavily tarnished by Stalin's tyrannical leadership. There was therefore few apparent alternatives, even if the British proletariat held any inclination towards them.

The claims being made for the post-war settlement were that capitalism had been stabilized and could be successfully managed to ensure constant growth. This would help increase opportunities for the mass of the population, and ensure high employment and rising living standards. Moreover, it was claimed that a tendency towards greater equality was built into this such that extremes of poverty would cease to exist. This, it was widely believed, would sustain a high level of legitimacy for the state. Now it would be wrong to attempt to prove with the benefit of hindsight that this was necessarily false, but such hindsight does at least help clarify the issues. Perhaps most importantly it is clear that the nature of the capitalist social formation had not been fundamentally changed. Keynes was no revolutionary, his aim had been to provide a means of socialising demand and expenditure, rather than supply and ownership. As Gamble notes:

> As understood and practiced by the Treasury, Keynesianism meant a policy of manipulating the total level of demand to correct the tendency that markets had, if left to themselves, to produce unemployment and stagnation. Beyond such 'fine tuning' no interference with individual decisions on investment, prices or output were contemplated (Gamble, 1981, p.121).

In as much as British capitalism had been subject to cycles of boom and slump, and no fundamental changes had been wrought, this suggests that the legitimacy enjoyed was unstable, and would require maintenance by the state if it was to endure.

Further to this, we should also avoid simply accepting the optimism of the 'end of ideology' theorists concerning the stability of the political system. On re-examining the data collected in the 1950s and 1960s, Held questions whether it really warrants the conclusion that consensus was the dominant feature of British political life (Held,1984). He notes for example that in the study conducted by Almond and Verba only 46% of British respondents expressed pride in the system of government, and of these it might easily be the case that they would wish for something better. Thus he argues that '...any claim about widespread adherence to a common value system needs to be treated with the utmost scepticism.' (Held, 1984, p.308), and concludes that the consensus of the immediate post-war period is best characterised as 'instrumental consent'. This involves no more than compliance with the social order providing that expectations of an improving quality of life are met (Held, 1984, p.308). This implies that people did not simply accept political authority without question. Rather, acceptance was conditional and liable to be withdrawn if and when the promise of reform failed to be realized. With economic growth in the 1950s and 1960s this condition was adequately met; 'Prosperity helped sustain the illusion that the acquiescence of the mass of people meant legitimacy of the political and social order.' (Held, 1984, p.310). But of course the implication of this is that should the government fail to maintain economic growth, then the legitimacy of the political system might rapidly diminish.

Motivation crisis tendencies

The concept of a motivation crisis concerns the extent to which patterns of meaning are constructed and accepted within the general population, with which social roles and purposeful action are maintained. At all times it might be expected that patterns of both fragmentation and integration are occurring as societies develop and change. Moreover simply to identify changes in patterns of motivation may not necessarily indicate any necessary tendency to crisis, in terms of threatening the organization principle of a society. We need therefore to be cautious about the propositions that we develop. However in the 1948-63 period there was clearly considerable change occurring, which had demonstrable effect upon motivation patterns. As we shall see below there are two clear phases in this process; the first witnessing the end of an older moral order, and the second the beginning of a new and more diverse set of moral codes.

In an analysis of the 1914-55 period Bedarida argues that the experiences and attitudes of different social classes varied considerably. He suggests that until the mid-1950s the lower middle class were characterised by a desire to belong to the established order.

In spite of their central position in the social scale they were acutely conscious of having no influence in the world of politics, society or the press, where all the seats of power were preempted by the middle of upper middle classes. They were conscious too of their powerlessness in the face of economic forces which they were quite unable to influence...Their reaction to these frustrations was a wide adoption of various kinds of conformity: political-hence their unfailing support for the Conservative Party between the wars; social-the cult of respectability was a fetish; moral-their strict adherence to a puritanical strictness of behaviour; religious-assiduous attendance at an Anglican church or a Nonconformist chapel (Bedarida, 1979, p.209).

The working class in contrast was constituted by the place it held in the relations of production.

Their outlook was confined by factory discipline to the dull performance of dull repetitive tasks. In this world of unchanging monotony consciousness of class, or belonging to a community that shared identical work, and even more, identical destiny, was keen and enduring (Bedarida, 1979, p.209).

While such attitudes persisted into the 1950s (Bedarida, 1979, p.208) there was nevertheless fundamental change occurring in the experiences of working class people. In the 1940s full employment returned, there was some increase in the level of real wages, and some increase in security provided by increased welfare provision. In the interwar period the working week remained at around 48 hours, but after the Second World War fell to 44 1/2 hours and by 1968 had fallen further to 40 1/2 hours (Bedarida, 1979, pp. 212-213). For both the working and middle classes, other changes in society were also affecting their outlook on life. The increasing use of methods of birth control was giving women greater control over their own lives. In the middle of the 19th century one married women in six used some method of contraception, whereas between 1920 and 1940 it had increased to three out of four (Bedarida, 1979, p.228).

Other fundamental changes in personal life included the increasing numbers of broken families. Rates of divorce had shown a tendency to increase throughout the first half of the 20th century. In the last quarter of the 19th century the annual average of petitions filed did not exceed 700, but by the early 1920s this figure had increased to 3,000 and by the early 1940s to 16,000. This trend continued after the Second World War, reaching a peak of 47,041 petitions filed in 1947, whereafter the numbers dropped to between 26,000 and 30,000 through the 1950s. Only in the early 1960s did the trend once more start to rise, by 1962 reaching 34,625 (Marsh, 1965, p.36). A further important change in personal life was the impact of religion which had over the first half of the twentieth century greatly diminished; 'The great 'sea of faith', which once covered the country, had ebbed until nothing was left but little pools in the midst of deserts of indifference or of marshlands where religion survived only in the shape of religiosity.' (Bedarida, 1979, pp. 241-242).

Until the mid-1950s there was little evidence of any great changes in patterns of motivation; patterns of integration were as apparent, if not more so, than patterns of fragmentation. This balance was however to swing dramatically over the next few years; 'Around 1955-6 English society was suddenly hit by a wave of change and from then onward driven on a new course that was to transform the atmosphere of the country within a few years. This happened without warning.' (Bedarida, 1979, p.249). With improving standards of living British society moved from an 'age of austerity' to an 'age of affluence', and with it came a new set of cultural influences that contrasted strongly with preceding decades.

In a review of the cultural forms of the post-war period, Marwick indicates a number of changes that might be considered significant. In novels and poetry he detects a trend toward a more introspective mood, and a concern with the 'trivialities of daily life' (Marwick, 1982, p.84). The theatre and cinema enjoyed a revival with some new modes of expression emerging, perhaps the most well known being the 'angry young men' who through their work '...cocked a snook at the comfortable and flowery conventions of the post-war literary scene and also at the comfortable platitudes of consensus politics...' (Marwick, 1982, p.101). John Osborne's play 'Look Back in Anger', first performed in 1956, is perhaps the best known of this genre. In the late 1940s and the early 1950s theatres in London had been dominated by American musicals and plays, but with the performance of this new work this dominance was broken, with increased emphasis being given to plays focussing on social issues of the day. (Lloyd, 1970).

A common theme in these areas of social life does seem to be an interest in questioning the nature of social values and roles; to examine the political nature of the personal. Such a theme, though, can only be considered important if it finds a more general representation in society, and certainly there is some evidence to suggest it did. An important example of this was the changes in youth groups;

> Gangs of adolescent, and even younger children, were nothing new; but the post-war years provided a jagged, brittle world,

with the sanctions of war removed...With the early 1950s there came the first nationally recognised figure representative of youths detachment from the rest of society and representative also of the fact that for the first time working class youth could take the initiative: the Teddy Boy (Marwick, 1982, p.76).

This laid the ground for further developments in youth culture in the 1960s. The mods, followed by the rockers in the early 1960s, were themselves passed over by the hippies and skinheads in the mid to late 1960s.

And if that represented one form of protest and change, so to did the formation of the Campaign for Nuclear Disarmament in 1958, which enjoyed much initial success in its protest about nuclear weapons. Although very different in nature, being a more middle class phenomenon, Bedarida maintains that '...it made a deep impression on the whole generation.' (Bedarida, 1979, p.259). Also within the middle-class, the late 1950s saw the emergence of the New Left. Based in the universities, this was a group of young left-wing intellectuals who sought to open up new ground to social and political thought. Ethical and aesthetic, as well as social questions, were increasingly opened up to a process of public questioning. Reflecting this less self-assured view of the world, Bedarida maintains that a substantial decline in national pride and patriotic feeling occurred in the 1950s; '...as the memory of the war faded, as the nature of world problems changes, as a new generation knowing little of the glory of the past grew up, the accumulation of self-confidence began to drain away and self-doubt took its place.' (Bedarida, 1979, p.252). In this respect the Suez crisis in 1956 was a turning point, as the limits of Britain's power on the world stage was dramatically brought to prominence.

At a variety of levels the motivation patterns of society were being opened to question, with old assumptions about social roles losing their aura of solidity. Overall, on reviewing these changes, Marwick concludes that 'In absolute terms there was an expansion at all levels of society in opportunities for entertainment, for intellectual stimulus, and for refreshment of the spirit.' (Marwick, 1982, p.101).

It would be a mistake however to suggest any unilinear pattern of development in all of this. For example, the new popular music industry which might have posed some threat was quickly absorbed by capital as a profitable money-spinning venture. Respect for the civil authority of the state remained strong. A study conducted int he early 1950s found some 73% of men and 74% of women thought highly of the police, and few were critical of the force as an institution (Marwick, 1982, p.110). Although Lloyd does suggest that respect for the police did tend to decline amongst the middle class in the 1950s. In particular, with the increasing number of cars on the road, 'This friendly relationship was weakened by the problem of motoring offences...' (Lloyd, 1970, p.360).

Perhaps of greatest importance however when examining patterns of integration in the immediate post-war period is the emergence, associated with the 'age of affluence', of a strong consumerist ethos in the mid-1950s. Hoggart argues that the growth of the mass media in the 1950s, including the rapid increase in publications and the introduction of commercial television, tended to erode local, working class culture, and to replace it with a shallow cultural form that lacked roots in people's experience of life; 'Most mass-entertainments are in the end what D.H. Lawrence described as 'anti-life'. They are full of a corrupt brightness, or improper appeals and moral evasions.' (Hoggart, 1958, p.282). The result, he contends, is a tendency towards uniformity within working class culture based around a passive acceptance of manufactured images; '...at present the older, the more narrow but also the more genuine class culture is being eroded in favour of the mass opinion, the mass recreational product and the generalized emotional response.' (Hoggart, 1958, p. 285). Such an image is captured by C. Wright Mills in his analysis of the evolution of the 'cheerful robot' (Mills, 1959).

Hoggart does not argue that this new form of mass culture is simply assimilated by working class communities; '...the old social-class distinctions still has some force.' (Hoggart, 1958, p.284). But he does maintain that considerable cultural change is occurring, resulting in increasing tension in how people organise their lives. This, he maintains, gives rise to '...the peculiarly inner and individual nature of this crisis.' (Hoggart, 1958, p.287).

Perhaps the clearest point to emerge from this review of changes in patterns of motivation in the immediate post-war period is that varied forces were at work, which had varied effects. Changes in patterns of motivation were multilinear; we can identify both increasing fragmentation and increasing integration. Furthermore, it is not altogether clear how the evidence of changing patterns of motivation should be interpreted. Habermas, as we saw earlier, places considerable importance upon such developments, arguing that they help generate the space for critical reflection on capitalist social relations. But Hearns in a review of the evidence, argues that although there is strong evidence to support the view that motivation patterns are subject to erosion in late capitalism, the assumption that this undermines social integration is erroneous. Rather, he contends that it tends to result in 'adaptive narcissism', where 'Social conflicts and problems are shifted to the level of psychic conflicts and personal problems, and the legitimacy of the self rather than the legitimacy of the prevailing socio-political arrangements is called into question.' (Hearns, 1979, p.133).

However, rather than attempt to develop a unilinear analysis of just what is implied by the erosion of patterns of motivation, it is perhaps more realistic to expect to see a variety of responses deriving from individuals own social construction of their existence. Following this through, a range of responses including adherence to a consumerist ideology, narcissistic conditions as suggested by Hearns, or further alternatives, might be expected to develop.

The compatibility problem

Having examined the nature and extent of threats to social and system integration we now need, following the model developed in Chapter 2, to begin to focus our analysis upon the pressures acting upon the state when making mental health policy. We need, therefore, to review the importance of the three exigencies of cost, control and legitimation. This will provide us with a basis on which to assess the nature of the compatibility problem facing the state.

Cost

The questions we are seeking to answer here are what financial pressures did the state find itself subject to in the 1948-63 period? was there a lack of finance to meet its commitments? and of course in particular, what implications did this have for the financing of mental health services? A major characteristic of all advanced capitalist societies in the 20th century has been the growth in the share of gross national product (GNP) appropriated and spent by the state. Furthermore, within this growing expenditure there has been a tendency for expenditure on social services to take an increasingly large proportion, and in this Britain is no exception.

Now as we saw earlier,this rising trend in the costs of welfare expenditure, and in state expenditure generally, led Scull to argue that a growing 'fiscal crisis of the state'impelled the state to desert institutional care in favour of community care. Yet, as Table 3.2 demonstrates, while the overall trends are towards ever increasing burdens upon the state, the immediate post-war period did actually provide some respite with social service expenditure only slightly rising, while the share allocated to industry between 1951 and 1961 actually fell by 2%.

Table 3.2
Expenditure on social services (percentage of
GNP at factor cost) 1910-1975

Year	Social services	Industry	Infrast- ructure	Total state expenditure
1910	4.2	1.8	0.7	12.7
1931	12.7	3.2	1.0	28.8
1951	16.1	6.9	3.6	44.9
1971	23.8	6.5	6.3	50.3
1975	28.8	8.3	6.8	57.9

Source: Gough 1979, p.77.

However, although it may not have been facing fiscal crisis, the state was of course facing certain financial limits and we should therefore still seek to establish the costs of health service provision. In cash terms there was an almost 60% increase in the net total cost of the health service during the 1950s. In the late 1940s and early 1950s this rapid increase provoked considerable concern within government circles. However as the 1950s progressed the real costs of the NHS appeared less threatening to government finances. The Guillebaud Report noted that when taking into account the effect of inflation there was little increase in expenditure (Guillebaud,19-56). Moreover, in the context of the growing economy, the economic burden of the National Health Service remained virtually static.

Table 3.3
Net total cost of the National Health Service
1949/50-1960/61

Year	(£Millions)	Year	(£Millions)
1949/50	305	1955/56	423
1951/52	348	1957/58	480
1953/54	372	1959/60	496
1954/55	388	1960/61	559

Source: Annual Reports of the Ministry of Health.

Table 3.4
The cost of the National Health Service
as a percentage of GNP 1949-1960

Year	%	Year	%
1949	3.7	1955	3.3
1950	---	1956	3.3
1951	3.5	1957	3.3
1952	3.6	1958	3.4
1954	3.3		

Source: Parliamentary answer given by the Minister of Health, reported in the Lancet, 1960, 1, 709.

These statistics demonstrate that the overall cost of the health service in the 1950s was not posing any insurmountable problems for the state. Indeed in a review of the cost of the National Health Service, the Guillebaud Report concluded in 1956 that '...the Service's record of performance since the appointed day has been one of real achievement. The rising cost of the service in real terms during the years 1948-54 was kept within narrow bounds...Any charge that there has been widespread extravagance in the National Health Service, whether in respect of the spending of money or the use of manpower, is not borne out by our evidence.' (1956, p.269). The concern that existed in the early 1950s was more to do with expectations within government circles that after an initial rush of demand health expenditure would tend to fall, rather than with any real threat to state finances (Klein, 1983, p.35). However, within this general state of affairs, we might also examine the scale and trends in the cost of mental health services.

For the first half of the 1950s a study by Abel-Smith and Titmuss found that mental hospitals received a relatively small percentage of the hospital budget. Mental and mental deficiency hospitals absorbed only 20% of the hospital budget, despite the fact that they held over 40% of in-patient beds. By 1957/58 the total cost of mental hospital provision was £58.5 million, approximately 11% of the National Health Service budget (Lancet, 1958,ii, p.161). Measured in 1950/1 prices the average cost of treating a mentally distressed in-patient in 1950/1 was £3 15s 11d and £4 13s 11d in 1959/60. For the same years the average costs of in-patients in maternity hospitals were £6 9s 5d and £16 11s 3d, and for the prestige London teaching hospitals £23 16s 10d in 1950/1 and £22 16s 9d in 1959/60 (Ministry of Health, 1960, pp.46-47). These figures clearly underline why the mental health services have earned the tag of a 'Cinderella' service, as the average weekly cost of in-patients in London teaching hospitals in the 1950s was at least five times that spent on mentally distressed people. The gap was slowly closing, with the costs in real terms of mental patients rising by a quarter while those in London teaching hospitals fell slightly, although when compared to the gross differences in expenditure this convergence is negligible.

Table 3.5
Current net expenditure in respect of different types of hospital in England and Wales 1950/1-1953/4 (£m. in actual prices)

	1950/1	51/52	52/53	53/54
Teaching	22.5	22.2	23.0	23.6
Non-Teaching	78.5	84.8	91.6	95.5
Tuberculosis & others	45.4	50.6	56.2	60.0
Mental and mental deficiency	35.0	37.4	41.9	44.7

Source: Abel-Smith and Titmuss 1956,p.28.

In the immediate post-war period local authority expenditure upon mental health services was minimal. In 1958/59 expenditure on services for mentally distressed people by local authorities totalled just £4.1 million (Lancet, 1958,ii, p.1376). The amount spent per head upon local authority mental health service provision actually fell during the 1950s (Titmuss, 1963, p.224).

These figures suggest that the cost of statutory mental health services in the 1948-63 period was not a great proportion of the total National Health Service budget, of total state expenditure, or of GNP. There is little evidence that this expenditure was the source of any great threats to the integrity of the economic sub-system. Thus, simply in terms of the structural space available to the state within British capitalism at this time, it seems clear that its room for manoeuver in terms of the size and the scale of mental health services it provides, was quite considerable.

In the immediate post-war period we can detect within the state and its related agencies a growing concern with control; or rather, the lack of it. At a general level, there was concern with the breakdown of family life. In 1949, the Departmental Committee on Grants for the Development of Marriage Guidance issued a report in which it recognised the need to sustain family life in the context of increasing social disintegration. Indeed the scale of the problem perceived leaves the impression of impending social collapse:

> Behaviour between class and class and between husband and wife is no longer governed by custom and convention, and the strain on the individual, deprived of the support given by a more active and healthy public opinion, is too great to be relieved by a mere palliation of the most acute of the symptoms...the country is faced with a social problem of considerable magnitude, going to the roots of its national life...some way must be found of creating new values and new standards of behaviour (Home Office, 1949, p.5).

A concern with social breakdown is also apparent amongst the psychiatric profession. In his presidential address to the Psychiatry section of The Royal College of Medicine in 1948, Masefield argued that the role of psychiatry is crucially important in maintaining social cohesion 'In these days when broken homes and unfortunate or indifferent parental influence are so common'. Such changes are, he argued, producing an '...increasing number of adolescent and young adult anti-social personalities which have caused so much concern in the Services. I look upon these young men and women as being sentimentally immature and without any true character formation.' (Masefield, 1948, p.221).

This perception of threats to social integration is a common theme within the psychiatric literature in this period. It is frequently noted that mental distress is more prevalent than was once thought. In particular the 'milder' conditions which in the past had gone untreated were identified as areas where psychiatric practice should be expanding (Sands, 1948, p.799). This concern is reflected in support given for 'mental hygiene', where it was argued that preventive work and the positive encouragement of good mental health would aid social integration. People would benefit from such intervention by being helped to '...find something that makes life worth living, some kind of philosophy for themselves.' (Rees,

1949, p.334).

Concern was also expressed over the effects of mental distress on industrial efficiency. In 1938 with unemployment still at high levels 47% of all mental patients had been regarded as unemployable, yet by 1953/4 with full employment some 75% were employed (Lancet, 1954,i, p.1087). It was considered important that mentally distressed people not held in mental hospitals remained at work. It was often suggested that approximately one-third of absence due to illness was due to neurosis (Lancet, 1955,i, p.858), which amounted to twenty times more days work lost than through strikes (Lancet, 1957,i, p.930). As the Chair of the Board of Control noted at the time, 'This is a very serious economic problem...' (Lancet, 1957,i, p.1031).

This concern with the scale of the problem was fuelled by an increasing number of people being treated for mental distress. Prior to 1948 there had been a long established pattern of increasing numbers of people being contained in mental hospitals. The increase in the mental hospital population in the mid-twentieth century was levelling off; a pattern continued until 1954 when it peaked, and subsequently declined.

Table 3.6
Persons under care and treatment in mental hospitals 1860-1948.

Year	Population of England and Wales	Number of resident patients	Resident patients per 1,000 pop.
1860	19,902,000	38,058	1.91
1890	28,764,000	86,067	2.99
1930	39,801,000	142,387	3.57
1948	42,800,000	145,779	3.41

(Excluding armed forces)

Source:Annual Report of the Chief Medical Officer, 1948.

But while the initial impression is of a declining use of mental hospitals, this is in no way contradictory with the numbers being diagnosed mentally ill, and the numbers of people entering mental hospital rapidly ascending. Despite the stabilization in the number of beds the number of admissions to mental hospital continued to rise.

Table 3.7
Resident population of mental hospitals
and other institutions 1950-1961

Year	Total	Year	Total
1950	147,546	1956	149,480
1951	148,071	1957	146,962
1952	149,353	1958	141,687
1953	151,378	1959	136,138
1954	152,144	1960	-------
1955	150,856	1961	137,094

Source: Annual Reports of the Ministry of Health.

Table 3.8
Direct admissions to mental hospitals
and other institutions 1948-1963

Year	Total	First Admissions	First Admissions per 10,000 Population
1948	51,227	36,028	----
1949	53,921	40,551	12.1
1950	60,266	40,829	12.1
1951	63,953	42,175	12.6
1952	66,773	42,749	12.7
1953	72,069	46,278	13.8
1954	76,650	46,612	13.8
1955	83,289	49,173	14.5
1956	88,542	50,405	----
1957	93,306	51,398	----
1958	------	------	----
1959	98,237	------	----
1960	------	------	----
1961	------	------	----
1962	146,458	------	----
1963	60,405	------	----

Source: Annual Reports of the Ministry Of Health.

Between 1928 and 1948 the average number of direct admissions to County and Borough mental hospitals each year had risen by some 25,000 (Chief Medical Officer, 1948, p.131), but as Table 3.8 demonstrates, the admission rate subsequently escalated in the immediate post-war period. The declining percentage of first admissions does indicate that the actual number of persons treated did not rise quite so quickly as the admission rate itself, but it is still undoubtedly the case that mental hospitals attended to a far greater number of people in this period than ever before in their history. This reflects in the increasing number of letters received by medical journals in the late 1950s from psychiatrists about the enormous workload they faced, and the strains that was causing (e.g. Lancet, 1957, i, p.930 and p.1143).

Furthermore, the number of out-patients also increased rapidly. Figures available are for mentally handicapped as well as the mentally ill, nevertheless the rate of increase is striking.

Table 3.9
Number of new out-patients 1950-1963

Year	New Out-Patients	Total Attendances During the year
1950	102,791	523,218
1951	106,518	545,114
1952	107,689	567,593
1953	111,326	599,645
1954	119,723	666,052
1955	122,304	696,799
1956	127,927	775,228
1957	134,039	833,764
1958	136,000	891,400
1959	144,300	1,026,900
1960	170,000	--------
1961	170,000	--------
1962	159,000	1,189,000
1963	166,000	1,227,000

Source: Annual Reports of the Ministry of Health.

These statistics however, only measure the more serious conditions, where hospital treatment was required. Further evidence in studies of psychiatric morbidity in general practice provides some guidance as to the number of people suffering mental disabilities in the wider population. However, while the difficulties of measuring the scale of activity of mental hospitals is considerable, these problems are compounded when examining general psychiatric morbidity. Firstly, which conditions should be considered psychiatric disorders is not entirely clear. For example, while psycho-neurotic disorders might generally be expected to be included in this category, there is a range of other diagnostic categories such as disturbances of sleep, nervousness, headache and peptic ulcers, where it is somewhat arbitrary as to whether they are classified as physical or psychological complaints (Watts, 1962, p.35). Furthermore the rate of consultation does not necessarily reflect the incidence of an ailment. The period we are considering is of course at the beginning of an almost free at point of use National Health Service, and it may well be that this encouraged an increased reporting of ailments (Ramon, 1985). However, taking these qualifications into account we should at least attempt some assessment of the available evidence.

In a review of the evidence Watts (1962) found that surveys in the 1950s of the incidence of psychiatric disorders reported by general practitioners varied enormously. As a percentage of total cases seen, the number of patients thought to be manifesting psychiatric symptoms varies between 6.5% and 70%, although as the Royal College of General Practitioners commented, 'The true incidence is probably more uniform from practice to practice than these figures suggest...' (Royal College of General Practitioners, 1958). This reflects in the morbidity survey for the General Register Office where it was found that 'Most practitioners find between 30 and 60 psychiatric patients per 1,000 with a mean of 45.' (Watts, 1962, p.35).' In the classic study of the time, a survey of 76 London family doctors reached the conclusion that 14% of the population displayed psychiatric problems (Shepherd et al.,1966).

Because of these difficulties the Royal Commission On the Law Relating to Mental Illness and Mental Deficiency concluded that the numbers of psychiatric patients seen by general practitioners is unknown. It further notes that in any case the same patients will appear in different sets of figures as they are referred from one part of the mental health services to the next, with no comprehensive records being kept to trace people through the system. However, while we may not be able to establish the exact incidence of mental distress in general practice, it does appear that it constituted a large part of the work load.

In total, the evidence suggests that the incidence of mental distress was rising, or at least that the diagnosis of psychiatric morbidity was increasingly sensitive to mental health problems. Perhaps most likely, is that both were occurring. In terms of control, this suggests that as a threat to social integration the importance of this area was rising for the state. Such a threat was certainly perceived by the psychiatric profession, and we might expect to see a concern with regulating social behaviour to have an increasing effect upon the policy making process.

Legitimation

To assess the legitimacy of mental health services in the immediate post-war period we will review the attitudes, interests and concerns of a variety of groups concerned with or involved in their provision. Of these the most important group is the psychiatric profession. Their power and status by the mid-20th century was considerable, in terms of their ability to define the nature of the problem of mental distress and how it should be addressed (Busfield,1986). For this reason we need to examine in some detail the development of the psychiatric profession through the first half of the 20th century in order to understand the position it takes up in the 1950s. Perhaps the most obvious of the changes that occurred was development of new therapies. In 1918 Wagner Jauregg was the first to describe a successful cure for syphilitic insanity by malarial therapy (Chief Medical Officer, 1948, p.128). As this began to be used this once incurable condition was found susceptible to treatment;

Table 3.10
Deaths from general paralysis of the insane in hospitals
for mental disorder 1923-1948

Year	Number of Deaths
1923	1,353
1933	733
1943	416
1948	164

Source: Annual Report of the Chief Medical Officer 1948, p.128.

In the 1930s a number of new physical treatments were developed. These included insulin coma therapy, involving the administering of large doses of insulin, resulting in coma that would normally be maintained for between thirty and fifty hours, and was thought particularly suitable for excited psychotic patients (Baruch and Treacher, 1978). Elctro-convulsive therapy (ECT) was also developed in this decade. Initially it was used to treat schizophrenia, but was found ineffective, and was found more useful in treating depression. The third major change in physical treatments in the 1930s was in the field of psychosurgery. This was practiced in England from 1940, and was argued to bring considerable relief of symptoms to some mentally distressed patients by making them more placid. Finally, as discussed in Chapter 1, the 1950s saw the discovery and use of the neuroleptic drugs.

A result of this development in physical treatments was to greatly increase the confidence of the psychiatric profession to deal with the mental ills of society. As Harris stated in his presidential address to the Royal Medico-Psychological Association in 1955:

> In these days it is necessary not only to have the efforts of the individual but the force of combined operation such as a united society gives. Who better than the Royal Medico-Psychological Association can see to it that this much desired end is attained (Harris, 1955, p.10).

There were also a number of important developments in psychiatric theory with regard to how the concept of mental distress was understood. Perhaps the most important of these was the tendency to integrate the concept of mental distress with the concept of physical illness. This is not simply a case of understanding both by the same conceptual model-the medical model-but also a process of arguing the two are more closely related entities than was once thought, where for example mental illnesses may have physical effects and vice versa. The development of this trend in psychiatric theory was noted by the Royal Commission on Lunacy and Mental Disorder in its report in 1926:

> It has become increasingly evident that there is no clear line of demarcation between mental and physical illness. The distinction as commonly drawn is based on a difference of symptoms. In ordinary parlance, a disease is described as mental if its symptoms manifest themselves predominantly in derangement of conduct, and as physical if its symptoms manifest themselves

predominantly in derangement of bodily function. A mental illness may have physical concomitants; probably it always has, though they may be difficult of detection. A physical illness, on the other hand, may have, and probably always has, mental concomitants. And there are many cases in which it is a question whether the physical or the mental symptoms predominate (Quoted in Jones, 1972, p.240).

A further tendency towards integration to be found in psychiatric theory is between the concepts of sanity and insanity. To trace this trend fully, we have to go back to the 17th century when the mad tended not to be segregated. But with the coming of the Age of Reason, madness came to exist as a direct threat to the new dominant order and, as Foucault argues, the 'grand confinement' commenced where to deal with the problem the mad began to incarcerated (Foucault, 1971). At this point then, sanity and insanity were held to be totally unrelated. This reflected in the attitude of society to the mad; they were regarded as freaks to be stared and laughed at. At Bedlam, an early English mental hospital, visitors were charged a penny entrance fee which entitled them to tease and torment the inmates (Skultans, 1979, p.38).

Yet by the 20th century attitudes towards the nature of madness had changed. Of particular importance in this was the development of Freudian theory, which presented mental illness as something comprehensible (Rose, 1986, p.49). Rather than just reserve the mental illness label for the seriously disturbed, the concept of neuroses was increasingly used and applied to larger areas of social life. Thus no longer were the sane and the insane regarded as opposite types sharing no common ground. While still representing opposite ends of an axis, that axis had totally changed in nature. It was now gradated rather than dichotomous, and it could be more easily traversed.

These changes in psychiatric theory in the first half of the twentieth century represent a change from a custody to a treatment model of practice. An effect of this was to reduce the legitimacy of the asylum, which with its isolated and enclosed setting embodied the custodial model. The treatment of mental distress was increasingly perceived as something that required new administrative structures:

A fissuring was occurring in mental medicine. A certain hostility was growing between the long established sector of asylum superintendents, defenders of the need for separate and distinct institutions for the treatment of the mentally ill, who dominated the Board of Control, and the physicians who sought the integration of the practice, training and facilities of psychiatry with those of the general hospital. The events that presaged a brighter future for psychiatry were largely taking place outside the asylums, or at any rate outside their main-stream. They were happening in the insulin units of the mental hospitals, in out-patient clinics, in private practice, in psychotherapy and psychoanalysis (Rose, 1986, pp.59-60).

This is not to suggest that the old asylums were totally stuck in the old custodial model. The Mental Treatment Act, 1930 had renamed asylums 'mental hospitals' and had allowed them to take voluntary admissions. In the 1940s some early moves towards developing an 'open door' policy had been made with the unlocking of some wards of a few mental hospitals. Nevertheless a considerable change was occurring in psychiatrist's views on appropriate sights for treatment, with the trend being towards diversification.

By the 1950s, the theory and practice of psychiatry had changed enormously. While still being based in mental hospitals, they felt that with improved competence and increased areas of need, their sphere of activity should be extended. Thus the legitimacy of their own base was being undermined to some degree by such develop-ments. Reflecting this, in its submission to the Percy Commission the Royal Medico-Psychological Association argued that there should be greater provision of 'treatment in the community'. This is not an argument for community care in the sense of involving a wider range of agencies in the treatment of mentally distressed people. As Martin argues, 'What is germane and scarcely disputable is that psychiatry (did not take) the initial lead in community care.' (Martin,1983, p.137). Rather, 'treatment in the community' is an argument for modernising institutional provision and for increasing the availability of treatment in local settings.

General practitioners showed little interest or concern in issues of psychiatric care. They lacked skills in counselling and psycho-therapy and had little to offer patients. Particularly in the years following the establishment of the National Health Service, general practitioners were most concerned with their own status within the new organisation and little attention was paid to what such a service might offer mentally distressed people (Martin, 1983, p.123).

In a review of the attitudes and actions of psychiatric nurses in the 1950s Ramon argues that their principle concerns were with there own conditions of service rather than any particular disquiet about the nature of service provision. She notes that concern was frequently expressed about overcrowding of mental hospitals, the lack of co-operation between doctors and nurses, and using nurses as domestics. While some anxiety is expressed about the status and duties of psychiatric nurses this does not extend into a critique of styles of intervention or of the conceptual basis of psychiatric practice (Ramon, 1985, p.188).

Psychiatric nurses demonstrated little interest in the development of community care. Of the associations representing nurses, only the Confederation of Health Service Employees submitted evidence to the Royal Commission on the Law Relating to Mental Illness and Mental Deficiency in the mid-1950s, and examination of their evidence reveals little that was radical or original. They supported the development of voluntary status for most mental patients, and also support the view that mental hospitals should provide treatment on a similar basis to that given to patients with physical complaints in general hospitals. The trend towards mental hospitals being used principally as treatment centres is recommended, but it is also noted that the implications of this are that local authorities will have to provide residential accommodation for those still recovering after a spell in a mental hospital. Other than this, however, no recommendations are made for the development of community care facilities.

Of all the professional groups psychiatric social workers were the most interested in, and keen upon the development of community services. This reflects in the considerable attention the changing emphasis of the mental health service towards community care received in their professional publications. While no single view emerges as to exactly how services should evolve, there is a general emphasis upon the provision of social support, with the psychiatric social worker liaising with mental hospitals but undertaking a relatively autonomous role in the community of providing support for mentally distressed people (Ramon, 1985, p.214).

This support for, and we might add self interest in, the development of services in the community emerges clearly in the submission made to the Royal Commission on the Law Relating to Mental Illness and Mental Deficiency by the Association of Psychiatric Social Workers. They note that 'There are certain people who although mentally ill would not need in-patient care and treatment if they could be given adequate help and supervision outside.'. They go on to argue for the need to provide a range of services, including domiciliary services, hostels, sheltered employment and rehabilitation centres, attendance centres and social therapy clubs and out-patient clinics. This view reflects psychiatric social workers value preferences. They tended to support psychotherapeutic rather than physical methods of treatment, and in particular favoured a psychoanalytic model of mental illness (Ramon, 1985, p.210). In pursuing this however there is no intention to confront the psychiatric profession. The argument made is that emphasis upon the social aspects of mental illness is complementary to the medical model, and is not intended to undermine it.

A further group that we might consider is Members of Parliament. A number of them participated in the debates over the changing nature of mental health service provision that occurred in parliament from 1954 through to 1959, and by reviewing these contributions we can establish there interests and concerns. Ramon has comprehensively reviewed the contributions of M.P.s to parliamentary debates preceding the 1959 Mental Health Act, and much of what follows is based on her work. She notes that several M.P.s were interested in the changes being made in the mental health services, including principally Mr. N. Dodds, Dr. D. Johnson, Mr. C. Mayhew and Mr. K. Robinson. These four were active in raising problems and questions relating to the changing service, although did not actively work together. Particular concern was expressed about the numbers of people being held unnecessarily in mental hospitals and about abuses of power by psychiatrists when detaining patients. It was generally accepted in Parliament that around one-quarter of the mental hospital population should not be there (Ramon, 1985, pp.234-236). Other areas of criticism included concern about the low level of funding being received by mental health services, and the poor conditions and overcrowding that then existed.

However there was also considerable praise given for many of the changes being made in service provision. The rising percentage of voluntary admissions was noted as a progressive development, as were the improvements being made in mental hospitals conditions. The professional competence of psychiatry was generally held in high regard, and the developments made in treatments were praised (Ramon, 1985, pp.238-239). Overall M.P.s were in support of the changes being made in the way mental health services were provided, with criticism being either relatively marginal or in terms of an insufficient level of funds being provided. While discussion took place over specific aspects of the proposed new legislation, the central principles and assumptions upon which it was based went unchallenged (Jones, 1972, p.310).

Very little evidence is available regarding the attitudes of the general public towards mental health services in the immediate post-war period. The most important single piece of evidence came in 1957 when the BBC screened 'The Hurt Mind', a series of five programmes on mental distress. Some twenty-five thousand letters were received in response and these were then analyzed by Carstairs and Wing. They found that the letters tended to be sympathetic to mentally distressed people, and hostile towards the professional groups. Overall, the scale and type of response indicated that there was considerable public sympathy for mentally distressed people, but whether this was a new phenomenon could not be estimated (Carstairs and Wing,1958). In contrast however, at the 1961 Annual Conference of the National Association of Mental Health the editor of the 'Woman' magazine told of how only 14 replies had been received about an article on the care of mentally distressed people whereas other articles on health issues had prompted reply by many thousands of readers (Jones, 1964, p.201).

In a recent review of the development of community care for mentally distressed people Jones notes that 'The policies of the early Sixties...were based on assumptions, none of which were empirically tested. There was no research to build on, no model schemes.' (Jones, 1981, p.19). And within this analysis, she includes the 'wonderfully romantic' (Jones, 1981, p.21) assumption made that the public was becoming more enlightened, tolerant and supportive of mentally distressed people. This view is also supported by Scull. He notes that while assumptions have been made about an increased tolerance of mental distress by the general public, '...where this increased tolerance comes from is not explained; nor is evidence offered to demonstrate its existence...'(Scull, 1984, p.99).

By the mid-20th century the legitimacy of mental health services had in various ways been undermined. Changes and development in knowledge bases and practices of the professional groups had not been matched by changes in the physical structure of the service. This was causing some tensions, where it was difficult to organise a service based around treatment when the system was predominantly designed for custody. Within the discussion around what changes were considered appropriate by different professional groups, we have found some tension between simply modernising and increasing the availability of treatment, and developing a more diverse range of supportive services. We have also noted some indifference to how services are organised. But out of this two central points emerge. Firstly, there was no particular support for, or even clearly thought out ideas around, the concept of a community care service. While the legitimacy of the old asylums was slowly eroding, no consensus existed on what should replace them. Secondly, the authority of the psychiatric profession is undisputed, giving them the power to define the nature of the problem being addressed and how best to deal with it.

Conclusion

Having reviewed the economic, political and social forces relevant to understanding the development of mental health services in the immediate post-war period, we are now in a position to assess the level of difficulty the state faced in reconciling the various aspects of the compatibility problem. In terms of the pressures we have identified the problem for the state is whether the existing institutional system, in place for over 100 years, would continue to prove adequate; whether it could continue to adequately reconcile the various aspects of the compatibility problem. The problem faced can be specified as follows.

Cost and control

We have argued that the cost of mental health services, in the context of a growing economy, posed no great threat to state finances. At the same time however the scale of the problem of control was rapidly growing. Increased emphasis was being placed upon the psychological nature of social problems, and the expanding role of psychiatric treatment to deal with these problems. There was therefore growing tension on this axis of the compatibility problem. The state was faced with a decision whether to make psychiatric services more widely available, and at what cost.

Cost and legitimation

With old, large and isolated asylums increasingly perceived as inappropriate places for the care and treatment of mentally distressed people, the state was faced with the problem of existing mental health services steadily losing legitimacy. This implied additional expenditure was required in an attempt to address criticisms being made; either to modernise existing facilities or develop alternatives.

With increasing emphasis being placed on the range of milder mental problems, and the prevalence of these within the community, institutional care was perceived as less appropriate to meeting the needs of mentally distressed people. Institutions built for removing and incarcerating 'lunatics' on a long term basis could not readily adapt to the change in emphasis from a custody to a treatment model of provision.

It is this range of problems that constituted the compatibility problem facing the state in the immediate post-war period. We might now move on to examine how the state perceived these issues, and how it responded to them.

4 The policy making process, 1948–1963

It would be difficult for any Government to attempt to lay down a precise and permanent relationship between Exchequer expenditure on the National Health Service and the gross national product. There are many factors which the Government of the day has to take into account in deciding what proportion of the national resources it is reasonable for the National Health Service to absorb at a particular time.

(Ministry of Health, 1955, p. v.)

We can examine the state's perception of the compatibility problem and policy responses in the following terms. Cost, as we have termed it, is understood as the need for least-cost efficiency; the state seeks to achieve certain policy goals using minimum financial expenditure. This is perhaps the easiest criterion to identify within the perception of the state, where service provision is seen as a drain upon valuable and limited resources. Control is understood by the state as the need for effectiveness. This is more difficult to elucidate, because the language of reform so obscures the control process going on. Moreover policy makers need not understand what they do in terms of control as presented here. Nevertheless, it will be shown that what the state thought effective was strongly influenced by the control criterion. Finally, the criterion of legitimation is understood by the state in terms of acceptability. This concerns negotiation with interest groups, to find a policy which receives sufficient political support such that it can be implemented.

Our analytical model suggests that cost, control and legitimation are the criteria the state must address in its mental health policy making process. These the state understands in terms of efficiency, effectiveness and acceptability respectively. The (potentially) antagonistic processes that it must then address are between efficiency and effectiveness, efficiency and acceptableness, and effectiveness and acceptability. The argument to be pursued in this Chapter is that we can indeed understand the state's mental health policy in these terms in the 1948-63 period. To examine this, we will sub-divide the period into four; 1948-52, 1953-56, 1957-59, and 1960-63. In each of these we can, by using the analytical model developed in Chapter 2, develop an explanation of how and why the state proceeded as it did with its mental health policy. Our concerns are with how the state perceives and responds to these forces; what it accepted, what it denied, what it ignored, what it invented, and what it did. It is this that constitutes the subject matter of internal rationalisation.

Before undertaking this analysis however, we might first briefly describe mental health services as they stood in 1948. There were 102 mental hospitals in England and Wales, which prior to the creation of the National Health Service in that year had been the responsibility of the County Councils (Chief Medical Officer, 1953, p.123). These provided the vast bulk of mental health services although there were some other forms of provision, including private nursing homes, neuroses hospitals, out-patient clinics and some other small scale services. But all of these were peripheral to the size and status of the mental hospitals.

Under the National Health Service Act, 1946 the Minister of Health took on principal authority for mental health services. He or she appointed Regional Hospital Boards to oversee the administration of mental hospitals, as well as all other hospitals. This was to be achieved by setting up Hospital Management Committees, each of which would be responsible for a small number of hospitals. The teaching hospitals were exempt from this, instead being accountable to a Board of Governors who in turn reported to the Minister of Health.

Local authorities had wide but permissive powers to develop services in the community for the 'prevention, care and after-care' of the mentally ill, this being acquired under section 28 of the National Health Service Act, 1946. They were also charged with a duty to provide for people being admitted to mental hospital. The third and final leg of services was to be provided by General Practitioners, who would be supervised by Executive Councils, and would continue as before to provide the first point of contact for health services.

Problems without solutions: 1948-1952

Efficiency and effectiveness

After taking authority for mental hospitals, the Ministry of Health soon came to realize that several problems existed with the service provided. The stock of mental hospitals were generally old and dilapidated. Only 28 of the former County and Borough asylums had been built in the 20th century and of the remaining 74, 30 had been built prior to 1854 (Chief Medical Officer, 1953, p.123). Moreover with rising admission rates, and the bed stock remaining static at around 120,000, a serious problem of overcrowding had developed with the number of patients held in mental hospitals being 11.7% over the numbers they were designed for in 1948, while by 1952 this had risen to 14.7% (Ministry of Health). Worse, the problem was geographically concentrated, with some hospitals experiencing over 60% overcrowding.

Although the Ministry of Health was faced with this problem of lack of capacity, it nevertheless sought to increased the orbit of psychiatric practice. Concern was held about an increasing range of conditions that, it was argued, were suitable for psychiatric treatment:

> The isolation of the mental hospitals and the ignorance of the medical profession have led to failure to recognise or diagnose properly the milder forms of mental disorder; 'anaemia', 'debility', 'rheumatism' have concealed a large amount of neurotic illness...investigators...have estimated that 30 per cent. to 50 per cent. of all cases seen by general practitioners and in general clinics are neurotic or have a large neurotic component (Chief Medical Officer,1948, p.128).

Where previously the orbit of psychiatric practice encompassed at most a few hundred thousand people, composed of the most seriously deranged, there were now a range of 'milder' conditions recognised as legitimate areas of psychiatric practice and concern, composed of people who might appear 'apparently normal' (Chief Medical Officer, 1950, p.123). Indeed, when taking the Chief Medical Officer's estimate of the incidence of such conditions, noted above, the orbit of psychiatric intervention increases to include millions of people; a number far greater than ever could be catered for in mental hospitals.

This increased concern with the scale of the problem of mental distress resulted in greater efforts to increase the availability of treatment services. An improved scale of payment for mental nurses was agreed in September 1949, which it was hoped would improve rates of recruitment (Ministry of Health, 1949/50, p.71). This however had little effect. In 1949 there were 19,195 full-time and 5,570 part-time psychiatric nurses, and by 1952 these figures had only risen to 19,394 and 6,817 respectively. While there was sufficient number of people entering the job, there was considerable wastage during training. Amongst other groups of workers there were also staff shortages. In 1949 there was just 202 full-time and 37 part-time psychiatric social workers, and in 1952 there numbers had only risen to 260 and 40 respectively. Amongst consultant staff only 405 worked with the mentally ill and mentally deficient, and many of these were only part-time posts. By 1952 their numbers had risen to 515, a 25% increase which was in fact greater than the average in all other medical specialisms.

Although the scale of the problem of providing sufficient psychiatric treatment was recognised to be increasing, resources with which to make improvements in service provision were limited. Between 1948 and 1952 the cost of the National Health Service had in cash terms doubled, giving rise to considerable concern within the Ministry of Health about the cost of health services. In 1950 this resulted in a cash ceiling being imposed on health expenditure (Ministry of Health, 1950/1, pp.1-4). Also, severe restrictions were placed upon new building with capital expenditure on mental and general hospitals amounting to only £9.1 million in 1949/50 (Ministry of Health, 1962, pp.1-2). Of this money mental hospitals did receive an ascending share, rising from 13% in 1948/49 to 15% in 1949/50, 17% in 1950/51 and 21% in 1951/52. But with the absolute amounts available being so small little impact could be made on improving conditions within mental hospitals. Abel-Smith and Titmuss estimated that the capital expenditure levels of 1952/53 would only allow rebuilding of the total hospital stock once every 220 years (Abel-Smith and Titmuss, 1956, p.53).

The state was faced with, and recognised, rising tension on this axis of the compatibility problem. Although we have argued that the cost criterion was, 'objectively', not of overwhelming import- ance, the Ministry of Health nevertheless lacked sufficient resources to consider any great expansion of facilities. Yet at the same time it recognised that increased capacity was required. It notes with dismay, for example, the serious level of overcrowding such that some mental hospitals were refusing to admit voluntary patients in order to control numbers taken in. The result of this, the Ministry of Health suspected, was that some patients were being certified simply to get them admitted. This it considered highly unsatisfactory, as its concern was to increase the accessibility of mental hospital treatment - an aim that it considered incompatible with the certification of patients.

Yet while recognising the problem, the Ministry of Health was uncertain what to. Some developments in service provision were being made such as out-patients departments and day hospitals but, while the state supported such innovations, it did not perceive them as a solution to the problem of finding a policy to make the needs and demands of efficiency and effectiveness compatible. The efficiency gains made by mental hospitals, as represented by the increasingly rapid turnover of patients, was praised, but this was no more than a 'relieving feature' of the overcrowding problem (Ministry of Health, 1950/1, p.28). Rather, perhaps because institutional care had been the dominant form of service provision for so long, the Ministry of Health looked to the development of more modern mental hospitals to provide resolution of the problem. It argued that mental hospitals as they stood were out of date because their large wards and isolated settings were inappropriate to modern times; they were built for custody, not treatment. Hence the future planning of mental health services should reflect this change, with new villa style mental hospitals being built that have a greater variety of rooms that a patient might use during his/her day, and situated nearer to centres of population.

By 1952 the Ministry of Health's attempt to internally rationalise its policies, such that the criteria of effectiveness and efficiency were made compatible, was in disarray. On the one hand, it stressed that '...one of the biggest problems that faces the service in the future is the provision of more accommodation in mental hospitals.' (Ministry of Health, 1952, p.iv), for this 'alone' (Ministry of Health, 1952, p.10) could solve the problems faced by the mental health service of providing an effective service. Yet on the other hand, the stress on the need for efficiency at this time was considerable. In a letter from the Minister of Health to the chairperson of each of the Regional Hospital Authorities, he drew '...their attention to the general financial position of the country, and (asked) for their help in securing every possible economy in the hospitals under their control.' (Ministry of Health, 1952, p.34). Plans were made in the Ministry of Health to build new mental hospitals, but these were only to be implemented when money was available (Chief Medical Officer, 1959, p.129). In the short term at least policy proposals were acknowledged to be unrealistic.

Efficiency and acceptability

The problem that arises on this axis is how to provide a service that meets acceptable standards of care, yet remains efficient. In contrast to the importance to the state of maintaining efficiency, that we noted in the previous section, there was far less stress given to making the service acceptable. It was acknowledged that mental hospitals were generally old and decrepid, and that the quality of life within them was impoverished (Ministry of Health, 1950/51, p.28; Chief Medical Officer 1952, p.180). In a memorandum written to the Cabinet in 1950, Bevan noted that '...some of the old mental hospitals are very near to a public scandal and we are very lucky that so far they have not attracted more limelight and publicity.' (quoted in Klein, 1983, p.36). Yet at the same time the Ministry of Health had limited funds with which to redress this problem. Klein notes that by the early 1950s the Ministry of Health had gained a reputation for financial extravagance within government circles:

> From the point of view of the treasury, vice had been rewarded in the 1940s, and the 1950s were marked by a determination not to allow history to repeat itself. In the assumptive world of the Whitehall policy-maker, the NHS remained for most of the decade an undeserving case (Klein, 1983, p.40).

The Ministry of Health did make some attempt to reconcile these two opposing demands. Efforts were made to improve the standards of mental hospital wards by re-decoration and modernisation. It was acknowledged that maintenance work tended to lag behind, and more resources were needed to improve conditions (Ministry of Health, 1950/51, p.28). This view in itself tended to marginalise the problem, as in fact mental hospitals were reaching the point where a massive overhaul was required. Yet at times the Ministry of Health would defend its corner even more strongly and claim that mental hospital conditions are adequate:

> The reports of the Visiting Commissioners of the Board of Control reflect that, despite the many restrictions at present operating, a satisfactory standard of care and treatment in most

mental hospitals is generally being maintained (Ministry of Health, 1950/51, p.28).

Although the Ministry of Health was making some attempt to address the loss of legitimacy of an old and antiquated institutional system, at the cost of some of loss of efficiency, it faced little prospect of long term success. The provision of full board and lodgings, with attendant staff, is an expensive way of dealing with mentally distressed people and there were few avenues for reducing the cost per patient. The role of voluntary workers within mental hospitals for example is praised (Ministry of Health,1950/51, p.31), but is viewed only as a marginal addition to paid labour. By 1952 the Ministry of Health was maintaining a position of making minor improvements to mental hospital conditions, but with little idea as to what should be done in the long term; on this axis of the compatibility problem the state was involved in a holding operation, with no clear longer term policy objectives.

Effectiveness and acceptability

We have argued that the opposing criteria on this axis are firstly the increasing need for control, and secondly the demand for treatment provided by mental health services to be, ostensibly at least, humane and benevolent. The problem faced therefore, was how to reconcile these two facets within the context of services as they existed in the 1948-52 period. Perhaps the most obvious way the Ministry of Health sought to legitimate the mental health service was by praising the advances made in therapeutic technique within psychiatry. The Chief Medical Officer in particular charts this. Malarial therapy for general paresis is considered to be a major advance in treatment. Therapeutic convulsion treatment (ECT) is acknowledged to be '...a potent weapon...' (Chief Medical Officer,1948, p.128). Insulin shock treatment too is considered very effective, and even psychosurgery is held to be of value in certain cases. These developments in practice are argued to have greatly increased the legitimate role of psychiatric intervention:

...they have given a great impetus to psychiatry by showing that something active can often by done and that there is a need for integration of psychiatry with other branches of general medicine and surgery (Chief Medical Officer, 1948, p.128).

Advances in psychotherapy too are considered a useful addition to the psychiatrist's tools. In particular, Freudian theory is thought useful:

> The concept of the unconscious and recognition of the importance of past experience and of instinctual drives have lead the way to a vastly increased interest in and understanding of psychopathology and the role of psychotherapy (Chief Medical Officer, 1948, p.128).

Thus the state sought to recognise both physical methods of treatment as well as psychotherapy as valuable advances in the treatment of mental distress. In total, such developments are presented as social progress, where mentally distressed people instead of simply being incarcerated can now be effectively treated with a range of new therapeutic techniques. Moreover, it is argued that these therapeutic advances have tended to increase the acceptance of a view of mental distress as an illness. There is, it is claimed, a '...wider acceptance, both by the public and the medical profession of the idea that the whole organism reacts to illness rather than the body and the mind separately...' (Ministry of Health, 1949/50, p.69). This integration of mental and physical illness, as we saw in Chapter 3 in our discussion of psychiatry, is a key feature in the medicalization of mental distress; something the state clearly wants to encourage and present as acceptable.

The Ministry of Health was in the late 1940s already considering new legislation, allowing for the informal admittance of mental hospital patients, in order that more people might receive the benefits of advances in therapeutic technique. By 1951 officials within the Ministry of Health were preparing a comprehensive Mental Health Bill, and envisaged presenting their proposals to the Minister in January 1952 and presenting a Bill to Parliament in November 1952 (Public Records Office,MH51/610). The problem with such proposals however were that no administrative solution had yet been found for the overcrowding within mental hospitals; it was difficult in such circumstances to deliberately foster increased levels of admission, although the explanation offered at the time for shelving the proposed Bill was lack of parliamentary time.

Overall the Ministry of Health was faced with little difficulty in reconciling antagonisms within this dimension of the compatibility problem. The psychiatric profession's authority went unchallenged by other groups in society, and with the state's support for their activities held a position of considerable power in determining the nature and treatment of mental distress. There were however a limited range of problems with this 'internal rationalisation'. This principally concerns the rising rate of admission to mental hospitals, which implied that the psychiatric service was not providing relief or cure-something that would undermine its acceptability as had happened once before in the second half of the 19th century (Scull,1979). However, explanation was provided:

> A growing appreciation by the public of the value of early treatment and the possibility of admission to hospitals on a voluntary basis have led to increasing demands being made on the mental hospitals... (Chief Medical Officer, 1948, p.131).

Thus, the rising levels of treatment being provided does not reflect an increased incidence of mental distress in the community or the failure to cure it, but quite the opposite, where improved and more accessible treatments are being increasingly sought after by the general population.

This argument is taken further, to explain the rising turnover of mental hospital patients. It is held that because of the increasing readiness of people to enter mental hospitals, they are being treated earlier for their illnesses than occurred previously and hence are more rapidly returned to health (Ministry of Health, 1950/51, p.28). Yet at the same time, as we noted in Chapter 3, the rate of re-admission was rising (that is, of those admitted to a mental hospital each year, an increasing percentage had been admitted before). So if treatment was considered more effective, why are people returning in rising numbers? This is acknowledged to be somewhat peculiar, but can be explained. Mainly, it concerns the rising numbers of voluntary patients being admitted, for amongst these, '...there is always a proportion of psycho-neurotics...' (Chief Medical Officer, 1951, p.153) who make a habit of returning to mental hospital only because they think they are once more mentally ill. Additionally, there is a tendency for voluntary patients to discharge themselves before treatment is completed, resulting in a high rate of relapse.

These arguments were little more than unsubstantiated assertions. The support for recent advances in psychiatric therapies, and the argument that these were finding general acceptance within society, were based on no evidence. As we noted in Chapter 3, little evidence existed to allow assessment of public opinion. Furthermore evidence existed that conflicted with the Ministry of Health's view regarding the efficacy of new treatments. Its own figures indicate that during this period the rate of cure of mental hospital patients as reported by psychiatrists was in decline, from 41.3% in 1948 to 31.5% in 1952 (Ministry of Health). This tends to undermine the key proposition concerning the newly found success of psychiatric technique. In effect, the position being maintained with regard to this axis amounted to a combination of speculation and kite-flying. The advantages of an alliance with the psychiatric profession is clearly identified, and the Ministry of Health sought to support its activities by creating an image of effective and acceptable therapeutic intervention. With the lack of alternative viewpoints on the political agenda it was able to achieve this.

Overall, we have identified a number of problems facing the Ministry of Health in its mental health policy. In our discussion of the cost criterion in Chapter 3 we noted that it was not a compelling restraint on mental health service expenditure in the immediate post-war period. But of course the 'long boom' was still in its infancy, and was not providing the state any great confidence about its anticipated available funds for social expenditure. Because of this the importance of the cost factor in this discussion of the 1948-'52 period takes on a greater importance than it might 'objectively' warrant, and reflects in the perceived lack of funding to adequately maintain mental hospitals. Secondly, on the question of acceptability, levels of care for mentally distressed people were recognised to be inadequate, and some efforts were being made to address this problem. Advances in treatment were held to be legitimate, with no groups able or willing to challenge psychiatric authority. Thirdly, because of therapeutic advances, mental health services were considered increasingly effective in treating mental illness. The major problem that arose however was that with rising admission rates, and overcrowding within mental hospitals, a perceived lack of capacity existed. The Ministry of Health was concerned about how treatment could be made more readily available to more people.

This set of conditions created for the existing institutional system of treatment and care a number of apparently insoluble problems. Insufficient funds were available for the Ministry of Health to increase the capacity of mental hospitals to the levels required. Furthermore the old isolated mental hospitals were increasingly perceived as inappropriate sites for therapeutic intervention. They had been built to provide custody of relatively few, more seriously disturbed people, where the problem now was seen in terms of how to provide treatment for increasing numbers of people displaying a range of mental illnesses, some serious but many being of a temporary and mild nature.

What we have here then is the physical, and conceptual, break-down of institutional care for mentally distressed people. The system was in decline because it was wearing out, failing to increase its capacity at a sufficient rate to match rising demand, and in any case was considered antiquated and increasingly inappropriate to the modern needs of mental health services. This was the situation facing the state as it went into the second half of the 20th century. Yet, as we have seen in discussing its attempts at internal rationalisation of the compatibility problem, the state was aware of a problem but had little insight into its nature or of how to deal with it. In short, institutional care remained hegemonic even though cracks within it were appearing. It was only to be in subsequent years that that hegemony was to be broken.

A state of flux: 1953-1956

We have established so far that mental health services in the form inherited by the Ministry of Health in 1948 were not adequately addressing the compatibility problem. Furthermore, we have examined the response of the Ministry of Health and found its policy initiatives and ideas to be inadequate to deal with the problems being faced. It is this context that provides the basis for analysis of the next four year period, when new strategies were actively sought out. We review this period using the same format as in the last section.

Efficiency and effectiveness

By 1952 this axis was under severe strain; with the scale of the problem faced growing, and limited funds available to address it, the institutional care system was not meeting the needs of the state. But from 1953 onwards solutions began to be sought. To examine these we need to look at two areas, flux within the organisation of mental hospitals, and flux within the organisation of new and developing services.

Constraints upon social services expenditure began to lift and this made available more money to improve mental hospital conditions. There was, in other words, a slight lessening of the requirement for efficiency which left scope for effectiveness to be more adequately addressed. In 1953 shortages of staff and accommodation in mental hospitals were highlighted by the Ministry of Health as one of three priority areas. Over the next three years some improvements were made in addressing both these problems with almost 2,000 more beds being in use in 1956 compared to 1952, 1,000 more full time psychiatric nurses, and 77 more consultant staff (this latter group covering both mental illness and mental deficiency). Some new wards were built and others refurbished. It was accepted that the '...need for a substantial proportion of the available capital resources to be devoted to the mental health services continues unabated.' (Ministry of Health, 1954, p.13), and this commitment reflected in the rising percentage of capital expenditure on hospitals devoted to mental hospitals, helped partly by some monies being earmarked by the Ministry of Health (the 'mental million' scheme) to ensure that mental hospitals were upgraded. By 1956 the percentage of capital expenditure on all hospitals that was devoted to mental hospitals reached 28.1% (Ministry of Health, 1956, p.13).

This activity clearly indicates a continuing concern to maintain, indeed improve, the effectiveness of mental hospitals.   Such improvements can largely be understood in terms of how to reap the greatest increase in effectiveness at the least cost; that is, with the least detriment to efficiency. For there was little new building and no totally new mental hospitals. Rather it was mainly a case of patching up existing stock and raising staff numbers in order to make full use of existing capacity. The intention was to maximise the ability of mental hospitals to provide treatment at minimum additional cost.

Increased emphasis upon raising the numbers treated can also be detected in other changes made.   Firstly, there was a tendency towards specialization within mental hospitals.   This involved initially a concern with the 'chronic patient', and how developments in treatment might reduce the numbers incarcerated (Chief Medical Officer, 1955, p.122). For even with recent improvements in turnover, mental hospitals still only took 3% of all hospital admissions, yet held some 44% of all hospital beds (Royal Commission On The Law Relating to Mental Illness and Mental Deficiency, 1957).   While many new admissions were subsequently discharged within a few weeks, there were a large number of people for whom the mental hospital had become home, and this was now perceived as a problem to be tackled with more intensive treatment.

By 1956 this analysis had been further developed (Chief Medical Officer, 1956, p.110). It was argued that developments in treatment allowed three patient groups to be identified. The first group consisted of those with less serious conditions who need not enter mental hospital at all, the second group consisted of the more seriously mentally ill who needed a short stay in hospital, and the third group consisted of the most seriously deranged who need long term accommodation. It was this latter group which was to be reduced as much as possible, in particular by moving the elderly out because, so the Ministry of Health now decreed, mental hospitals were not suitable for them (Ministry of Health, 1954, p.13). In practice, this policy was difficult to implement, for although 'Much effort was put into the rehabilitation of the long-stay patients in the 1950s and '60s...there was in practice rarely any possibility of discharge to the community...' (DHSS, 1975, para.214). However, although the policy may not have succeeded, this attempt at specialization in the mental hospitals represents an effort to make the service more effective by concentrating resources upon providing treatment to those who would be most likely to respond.

In addition to this tendency towards specialization, there was also further administrative change to make mental hospitals more accessible. This principally concerned the 'de-designation' of a number of mental hospital beds, starting in 1953, which meant that some beds would be exempt from the 1890 Lunacy Act regulations concerning admission. As an experiment, the number of beds so designated grew to only a few thousand. However, it represented an important step towards making treatment more accessible by making the admission procedure less formal; a trend that was gaining increasing momentum in the mid-20th century.

These changes in the organisation of mental health services were intended to gain maximum increases in the effectiveness of mental health services, in terms of treating larger numbers of people for mental illnesses, at minimum additional cost. The aim, of course, was good mental health:

> For good mental health one would postulate good physical health, a modicum of intelligence, lively instincts with a sufficiency of reasonable control, full participation in family and social life, giving and receiving in a warm-hearted way; an eye to the welfare of the self, the family, the community and the nation (Chief Medical Officer, 1954, p.104).

Yet, as we noted in our discussion of the socio-economic context of mental health policy making in this period, it was precisely the validity of some of these issues as guidelines to personal behaviour which were, particularly in the mid-1950s, beginning to be questioned. But while the objectives may have been clear, the method of achieving them were less so. The problems within the mental health service were too serious to be resolved by relatively minor organizational changes within mental hospitals. Rather what was needed, as the state came to realize in this period, was the re-focusing of service provision towards a wider audience;the community.

The first point to consider in this analysis is that even despite the apparent reinforced commitment to mental hospital services, the state's rhetoric began to turn against them. In its 1953 annual report, the Ministry of Health reviews the first five years of the National Health Service. We noted earlier that it identified major problems as being the lack of mental hospital accommodation and the shortage of nurses. But now we find that the definition of the problem begins to shift. Firstly, on accommodation; 'The problem is not so much one of shortage of beds but rather the more intensive use of those already existing.' (Ministry of Health, 1953, p.14). As for nursing staff; 'There may, however, be room for adjustment of the estimate of trained nurses needed. The character of mental hospitals is changing.' (Ministry of Health, 1953, p.15).

By 1955 this argument had developed further. The Ministry of Health maintains its emphasis upon upgrading mental hospital conditions, indeed this goes so far as a commitment in the Conservative Party Manifesto of 1955, 'United for Peace and Progress', to the building of new mental hospitals and the refurbishment of the existing stock where needed. But equally, the dilapidated and inappropriate nature of such provision is emphasised; they are held to be unsuitable to modern methods, treatments and social attitudes (Ministry of Health, 1955, p.13). In addition, the potential contribution of mental health services based outside hospital grounds begins to be realized. Thus by 1956 the Ministry of Health had begun to envisage an alternative to a predominantly institutional based mental health system (Ministry of Health, 1956, p.17).

The Ministry of Health appears to want to move away from the emphasis upon institutional care and treatment, but is not altogether clear what change is required. This confused picture continues through the mid-1950s, in 1955 for example it chides Regional Hospital Boards for failing to allocate a sufficient part of their capital budget to mental hospitals, but also states that mental hospitals are unsuited to modern methods of treatment (Ministry of Health, 1955, p.14). What we have here, then, is a stage of transition where mental hospitals are still needed but are of diminishing importance as the state's support of an institutional care policy for mentally distressed people begins to give way. Furthermore, as Bennett and Morris note, the impetus towards developing community resources was by no means a coherent policy development, but rather in large measure a response to the problems being faced within the mental hospitals:

> The changing pattern in the life of the hospital and the development of community facilities anticipated the future trend towards community care. But...although the elements of community care had been established...(these) were still viewed as complementary to the mental hospital. Mental hospitals were criticised and improved, but their existence was not questioned. The innovation of facilities in the community was not a response to attempts to deinstitutionalise, but rather a response to the needs of a newer and larger population that was willing to use the mental hospital (Bennett and Morris, 1983, pp.7-8).

Efficiency and acceptability

By 1953 this axis was, as we have argued, in an unsatisfactory condition as far as the state was concerned. Institutional care was expensive, in terms of cost per person attended to, and yet conditions within mental hospitals were poor and would cost a great deal to rectify. But in the next few years this situation was to change, with the state adopting a variety of arguments and strategies with which to reconcile efficiency and acceptability. We can examine these in two groups; those based around institutional care, and those around newly emergent services.

We noted in the last section that the criterion of efficiency was felt by the Ministry of Health to be less pressing in this period than had been the case. And in the same way that this allowed effectiveness to be more adequately addressed, so too did it allow acceptability to be relatively prioritised. Now in part the spending we identified to make the service more effective-on extra staff and beds-might also be considered to make the service more acceptable. Inevitably, expenditure will not simply address just one or other of these criteria, but will have implications for both. However, it might be argued that the principal function of spending on increasing the capacity of mental hospitals is to make them more effective, while other expenditures more directly address the criterion of acceptability. And in reviewing what the state did, some such expenditure can be identified.

Conditions within mental hospitals were made more tolerable in a number of ways. The standard of the food given was improved, and the decor of hospital wards upgraded (Ministry of Health, 1956, p.13). In the financial year 1956/7 a special allocation was made by

101

the Ministry of Health to the Regional Hospital Boards for use specifically in mental and mental deficiency hospitals '...to help them make improvements and in particular to raise the nutritive value of the patient's diets.' (Ministry of Health, 1958, p.27). This increased attention to the comfort of mental patients reflects in the increased average cost of maintaining mental hospital patients. Between 1953 and 1956 it rose by over 20% while at the same time for example the average cost in real terms of maintaining maternity patients fell slightly (Ministry of Health, 1960, pp.46-47). Furthermore, the level of overcrowding within mental hospitals began to fall. Having peaked in 1953, at 15.7%, it subsequently fell in each year reaching 14% in 1956 (Ministry of Health). Thus, by the end of this period, conditions for patients in mental hospitals had been made more acceptable.

In addition to attempting to reconcile efficiency and acceptability within mental hospitals, the Ministry of Health also in this period began to argue that some emerging services might be of use in addressing tensions on this axis. It is stressed that integrated domiciliary services, provided by local authority and general practitioner services, should be developed. These would undertake preventive and after-care work and thereby - so it is hoped - help reduce the demand for institutional care. Furthermore, volunteer help would be important in developing such a service, and should be made greater use of (Ministry of Health,1953, p.ii; 1955, p.i).

The Ministry of Health also began to notice developments being made in new types of service provision in this period, and their potential gradually came to be realized. The new day hospitals were noted to be a useful addition to the mental health service because, it was argued, they are both cheaper and more therapeutic than existing mental hospitals (Ministry of Health, 1953,p.16). Out-patient clinics too are considered to be a useful addition to the service, as well as local authority initiatives such as the development of day centres. In all these cases it is argued, or implied, that they are better for the patient (for example, because family contact is maintained, and it is less disruptive to the patients life) and that they are cheaper than mental hospital treatment.

Between 1953 and 1956 the state's perception of and response to the competing pulls of efficiency and acceptability changed markedly. Where there was only confusion, there now existed a variety of new initiatives and ideas that the Ministry of Health was beginning to identify as providing a solution to this problem. In 1956, the Chief Medical Officer argued that the future of mental health services had three foci; a developing community service, an expansion of general hospital facilities for mentally distressed people, and the existing (but upgraded) mental hospital stock. The Minister of Health too held a similar view, although giving less emphasis to the provision of mental hospital facilities:

> The extent of the problem of overcrowded mental hospitals could probably be reduced considerably by further development of all the resources of hospital and community care in a comprehensive service (Ministry of Health, 1956, p.13).

Effectiveness and acceptability

By 1952, as we saw earlier, this axis was not causing the state any major problems. The individualization and medicalization of personal distress in terms of mental illness was both effective and acceptable (the problem of course was finding an administrative structure suitable for the implementation of this). Not surprisingly therefore this strategy was retained, although there were some extensions and refinements of it.

An argument increasingly deployed in the mid-1950s was that advances in treatment had made mental illness more socially acceptable. It was held that the public are better informed about what mental illness is, are increasingly tolerant of the mentally ill, and are more ready to have such people in the community and indeed to help them stay there (Chief Medical Officer, 1953, p.9). This, it was argued, would allow people to be more readily discharged from mental hospital as well as making possible the treatment of people on an out-patient basis. We noted in Chapter 3 that little evidence existed to support such propositions, yet they were of considerable importance in sustaining the argument for diversifying mental health services.

The Ministry of Health began increasingly to take the lead in this period in defining the nature of the mental health problem, and how it should best be dealt with. This was most clearly demonstrated by the setting up of a major exhibition in London in November 1955. It was opened by the Minister of Health, who noted that the problem of mental illness is a serious one and requires attention (Ministry of Health, 1956, p.12). The purpose of the exhibition was to '...explain the true nature of mental illness...(and) to show something of the modern methods of treatment.' (Ministry of Health, 1956, p.19). To enable the mental health service to function effectively, the community's attitude to mental illness needed to become more tolerant, and the stated aim of the exhibition was to engender within the community a sense of responsibility to mental hospitals and their patients (Ministry of Health,1955, p.38):

> Without any attempt to 'glamourise', a lively picture should be presented of modern psychiatry, of the advanced state of knowledge of mental illness and its treatment, of a modern service with up-to-date ideas, aided by new methods of treatment, new drugs and new electrical apparatus (Public Records Office, MH55-2193).

The overall emphasis of the exhibition was to encourage people to accept mental hospital admission as being an acceptable part of everyday life. To overcome prejudice against the old asylums an attempt was made to improve the image of what people could expect from them. Illustrative case histories were used, including a person admitted to an older institution 'recovering quite quickly', and compared to a person admitted to a newer facility yet taking slightly longer to recover. Photographs of older mental hospitals were included, with captions such as 'Some patients have their own rooms where they can keep their belongings', and 'Most mental hospitals have lovely grounds where recreation of all kinds is provided for patients and staff' being included. The exhibition closes with the comment; 'Mental hospitals, though often housed in old buildings which may look unattractive outside, are up-to-date in outlook and methods of treatment...inside restful colours, flowers and paints do much to produce pleasant surroundings and a peaceful atmosphere.' (Public Records Office, MH55-2193).

The exhibition was subsequently to go on tour around the country, and within its first year over 100,000 people had attended and some 22,000 copies of 'The Hurt Mind', a BBC publication on mental distress, had been distributed. The individualization and medicalization of personal distress clearly remains a favoured strategy by the state. The competing claims and requirements for effectiveness and acceptability are resolved within the idea of mental distress as individual pathology that can be treated. Also, it is equally clear that mental hospitals, once modernised, are considered appropriate sites for the provision of treatment; the assumption being that people would indeed be cured and returned to the community. And as we can see from the Mental Health Exhibition, the state was sufficiently confident of this to go on the offensive.

The new model emerges: 1957-1959

By 1957 mental health services were clearly entering a period of substantial change. The old institutional model with its emphasis upon custody was in retreat, and a new and more diverse range of services were emerging. As yet, it was not clear what the eventual outcome would be in terms of the relative importance of mental hospital and community services, but in the last years of the decade this was to be clarified. To examine this three areas need to be reviewed; firstly, the Report of the Royal Commission On The Law Relating To Mental Illness and Deficiency which was presented to Parliament in May 1957, secondly, the state's policy making process which made further advances in changing the nature of mental health service provision, and finally, bringing these two areas together, the Mental Health Act 1959.

The terms of reference given to the Royal Commission were:

> To enquire, as regards England and Wales, into the existing law and administrative machinery governing the certification, detention, care (other than hospital care or treatment under the National Health Service Acts 1946-52), absence on trial or licence, discharge and supervision of persons who are or alleged to be suffering from mental illness or mental defect, other than Broadmoor patients; to consider, as regards England and Wales, the extent to which it is now, or should be made, statutorily possible for such persons to be treated as voluntary patients, without certification; and to make recommendations.

This agenda was set in 1954 and reflects the concerns of the time, these being to enquire into administrative and legal changes that might be made in order to reduce the problems of an institutional care system facing a lack of capacity, a loss of legitimacy as an appropriate means of providing for mentally distressed people, and insufficient funds with which to deal with these problem. But when the Royal Commission reported three years later it had gone beyond these terms of reference by presenting a whole set of arguments and assumptions about the nature of mental distress and appropriate methods of treatment, that then provided a basis for a series of recommendations for changes in the administrative structure of mental health services.

The conceptual model employed by the Royal Commission reflected the medical domination of its members. Its opening line reads: 'Disorders of the mind are illnesses which need medical

105

treatment.' (Royal Commission, 1957, para.5). Moreover, this view of mental illness is held to be generally accepted throughout society; '...we believe that most people today would at least pay lip-service to the principle which has been repeated to us by witness after witness, that the mentally ill are sick people...' (Royal Commission, 1957, para.67).

The Report also supports the view that the notion of mental illness should be integrated with that of physical illness. Again, a nebulous and unsubstantiated reference is made to public opinion: '...most people are coming to regard mental illness and disability in much the same way as physical illness and disability.' (Royal Commission, 1957, para.3). Additionally, the tendency to integrate mental illness with mental health, where each represents opposite ends of one continuum, is supported. Thus we are told that 'Most mental illnesses can occur at any age.' (Royal Commission, 1957, para.83), and that 'Mental illnesses, even of the same type, may vary in their severity.' (Royal Commission, 1957, para 80). The Report advocates the use of the term 'mental disorder' to cover the spectrum of mental problems (including mental handicap, with which we are not concerned with here). This term has since been accepted by all governments and has informed debate on mental health services since. We might ask then why the Report chose the term:

> We prefer this term to either 'mental abnormality' or 'mental disability', as either of these other terms might seem to imply, erroneously, that all through his life everyone is either normal or abnormal, either fully capable or disabled, where as in fact many forms of mental disorder last only a short time (Royal Commission, 1957, para.74).

These three arguments, that mental distress is an illness suitable for medical treatment, that mental and physical ailments are similar in nature, and that sanity and insanity are more closely related than once thought, are all common themes that we identified in Chapter 3 as emerging in the first half of the 20th century. We find here a major endorsement of these arguments, with the implication being that they are largely accepted within society and should be reflected in the manner in which mental health services are organised. We might, therefore, now examine what the Report considered to be the administrative implications of such a model of mental distress.

A key notion in the changing conception of mental distress is integration, and so it is in the proposed changes in the administra-

106

tive structure of mental health services. The Report argues that the separate development of mental health services from other forms of social services needs to be overcome: 'We consider it essential that the services for mentally disordered patients should continue to be an integral part of the general health and welfare services.' (Royal Commission, 1957, para.44). This integration was proposed on two levels. Firstly, mental hospitals should operate in similar fashion to general hospitals. Rather than providing long term residential care, mental hospitals should specialise in the provision of treatment (Royal Commission, 1957, para.46). Out-patient clinics and domiciliary services too should be developed, to meet the needs of the mentally ill who do not require hospitalization. Secondly, mental hospital provision should be integrated with local authority services. A continuum of care and treatment, providing services for people at different points between mental health and mental illness, should be provided:

> We consider it essential that contacts between psychiatric and other general and special interests within the hospital service and within the local authority services should be developed and strengthened...There should be much greater administrative flexibility in deciding what forms of care are really appropriate to each person's individual needs (Royal Commission 1957, para.592).

To develop this more integrated mental health service, the Report fully recognised that the existing imbalance between mental hospitals and local authority services would have to be addressed. Existing powers of the local authorities to provide community care for mentally distressed people were argued to be inadequate. Only permissive legislation existed, allowing them to provide the range of services that the Royal Commission Report considered necessary. They recommend, therefore, that provision of community services - in particular residential accommodation - should be imposed upon local authorities as a statutory duty and that the Exchequer should make grants available to fund the capital costs of such ventures. The implication of this, as the Report fully recognises, is that the cost of mental health services is likely to rise:

> We have felt it right to assume that a fair share of our national resources will be allocated in future to the mental health services both by the central government and by local authorities, and that it is recognised that in many areas these services have

a considerable amount of lee-way to make up compared with some other parts of the country's health and welfare services (Royal Commission, 1957, para.609).

The third main area of administrative change proposed, is the abolition of legal formalities for the admission of patients to mental hospital. It is argued that the existing law, based on the 1890 Lunacy Act, is outdated. Its assumption that patients should be detained under custody before receiving treatment was now inappropriate to modern methods and conceptions of treatment of mental distress. Thus the Report recommends '...that the law should be altered so that whenever possible suitable care may be provided for mentally disordered patients with no more restriction of liberty or legal formality than is applied to people who need other social services.' (Royal Commission, 1957, para.7).

The intention of these changes is to increase the accessibility of mental treatment to people, by removing the (supposed) stigma of certification and by making admission procedures simpler. However there is no intention to remove compulsory admission for some people who might resist treatment; 'Some may be dangerous to themselves or others, or may be incapable of protecting themselves. if proper care is to be provided for such patients, it can only be done by using compulsory powers.' (Royal Commission,1957, para.6). As such the reasons for admission are not so much being changed, as being expanded.

The Report of the Royal Commission represented a collation of major themes of the previous fifty years. It provided formal approval of trends and developments in psychiatric theory and practice, and presented a model of provision that would allow these changes to flourish. In the 1948-56 period we saw how institutional care was in crisis, yet no clear alternative being presented to it. While some new ideas were being expounded, they lacked a coherent model of service provision in which to be situated. It was this that the Royal Commission sought to furnish. As such, it set the agenda for the debate to follow around how to develop an alternative to institutional care.

The new Minister of Health, Derek Walker-Smith, who was appointed in September 1957 and was to guide the changes in legislation in 1959, noted the Royal Commission's Report to be the most important single event in health matters in that year (Ministry of Health, 1957, p.iii). However, while the Report was clearly of considerable importance in influencing the development of mental health policy, we need also to examine the context in which it was received. This concerns, of course, the policy making environment as determined by the three criteria of cost, control and legitimation.

Efficiency and effectiveness

Through the 1950s we have seen that the cost criterion gradually diminished in importance. With the economy booming the state felt increasingly able to commit expenditure on social services. The demands made to economise within the health service, which had characterised policy statements in the early 1950s, was now replaced by a general satisfaction with the performance of the health services. For increases in effectiveness (in terms of patients treated) had far outstripped increases in the cost of services provision. There was, then, even a sense of satisfaction:

> While it is true that the increasing cost of the Service has given successive Ministers cause for concern, the rise during the decade was due predominantly to the inflationary trends in the economy, reflecting to the extent of approximately 70 per cent. the effect of higher prices and higher renumeration...no major change (is) needed in the general administrative structure to secure a more efficient and economical organisation (Ministry of Health, 1958, p.v).

With a diminished concern for efficiency there was greater scope for making mental hospitals effective, and they continued to receive priority treatment. Capital expenditure upon psychiatric hospitals rose both in real and percentage terms, reaching 29.8% of total capital expenditure by Regional Hospital Boards in 1959/60. The numbers of staff employed continued to rise, with the number of full-time psychiatric nurses rising from 20,903 in 1957 to 24,652 in 1959, and the number of consultant staff working in mental health (ie mental illness and mental deficiency) rising from 614 to 648 in the same period. The effectiveness of mental hospitals is still clearly of some concern to the state, and with increased resources is able to provide additional funding to improve their treatment facilities.

Other areas that we have identified as being concerned with this axis were efforts to make mental hospitals more accessible and more specialised, and these continued to be supported by the Ministry of Health. The increasing percentage of patients being treated on a voluntary basis, and the concomitant decrease in certified patients, are held to be progressive changes reflecting the increasingly effective nature of psychiatric treatment, as well as the general public's increased willingness to receive such therapies. Also the attempt to concentrate resources upon treatment rather than residential care is maintained. The failure to shift long term residents is acknowledged by the Ministry of Health, when it notes a growing bifurcation in the resident population of mental hospitals between short and long term patients. But this, it is argued, is only a temporary problem that will successfully be addressed by modern methods of treatment (Ministry of Health, 1958, pp.28-29).

Although the state continued to support and fund mental hospitals in this way, it was in part only dealing with old problems. It now had the resources to tackle a little more adequately the lack of capacity within mental hospitals which since 1948 had been a source of serious concern. Yet within mental hospitals, the overcrowding problem was now abating. Since 1954, the mental hospital population had begun slowly to contract. In 1957, the bed space in use had peaked at 121,412 and subsequently fell - by 1959 dropping to 117,576. Even with this reduction in the scale of the service the level of overcrowding fell rapidly; standing at 11.9% in 1956 it then dropped substantially to 7.6% by 1959. Thus, even though the rate of admissions continued to increase, the perception of the problems of institutional care on this axis began to diminish.

Although these problems were being more adequately managed, the perception within the Ministry of Health of the need to increase the orbit of mental health services remained. This concern is based upon the developments in psychiatric theory indicating that mental illness is a problem, or potential problem, for all. Without reference to source, it is claimed that some two million people a year receive treatment from general practitioners for psycho-neurotic disorders (Chief Medical Officer, 1958, p.126). This estimate is higher than any of the available statistical evidence suggests, including that of the General Register Office, that we reviewed in Chapter 3. As such, it appears that the state is actively seeking out areas of what had been private life in which to provide a service. As the Chief Medical Officer cogently informs us; 'The practice of medicine is not wholly a matter of the diagnosis and treatment of diseases as they occur in individual patients; its field extends into the world of everyday life.' (Chief Medical Officer, 1959, p.143).

The Ministry of Health was quick to recognise that the new administrative structure of mental health services proposed by the Royal Commission Report would enable services to become more effective. In a review of the Report, it enthuses about the increased accessibility of mental hospitals that is proposed:

110

Patients who are content to enter mental hospital should do so with no more formalities than are required when a patient enters a general hospital. Powers to detain patients compulsorily should only be invoked when this is positively necessary (Ministry of Health, 1957, p.9).

The proposal for an increased range of services to be developed is also welcomed. It is acknowledged that this '...would require a very considerable expansion of the services provided by local authorities for all groups of mentally disordered persons.' (Ministry of Health, 1957, p.9). Thus in total, the state welcomed the main recommendations of the Report.

But while such proposals were supported on the basis of their imagined effectiveness, the implied costs of such a service were less welcome. This wariness is clearly demonstrated in the interpretation made of just what the Report was saying:

It pointed out that even in the most favourable economic circumstances such expansion would take a considerable time, and recognised that it was recommending this expansion at a time when public expenditure is subject to strict limitation, especially in regard to capital development...It expressed the hope however that even in present circumstances a start could be made, and recommended that consideration should be given by the central government to means by which such expansion could be expedited as far as is consistent with general economic policy (Ministry of Health, 1957, p.11).

This interpretation of the Royal Commission's Report clearly demonstrates the importance of the cost factor in the state's thinking. It is wary of taking on responsibility for Exchequer funding for the newly developing services, and justifies its position on the basis of what the country can afford. For a Marxist analysis, it is perhaps tempting to accept this at face value and point to the imperatives of the capitalist economic system as the underlying reason for the government's stance. But of course, as we noted in Chapter 3, the economy was booming and considerable confidence existed over future economic prospects, while mental health services in total only represented a small fraction of overall state expenditure. The National Health Service only took up some 3% to 4% of GNP, and of this mental health services received just one-tenth. Thus, at this time what appears more important was the power of the treasury. Considerable pressure was being brought to bear on the Ministry of Health in the late 1950s to reduce its expenditure. Indeed the Minister of Health, Derek Walker-Smith, later admitted that in a cabinet battle in 1958, he had been on the point of resigning over demands for cuts in spending (Roth, 1970, p.230).

Efficiency and acceptability

As with our discussion of the efficiency/effectiveness axis, we need here to consider changes in the Ministry of Health's attitude to both institutional and community services. Taking the first of these, we find that there was still some concern with the poor quality of accommodation and general living arrangements within the mental hospitals. During a debate in the House of Commons in 1958, celebrating the tenth anniversary of the National Health Service, Bevan noted that '...some of our mental hospitals are in a disgraceful condition.' (quoted in Klein, 1983, p.31). As we saw in the last section, capital expenditure on mental hospitals continued to increase in real terms and as a percentage of the overall hospital capital budget. Such expenditure was not just directed at increasing effectiveness, by building new wards, admission units and so on, but was used in part to improve the fabric of existing buildings. The unit costs of maintaining mental patients continued to rise, as the conditions in which they were kept slowly improved as well as because of the increasing costs of treating patients. Thus, with some diminishing of the importance of the cost criteria the state was able to address the opposing criteria of legitimation by making conditions a little more acceptable. In 1958 further additional allocations were made to Regional Hospital Boards specifically to improve the diet of mental patients (Ministry of Health, 1958, p.27). Such improvements were minimal, but does provide the basis for the Ministry of Health to claim that '...great improvements have been made by up-grading, reconstruction and new building. The effect has been to make the hospitals both pleasanter places for patients and staff, and better suited for their therapeutic purpose.' (Ministry of Health, 1958, p.26).

But while recognising the short term need to make mental hospitals more acceptable, the Ministry of Health was of course in the process of attempting to alter the focus of service provision. Thus despite these increases in expenditure during this period, we find that at the same time it also mounts an attack against the appropriateness, or legitimacy of mental hospital services. Firstly, it's argued that mental hospitals as they currently exist are not wanted in a modern mental health service system:

> The shift to community care recommended by the Royal Commission is based on developments in medical treatment in recent years, and on increasing acceptance by doctors of the view that for many patients treatment is likely to be more effective if the patient's links with his own home surroundings can be kept intact. Long term residence in a hospital-resulting in 'institutionalisation'-may reduce the patient's prospect of eventual rehabilitation and discharge (Ministry of Health, 1959, p.7).

These arguments are repeated a number of times in the late 1950s, but really must be considered facile. The notion that links with the community should be maintained directly contradicts the views of psychiatry and the state over the previous century and more. The name, asylum, and the isolated settings in which they were built, reflects the overwhelming consensus that had existed that isolation from the community was necessary for effective therapy. The sudden realisation that the opposite is true goes unexplained. As for the dangers of institutionalization, a similar critique developed in the 1870s had had little effect upon state policy (Scull, 1984), and indeed this new critique in the 1950s was barely emerging. But now of course the nature of the problem was changing, and mental hospitals in their old form were ill-suited to dealing with it. The extension of psychiatric services into the community thus involved the Ministry of Health de-legitimating its own out-dated policies.

Secondly, on the basis that mental hospitals as they exist are not wanted, it's argued they are not needed. In 1957 we find the first textual reference in the Annual Reports of the Ministry of Health to the falling mental hospital population; 'The reduction in the number of patients resident mainly reflects increasing success in the rehabilitation and discharge of patients who have been in hospital for many years, and the shorter length of stay of newly admitted patients.' (Ministry of Health, 1957, p.22). Just one year later, its argued that 'So far as mental hospitals are concerned, there are grounds for hoping that the watershed has been crossed.' (Ministry of Health, 1958, p.28). And just one year after that, we are told that '...there is likely in the long run to be a marked decline in the need for long-stay accommodation in psychiatric hospitals...' (Ministry of Health, 1959, p.25).

The only evidence cited to support this is a statistical run between 1954 and 1959, which witnessed a reduction in the mental hospital population from 148,080 to 133,154. On the basis of this, we find that:

> ...it is clear that, in long term planning, it is now necessary to begin seriously to allow for the fact that we are likely in future not to need nearly so many beds as are now used for long-stay patients suffering from mental illness...during the next few years much careful thought will be needed before any large-scale new developments for long-stay patients in mental hospitals are embarked on. Similarly, difficult problems arise when major works of renewal or up-grading are being considered at existing mental hospitals, so as to avoid the danger of spending a lot of money on a hospital which in 10 or 15 years may be partly or wholly out of use or being put to some quite different purpose, and yet to provide all the amenities needed by existing patients (Ministry of Health, 1959, p.25).

The proposition defended by the Ministry of Health that it is following trends and developments, rather than trying to make them, cannot be sustained. The reduction of a few thousand mental hospital beds over a five year period, in the context of a hundred year period of expansion of mental hospital provision is not, as many were soon to point out, sufficient basis for major policy changes (Jones, 1964). Indeed even the Chief Medical Officer finds it impossible to support such arguments. He notes that with an ageing population, the lack of likely success in rehabilitating the 'hard core of organically deteriorated patients', and the possible future rejection by the community of 'eccentrics', that in fact there is a continuing need for mental hospital provision (Chief Medical Officer, 1959, p.131).

While the attitude of the Ministry of Health towards institutional care for mentally distressed people was to erode its acceptability, its attitude towards community care was conversely to attempt to increase its legitimacy. A key part of this is the argument that the public is now more tolerant of the mentally ill, and more prepared to accept discharged patients living amongst them. Between 1957 and 1959 it becomes a commonly stated theme that there had been 'A substantial change in the general climate of public opinion...' (Ministry of Health,1958,p.22) which made community care feasible and desirable; in short, 'People are more ready to tolerate mental disorder.' (Chief Medical Officer, 1958, p.121). No evidence was offered to support this contention, and as we saw in Chapter 3 very little evidence existed to support such a view. Yet, with frequent repetition, the idea that mentally ill people could expect to be more

114

tolerated and better supported within the community provided a major prop to the argument for developing a community based system of care and treatment.

The varied experimental developments in mental health services, that had been encouraged in the mid-1950s, were now increasingly argued to be able to provide a service that was both efficient and acceptable. One of the most important of these was a scheme started in 1957 at Graylingwell Hospital, Chichester, where by developing domiciliary, out-patient and day hospital facilities, it was found that in-patient admissions dropped substantially. Where the cost per hospital patient per week was running at £7.2.11d, the cost per patient of the new community based services was £0.9s per week (Lancet, 1959,i, p.668). At a day unit introduced at the Maudsley teaching hospital it was found that the running costs of providing thirty places were just one third of those of a thirty bedded ward (Lancet, 1957,i, p.732). By the end of 1958 some 35 day hospital units had been established, and these it was argued would help further the reduction in need for in-patient treatment (Ministry of Health, 1958, p.24). The Ministry of Health was all to aware of the advantages these developments offered in terms of meeting its own problem of reconciling efficiency and acceptability of service provision:

> The advantages to, for example, the housewife or the salary earner of being able to secure the needed treatment, while continuing to live an ordinary life, are obvious, and one should not overlook the economic advantages which accrues to the community at large (Ministry of Health, 1958, p.24).

The claim of the Ministry of Health then, was that these new community services, together with local authority, voluntary and community provision, were more acceptable because they offered a form of care more suited to patients needs. And when taking into account the fact that it was refusing to centrally fund local authority initiatives, and the evidence about the cost of developments such as at Graylingwell noted above, there is little doubt that it thought it could achieve an increase in acceptability of mental health services without incurring a commensurate increase in cost. Community care appeared the ideal solution to the tension between efficiency and acceptability, which institutional care had been unable to reconcile.

In our discussion of this axis so far we have seen how the Ministry of Health supported a model of mental illness as a medical condition suitable for psychiatric intervention. This we have argued almost ideally met the twin requirements of effectively providing control through the provision of treatment while being accepted as a legitimate activity. Not surprisingly, therefore, we find this argument being maintained.

In November 1955, the first of the Mental Health Exhibitions, that we discussed earlier, had been held in London. This was then repeated in subsequent years in different parts of the country. By the end of 1958 there had been 51 exhibitions (Ministry of Health, 1958, p.68). The aim of these was to spread greater understanding amongst the general population of the 'true' nature of mental illness, and the increasing effectiveness of the treatments available. The Ministry of Health also notes with approval the increasing media interest in mental illness, and its support given to spreading knowledge about the importance of the problem and of the therapies available. All of this '...did much to help forward the process of public enlightenment.' (Ministry of Health, 1957, p.26).

The true nature of mental distress presented by the exhibitions was very much based upon changes in psychiatric theory over the previous half century. We have examined in earlier sections the facets of this, concerning the integration of the concepts of mental and physical illness, and of sanity and insanity. The result of the campaign the Ministry of Health now claimed was that '...mental disorder is now very widely accepted as an illness like other illnesses, that people suffering from it are increasingly willing to seek treatment for it...' (Ministry of Health, 1958, p.22). And once coming forward for treatment, it is claimed that much can be done to help patients; 'It was only recently that powerful therapeutic weapons had been put into the hands of the medical staff, who for many years had had very limited prospects of curative work.' (Ministry of Health, 1958, p.22). By the end of the 1950s, then, the state is confident that psychiatric treatment for mental distress is acceptable, and effective.

It is difficult to reconcile this view of psychiatric treatment with what was actually happening. Although the confidence of the psychiatric profession to provide effective treatment was growing, some caution was still expressed about the extent to which mental distress could be cured. Psychiatrists acknowledged that the development of new drugs constituted an important therapeutic advance in the amelioration of the more distressing aspects of severe mental illness, but were still conducting trials to establish their curative value. This reflects in the reasons given for the discharge of patients from mental hospital. As we noted in Chapter 1, between 1948 and 1957 the percentage discharged as 'recovered' declined from 41.3% to 23.%, while the percentage discharged as 'relieved' increased from 46.5% to 65.5%. The numbers discharged as 'not improved' remained relatively static, declining from 12.3% to 10.7%. Moreover psychiatrists were well aware of the need for increased knowledge about the nature and development of mental illnesses, yet the amounts spent by the state on research in this field was minimal, amounting in 1957/8 to only £55,000 (Ramon, 1985).

Such evidence as this however only demonstrates the success the Ministry of Health had in presenting psychiatric treatment as effective and acceptable, for no pressure groups were able or inclined to contradict such a view. The psychiatric profession, seeing its own interests lying with accepting such arguments, allowed the state to pursue claims about the value of drug treat-ments, and about the value of maintaining people in the commun-ity, despite its own views having over previous years differed considerably from this position.

However the problem still unresolved was how to develop an administrative structure that would allow this changing emphasis in mental health services to develop. Some new measures had emerged, such as use of non statutory mental hospital beds (rising from 2,923 in 1953 to 8,246 in 1958; Ministry of Health, 1958, p.27), the increasing percentage of voluntary patients, and the develop-ment of alternative treatment sights such as day hospitals and out-patient clinics. But as yet they lacked a coherent administrative rationale; they helped address the problems the state faced but were random and unco-ordinated in their development. However, with the Report of the Royal Commission in 1957, such a rationale was found:

...there has been a general welcome for the principles upon which the Report of the Royal Commission was based...Two of these principles which well reflect the changes which have taken place are that the procedure for securing treatment for mental disorder should be as informal as it can be, and should, so far as possible, be the same as that for securing treatment for physical illness; and that there should be a reorientation towards community services... (Ministry of Health, 1958, pp.22-23).

The state was now in a position to legislate. The problems of institutional care, which had been long recognised, could now it was believed be overcome by changing the emphasis towards a community based system of care and treatment. This would allow more patients to be treated by making treatment services more accessible, as well as more focussed on the provision of treatment as increasingly the care of patients is transferred to the community. This increase in the provision of treatment would be achieved without a commensurate increase in cost, and the whole process could be presented as a legitimate reform intended for the benefit of mentally distressed people.

The Mental Health Act, 1959

By the end of the 1950s there was a consensus of opinion that new legislation on mental health was required although, as we saw in Chapter 3, not on what specific changes should be made. Existing provisions, based upon the Lunacy Act of 1890 and the Mental Treatment Act of 1930, were generally considered to be a fetter upon new developments in the treatment and welfare of mentally distressed people. And with a new model of provision now established, it was time to repeal old legislation that inhibited its development and replace it with legislative provision for the development of community care. The Mental Health Bill was introduced in the House of Commons on 17th December 1958, passed through all its stages in both Houses during the parliamentary session, and received the Royal Assent on July 29th,1959.

The Act repealed all previous legislation concerning lunacy, mental treatment and mental deficiency (provision for the latter in the Act is not discussed here). It defines its area of concern as 'mental disorder'; this being 'mental illness, arrested or incomplete development of the mind, psychopathic disorder and any other disorder or disability of mind'. Mental illness is not defined further, though it is made clear that a person may not be dealt with under the Act simply for reason of 'promiscuity or other immoral conduct'. Psychopathic disorder however is elaborated upon; it is 'a persistent disorder or disability of mind (whether or not including subnormality of intelligence) which results in abnormally aggressive or seriously irresponsible conduct on the part of the patient and requires or is susceptible to medical treatment'. A central principle of the Act was to encourage the development of community services for mentally distressed people not requiring hospital admission. It lays out in some detail the powers of local authorities to provide services. These include provision of residential accommodation, centres for training and occupation, and 'the provision of any ancillary or supplementary services'. 'Mental Welfare Officers', a term used in part to replace that of the 'duly authorised officer', could be appointed with powers to enter and inspect premises if having cause to believe that a mentally disordered person is not under proper care. They were also empowered to return to hospital a patient absent without leave and to retake patients escaping from legal custody.

Although the Act placed considerable emphasis upon developing local authority community services, it added few powers to aid such change. Local authorities were already empowered under section 28 of the National Health Service Act,1946 to provide community services and the Mental Health Act only provides greater definition of this. A direction from the Minister of Health to local health authorities shortly after the Act was passed made it obligatory that provision be made under section 28, and the National Assistance Act,1948 was amended to allow Part III accommodation to be provided for the mentally disordered. But the Act did not provide increased central funding to help in the development of such services; it provided considerable encouragement, and it provided slightly greater powers, but provided no additional resources to facilitate the development of community care services.

The second major principle of the Act was that treatment should as far as possible be provided on an informal and voluntary basis. The certification of patients and the need for a magistrate's order for patients to be admitted was replaced by applications to be made by the nearest relative or mental welfare officer, and supported by recommendations from two medical practitioners. This replaced what was perceived as the excessive legalism of the provisions of the 1890 Lunacy Act. The provisions of the 1930 Mental Treatment Act to allow voluntary admission by patients able to express their own wishes was replaced by informal admission, whereby people could be taken into mental hospital without the patient's own volition, provided they did not specifically object to treatment. Thus for most patients it was envisaged that entry to mental hospital would be on an informal basis, mirroring the practice of general hospitals. However, for the minority who could not be persuaded to enter voluntarily but for whom treatment was considered necessary, compulsory provisions were retained. The Act allowed for compulsory admission for observation, for treatment and emergencies. Also in relation to admittance of mental patients, the Act allowed for any hospital to receive patients. It was envisaged that this would allow a substantial increase in psychiatric facilities provided in general hospitals. Previously designated mental hospitals were no longer obliged to receive patients. In this way, the admission of patients was brought further into line with services for the physically ill.

In his Annual Report for 1959, the Minister of Health enthuses about the new legislation:

> The most important single event within the National Health Service during the year under review was the addition to the Statute Book of the Mental Health Act, 1959...This far-reaching measure gives effect to the enlightened and forward thinking of recent years, which was crystallised in the Report and Recommendations of the Royal Commission on the Law relating to Mental Illness and Mental Deficiency (Ministry of Health, 1959,p.iii).

We might, however, consider just how enlightened and just how close to the Royal Commission's Report the Act really was.

The Mental Health Act embodies the recommendations for access to mental hospital to be made less formal, and to mirror admission practices in general hospitals. We have seen through the 1950s continual state support for this, because it increases the effectiveness of the mental health service by making treatment more readily available. It also increases the power of psychiatry by making treatment the main criteria for admission, and doing away with legal involvement. It is the medical model of intervention in which the Ministry of Health places its faith in regulating mentally distressed people. But at the same time, we have seen that by the end of the 1950s it was attempting to reduce the scale of mental hospital provision. Despite increasing the ease of admission the argument pursued is that fewer beds will be needed, for the aim is to increase the efficiency of mental hospitals by raising the throughput of mental patients, and by lowering the number of chronic patients in mental hospitals. The intent of the new informal admission procedure is to increase the effectiveness of the service by providing treatment to many people, while their more general need for care is left to the community.

The Ministry of Health, as we have seen, perceives community care to be an efficient way in which to provide mental health services. But they need also to be acceptable; something that the

Royal Commission argued would require Exchequer funding for new community services. On this issue, the state chose to ignore such enlightened thinking, but this did make the resolution of efficiency and acceptability problematic. The defence made was that with a new general grant being introduced in 1959/60 to replace specific major Exchequer grants to local authorities, it would be inappropriate to introduce a specific grant for the development of community care services. However the need for additional resources is recognised, and for the first grant period the Ministry of Health claims to have included the estimated expenditure for community care services in the general grant (Ministry of Health, 1958, p.174). On this basis the Minister of Health maintained that community care was not a cost-cutting exercise; 'I yield to none in my desire for the steady progress and gathering acceleration of the local authority mental health services.' (Quoted in Ramon, 1985, p.273).

We have seen how the antagonism between effectiveness and acceptableness in the regulation of mentally distressed people was reconciled by the Ministry of Health through its support for the ability of psychiatry to deal with the problem humanely and appropriately. It is no surprise then to see the power of the psychiatric profession increased by the Mental Health Act. As we noted above, the role of the legal profession in regulating admission to mental hospital was removed, and greater emphasis placed on medical opinion. Furthermore the Board of Control, which since 1913 had had a 'watchdog' function in overseeing mental hospitals was wound up. There had in fact been since 1774 in one form or another an inspectorate to ensure compliance with mental health legislation (Hamilton,1986), but with the links between mental illness and physical illness becoming more apparent, it was argued that the administrative structure of mental and general hospitals should be unified; with medical authority taking precedence in each (Chief Medical Officer, 1960, p.97). Mental Health Review Tribunals with powers to review cases of compulsory admission were established by the new Act, but this represented less of a challenge to the dominance of a medical approach to mental distress.

A further endorsement of the central role of the psychiatric profession appears in the way psychopathy is dealt with in the Act. While the Royal Commission report had referred to the 'psychopathic personality', it had not given a definition of the condition. But, as we saw above, the Mental Health Act supplies this. The condition is defined only by the normative evaluation of 'abnormally aggressive or seriously irresponsible conduct'. The

121

association of mental illness and non-conformity is hidden here by only the thinnest veneer. As one M.P. noted, psychopathy concerns:

> ...the changeling and the waif. They are not so different from those who, in these days, pathetically and fantastically refer to themselves as the 'beat generation' and 'rebels' and all that sort of thing. There seems to be one thing which all these people have in common, they are incapable of forming real, lasting and valid relationships with the rest of society (Quoted in Ramon, 1985, p.256).

The Mental Health Act makes it clear that despite the lack of any mental illness that can be diagnosed, aberrant behaviour falls within the legitimate orbit of psychiatric practice. The association of psychiatry with social control is perhaps at its most obvious when dealing with the psychopath. As Ramon notes, 'Where such factors as deviation from norms of employment, sexuality and interpersonal relationships are involved, one is entitled to be somewhat suspicious of how such judgments operate in relation to the working-class psychopath.' (Ramon, 1986, p.229). But it is also a reflection of the confidence of the state in the power of psychiatry to effectively deal with individual dissent in acceptable ways, even when no medical grounds for intervention could be established.

In total, the Minister of Health maintained that 'This Act adds a notable Chapter to the story of our social progress...' (Ministry of Health, 1959, p.iii). The whole process of changing mental health service provision from a focus on institutional to community care is presented as one of reform. The analysis presented here however suggests that in fact two central processes were occurring, which need not be accepted as reform. The Mental Health Act legislated for the expansion of the orbit of psychiatric practice, where treatment was no longer to be confined to mental hospital in-patients, but could now operate in the community. This was supported by the Ministry of Health in its endorsement of medical intervention in an increasing range of 'psychological' problems, and in its support for the development of a range of locations for the provision of treatment. Secondly the twin facets of treatment and care that had been fused in the institutional care model, were now being separated out. Community care allowed the state to support with some vigour treatment in the community, but care was to be - as far as possible - by the community.

After the rhetoric, the reality: 1960-1963

With the enactment of the Mental Health Act the Minister of Health, Derek Walker-Smith, felt he had completed his work. After the General Election in October 1959 he expressed a desire to Macmillan to return to his work as a barrister, and eventually in June 1960 announced his resignation. In July he was replaced by Enoch Powell. Thus with the turn of the decade the context of mental health policy making had undergone substantial change. A major new Act was in place that provided a basis for large changes in service provision. The Conservatives were in office for a third term, without electoral worries for some time. And a new Minister of Health, known for his critical attitude to public expenditure, was in place. In this context the reality of community care was to emerge.

Efficiency and effectiveness

The community care policy laid clear emphasis upon the development of alternatives to institutional care. However, while this implies a diminution in the relative importance of mental hospital provision, we find that in the early 1960s the Ministry of Health still supports their activities. As in the 1950s, there is an emphasis on making such services more effective by emphasising the treatment role of mental hospitals. The number of psychiatric nurses continued to rise, from 31,719 in 1961 to 33,837 in 1963 (whole-time and part-time staff). By 1963 there were some 763 consultant staff in mental health, a rise of 115 since 1959 and almost double the level employed in 1948. Within mental hospitals some further developments were being made to treat patients. In 1957 just 1% of mental hospitals containing over 300 beds had occupational units. By 1961 some 64% had such units, which it was hoped would provide patients with '...training not only in work skill but also in earning money with a view to resettlement in open employment and independent living.' (Chief Medical Officer, 1961, p.101). Equally, the numbers of people being admitted to mental hospital continued to increase, and to do so at an accelerated rate. In 1959 there had been 98,237 admissions, in 1961 138,716, and by 1963 160,405 admissions. Although these statistics in part reflect the rising level of repeat admissions, it is still the case that mental hospitals had never treated so many people before.

Despite these developments, however, a decisive turn in the Ministry of Health's attitude to the role of mental hospitals occurs in this period. For while the immediate need for mental hospital provision is acknowledged, the overall trends towards care in the community and the inappropriateness of existing mental hospital provision is stressed. Right from the beginning of this period plans for a massive reduction in mental hospital beds occurs. On the basis of the fall in beds occupied since 1954 the state now argues that a '...substantial decline in the number of hospital beds required is to be anticipated and the figure may fall from 152,000 beds to 80,000 over a period of 16 years.' (Ministry of Health, 1960, p.1). It is estimated, on the basis of a survey conducted by the General Register Office in the mid-1950s, that a total of 1.8 beds per thousand of the population will be required. Half of these will be required for long-stay patients and half for acute admissions (Chief Medical Officer, 1960, p.95). In total, its estimated that the scale of mental hospital provision should be halved over the next 15 years. Moreover its suggested that these estimates may yet be subject to downward revision, because as community services develop and the effectiveness of treatments improves the need for mental hospital beds will be further reduced (Chief Medical Officer, 1960, p.96). As we saw earlier the statistical basis for such projections were at best tenuous, yet by the early 1960s they have provided the basis for policy developments.

In 1962 the 'Hospital Plan' was published, which laid out a major programme of hospital building for the next decade. Since 1948 capital expenditure on both mental and general hospitals had totalled £157m, but it was now planned that by 1970/71 a further £707.5 million would be spent. This was clearly a period of some optimism about the amount of money available for social expenditure, with the cost constraint on policy making being relatively unimportant. Yet, within the Hospital Plan a policy of reducing mental hospital provision is made clear; 'Because of the success of new methods of treatment combined with changed social attitudes, it may be expected that the recent decline in the number of hospital beds required for mental illness will continue.' (Ministry of Health, 1962, p.5). Further, the policy of developing psychiatric units at general hospitals is endorsed, and it is assumed that local authorities will develop adequate community services even if they do not already exist (Ministry of Health, 1962, p.11). Hence, 'In this new pattern there will be no place for many of the existing mental hospitals.' (Ministry of Health, 1962, p.8).

Rather than facing a fiscal crisis, the state's room for manoeuver is in fact if anything increasing. Yet a clear decision is being made to run mental hospitals down. This reflects in the capital expenditure programme. Between 1948 and 1961 27.3% of capital expenditure on all hospitals had been on mental hospitals. As we saw earlier this had gradually risen, and had reached 29.8% in 1959/60. This however was to be its peak, with a substantial fall occurring the following financial year with mental hospitals receiving just 25.7% of hospital capital expenditure (Ministry of Health, 1961, p.136).

A year after the Hospital Plan was produced a companion document, 'Health and Welfare:The Development of Community Care', was published. The contrast between the two is strong. Where the Hospital Plan made specific statements about the development of services for treatment, the care of the mentally ill in the community receives no specific undertakings. A comprehensive review of local authority plans for the development of community care is presented, and some encouraging words about the benefits to patients of remaining within the community are given. But as Jones notes, 'Those who looked for a rationale of community care and a positive lead from central Government were disappointed.' (Jones, 1972, p.326).

By the early 1960s we can see that on the efficiency/effectiveness axis a fairly complicated picture emerges, but which is nevertheless comprehensible. To recapitulate, the Ministry of Health sought to sustain the availability of treatment in mental hospitals, particularly as admission rates continued to rise. But it sought to substantially reduce the amount of care - in terms of the number of hospital beds - that mental hospitals could provide. Also it was concerned to eventually replace mental hospital treatment with provision in the community by psychiatric units in District General Hospitals, as well as by general practitioners, social workers and other ancillary staff. As far as possible, the service was to be treatment orientated by becoming integrated administratively and conceptually with physical medicine. This would maximise effectiveness by taking psychiatric care out of the asylum and into the community, providing a service that effectively provides treatment for considerably more people than might be held in mental hospitals. At the same time the provision of care is minimised. The intention is that only when mental patients are undergoing treatment will they be cared for, with their longer term needs for support being left to the community.

Now this is not to suggest that the service will be any cheaper. For while the aim is to reduce the cost of treatment for individual patients, there is considerable emphasis upon providing a service for many more people. Rather, the aim is to increase efficiency by focussing mental health services more directly on the concerns of the state. Extraneous expenses attached to the effectiveness of the service are, as far as possible, detached. What we have here then, is the administrative expression of the Mental Health Act's aim of treatment in the community and care by the community.

Efficiency and acceptability

A trend we have identified on this axis has been the steadily rising cost of in-patient care for mentally distressed people, and despite the proposed run down of mental hospitals this trend continues in the early 1960s. Between 1957/8 and 1962/3 the cost per week increase for mental in-patients was over 50%, although 30% of this was accounted for by increases in rates of renumeration for staff and inflation in the cost of supplies. Also the cost of treatments rose, as the emphasis within mental hospitals switched towards more intensive therapy. But nevertheless, the increase in revenue costs of hospitals for mentally distressed people was higher than for any other patient group which in part was accounted for by the continuing effort to improve the conditions in which patients were kept (Ministry of Health, 1963, pp.38-39).

The reduction in mental hospital provision had by the early 1960s become a firmly established principle for future policy making within the Ministry of Health. It was held to be acceptable on the basis that improving methods of treatment and increasing levels of care being provided in the community make the existing level of hospital bed provision too high; '...it is clear beyond any reasonable doubt that during the next 15 years there will be very large reductions in the need for beds for the treatment of mental illness...' (Ministry of Health, 1960, p.12). It is interesting to note that so keenly was the policy pursued that the Chief Medical Officer felt it necessary to give some warning about the implications of such a rapid reduction in numbers of beds. He stresses that with rates of admission and re-admission continuing to rise it is not yet clear just what level of provision is required. Thus he warns that 'It is clear that planning the future of the curative services for the mentally ill involves a great deal more than the application of estimates of bed requirements based on trends in hospital statistics.' (Chief Medical Officer, 1960, p.96). Within the Ministry of Health itself, then, we can see some tension between competing interests for what is efficient and what is acceptable. But overall the policy to reduce beds is well established, and some confidence is held that the reduction in bed numbers can be accelerated. The final task to be undertaken now was to sell the idea publicly; to make it generally accepted.

In 1961 at the Annual Conference of the National Association for Mental Health, Enoch Powell came to make the inaugural speech. He used the occasion to launch the new policy initiative in what has now become a famous speech. The estimated reduction of mental hospital beds by half was announced, and presented as a bold new initiative responding to modern developments in the care and treatment of mentally distressed people; '...if we are to have the courage of our ambitions, we ought to pitch the estimate lower still, as low as we dare, perhaps lower.' (Quoted in Jones, 1972, p.321). Moreover the implications of this were clearly spelt out, and done so in a manner that made criticism appear reactionary:

> Now look and see what are the implications of these bold words. They imply nothing less than the elimination of by far the greater part of this country's mental hospitals as they stand today. This is a colossal undertaking, not so much in the physical provision which it involves as in the sheer inertia of mind and matter which it requires to be overcome. There they stand, isolated, majestic, imperious, brooded over by the gigantic water-tower and chimney combined, rising unmistakable and daunting out of the countryside-the asylums which our fore-fathers built with such immense solidity (Quoted in Jones, 1972, p.322).

This policy was presented as a response to changes in the needs of mentally distressed people. As Powell informed the conference, 'A hospital is a shell, a framework, however complex, to contain certain processes, and when the processes change or are superseded, the shell must probably be scrapped and the framework dis-mantled.' (Quoted in Roth, 1970, p.250). Yet not one speaker at the conference supported Powell, and when a group of medical superintendents sought him out after his speech to urge caution, he had gone (Roth, 1970, p.250). Rather than responding to demand or need, Powell was clearly selling an idea that reflected the state's interests; it was efficient, and his job was to make it acceptable.

More was to follow. Three weeks later a Ministry Circular (HM(61)25) was issued which presented in detail much of the envisaged developments in policy. The estimated drop in the number of beds, from some 150,000 to 80,000 in sixteen years was presented as a basis for future planning by the Regional Hospital Boards. They were to '...ensure that no more money than is

127

necessary is spent on the upgrading or reconditioning of mental hospitals which in ten to fifteen years are not going to be required for some different purpose...' (Quoted in Jones, 1972, p.322). And shortly after this, an article was published in the Lancet by Tooth and Brooke (the Principle Medical Officer at the Ministry of Health and a statistician in the General Register Office respectively) in which detailed statistical projections in mental hospital beds were presented (Tooth and Brooke,1961).

Although this paper has since been taken as a major statement on the development of the policy of de-institutionalization, it really represented no more than a public statement on what was already firmly established within the Ministry of Health. The concerns of the Chief Medical Officer appear, with the warning that there are some reasons for increasing use of mental hospitals such as rising longevity. But more prominent is the use of statistical data on the run down of the mental hospital population in the late 1950s, the same as used by the Ministry of Health, which provided the basis for a projection that the bed requirement would approximately halve in 16 years. The paper ends with a compromise statement between these two views; 'It seems unlikely that trends of this magnitude based on national figures are no more than temporary phenomena; though many factors may modify the rate of change, the direction seems well established.' (Tooth and Brooke, 1961, p.713). This, Jones suggests is a more 'modest claim' (Jones, 1972, p.323) than being made by the Minister. But really it simply reflects a minor dispute between competing claims within the Ministry of Health for mental hospitals to be efficient or acceptable, and of course the main power base lies with the former.

If tension existed on this axis within the Ministry of Health, it is perhaps not surprising that reaction to the new policy initiative more generally was somewhat guarded. Firstly, the statistical projection of a rapidly declining mental hospital population was questioned. It was noted that a linear reduction is assumed, when it is more likely that the rate of decline would gradually slow (Letter to Lancet,22 April 1961). The use of a five year trend which went against trends of the previous century to base such major developments of policy was seriously questioned (Jones, 1972, p.325). Furthermore, the assumptions being made about the scale of community services that existed, and could be developed, was queried. Titmuss in particular suggested that the state was demonstrating a 'quite remarkable degree' of optimism over the likely future developments in services; 'Beyond a few brave ventures, scattered up and down the country from Worthing to

Nottingham, pioneered by statutory and voluntary bodies, one cannot find much evidence of attempts to hammer out the practice, as distinct from the theory, of community care for the mentally ill...' (Titmuss, 1963, p.222).

However, such criticism as this was within the context of accepting the overall changes in policy from institutional to community care. While reservations were held, it was more to do with the level of committment exhibited by the Ministry of Health, and the speed with which it was trying to move, rather than over the policy itself. This state of affairs reflects in the party manifestoes for the 1964 general election. The Conservatives, in 'Prosperity with a purpose', took some note of criticisms being made; 'There will be no question of closing any existing hospital unless or until there is satisfactory alternative provision.'. Labour, in 'Lets Go with Labour for the new Britain' is more critical; 'The Tories so called 'plan' is largely based on guesswork. It seriously underestimates the demand for beds in certain areas and for certain categories of need such as mental illness...The community care services run by local authorities-the most neglected of all the Health Services in recent years-will be given a new impetus.' In terms of our analysis, this reflects some tension between efficiency and acceptability. But providing the axis does not fissure, the Ministry of Health could sustain its position.

Effectiveness and acceptability

1960 was 'World Mental Health Year', and the Ministry of Health was fully in support of this attempt to publicise the importance of dealing with mental health problems. The Mental Health Exhibition, which had been touring since 1955 was made available to groups organising meetings around the issue of mental health, and a variety of other activities were undertaken by the state to promote 'true' understanding of mental illness:

> The Minister (of Health) played a prominent part personally, with a broadcast, visits to a mental hospital, an occupation centre and an address to a conference; Press and broadcasting support was stimulated; hospital and local authorities were invited to publicise their services for mental health and to hold open days, meetings, Brains Trusts and exhibitions; with the co-operation of the General Post Office postage stamp obliterators in 150 machines, covering the major areas of population in England and Wales, carried the slogan 'World Mental Health Year' (Ministry of Health, 1960, p.35).

This however, was to be the last part of the campaign by the Ministry of Health to promote a medical conception of mental distress. The selling of psychiatry as an agency with appropriate expertise had been successful, and with the passing of the Mental Health Act their role firmly established. Thus, by the end of 1960 the last of the Mental Health Exhibitions was withdrawn, and the state then took less interest in such publicity work.

As we discussed earlier, the Ministry of Health's presentation of the nature of mental illness, and of the effectiveness of psychiatry in dealing with it, had little empirical basis. Studies of the effectiveness of the new psychotropic drugs were finding that they tended to relieve rather than cure, while more generally it was recognised that further research was required before curative therapies could be developed. Moreover just what constituted mental illness remained ill defined, and also therefore any claims of psychiatry to expertise in treating it. A study for the General Register Office found that of 293 patients admitted on four occasions in a two year period 41% received two different diagnoses, 16% had three, and 2% were given different diagnoses on each admission. This included admissions to the same mental hospital, and the differences in diagnoses noted only concerned jumps across major categories such as schizophrenia and depression (Brooke, 1963, p.165).

But for the state, the concern with effectiveness is not solely about the accurate diagnosis and cure of mentally ill people. Rather, its primary concern is with sustaining the definition and treatment of problems of personal distress within society as individual pathology. Curing the mentally ill is less important than defining people as mentally ill, and by the early 1960s the second of these had been achieved.

With the conceptual model in place and generally accepted over how mental distress should be understood and treated, the Ministry of Health's concern in the early 1960s turned towards increasing the availability of treatment in the community. This was understood in terms of any provision made outside of the old asylums. Within the Hospital Plan, it was anticipated that the number of psychiatric units located within district general hospitals would be increased, providing an additional 4,000 beds (Chief Medical Officer,1963, p.128). In 1960 there were already 82 such units, providing approximately 5,000 beds (Rehin and Martin, 1968, p.10), but in the early 1960s few further psychiatric beds in such units were provided (Chief Medical Officer, 1963, p.128). If the plans were to go ahead the emphasis of provision would have to change substantially, for with the anticipated reduction in mental hospital beds the psychiatric units would by the early 1970s provide one-seventh of all psychiatric beds, compared to the existing level of less than one-thirtieth (Rehin and Martin, 1968, p.20).

Other developments in community treatment were also encouraged. By 1959 some 45 psychiatric day-hospitals and day centres had been established (Rehin and Martin, 1968, p.11), but this number was to treble in the next few years(Martin, 1983, p.19). The number of new out-patients attending clinics also increased, from 170,000 in 1960 to 190,000 in 1963. Emphasis was also placed on the development of community support. 'The effectiveness of the community care services for the mentally ill depends greatly on the recruitment and training of suitable staff, particularly mental welfare officers'. (Ministry of Health, 1960, p.76). But developments in this area proved to be slow. By 1963 just 106 psychiatric social workers (whole-time equivalent) were employed by the local health authorities (Ministry of Health 1963, p.21), and by 1962 only 545 residential places in local authority hostels and 423 beds in voluntary hostels existed (Ministry of Health,1962, p.70). There was, then, a policy of encouraging the provision of treatment for mentally distressed people by integrating mental health services with general medicine, and the provision of that service within the community. The importance of this was held to be considerable:

> If the opportunity for bringing psychiatry fully into the general pattern of medicine which now presents itself is grasped, the new attitudes created both within the profession and in the public mind will do more for mental health than any other single measure (Chief Medical Officer, 1960, p.97).

However, as we can see from the statistics noted above, in the early 1960s the speed of development of new services was fairly slow, particularly those provided by local health authorities. And this lack of development of community services, combined with the estimated rapid decrease in the mental hospital population, began to create some tension on this axis. The overall model of a modern psychiatric profession providing an effective service was not questioned, but the speed of change and lack of apparent co-ordination between the arms of the service was: '...it seemed that a greatly over-simplified and over-optimistic model of mental illness, its management and its social repercussions, had been embraced.' (Martin, 1983, p.19). Jones questioned the attempt to integrate mental and physical medicine. She argued that an overly medical

131

model of mental illness was being adopted, which tended to ignore the importance of the social environment when providing therapy. Hence she argued that too great an emphasis was being placed upon the role of psychiatric units in general hospitals, as there emphasis upon treatment failed to acknowledge the patient's need for a therapeutic environment (Jones, 1964, pp.208-211). As Jones noted at the time, the new policy of community care was perhaps not as enlightened as was being suggested; 'Developments in the next few years may show that the present proposals with regard to the mental hospital are retrogressive rather than progressive, and that we shall have to think again.' (Jones, 1963, p.71).

Conclusion

In this analysis of the state policy making process in the 1948-63 period we have identified a number of major changes being made to how mentally distressed people should be provided for. Where the assumption had been that mental hospitals provided the best place for their care and treatment, it came to be argued that in fact mentally distressed people would benefit from remaining within the community as far as possible. The overall emphasis was to be upon supporting people requiring care within community settings, with hospital admission to be used as far as possible only for the provision of treatment. In the main, the community care policy was yet to be implemented, but by 1963 it had largely been resolved just how services should change and develop.

The explanation offered here for this process shares little in common with either the Marxist or Social Democratic models reviewed in Chapter 1. The anti-institutional critique, the use of psychotropic drugs, and the fiscal crisis of the state have little bearing on how and why the model of service provision changed so dramatically. Instead, our starting point has been the problems experienced by the state and how it addressed them. Institutional care, by the mid-20th century, was failing to adequately solve the compatibility problem created by the exigencies of cost, control and legitimation. This reflected in the physical and conceptual decay of the old asylums; institutional care was in crisis.

Now this is not to suggest that a community care policy was in any way a necessary outcome of these problems. The state could, as indeed it initially intended, have maintained the institutional system by embarking on a massive overhaul of asylums. But such a policy would not have as effectively dealt with the problems faced as did the community care policy. In terms of cost and control, it allows for the extension of the sphere of psychiatric practice but without incurring large costs of providing additional in-patient accommodation. In terms of cost and legitimation, it allows for an increase in the legitimacy of mental health services because of its apparent reformist qualities, while some of the costs are dispersed into the community. In terms of control and legitimation, the 'therapeutic advances' of the psychiatric profession, and their general claim to expertise in the field of mental illness went unchallenged. The community care model was able to exploit this fully, by increasing the powers and responsibilities of psychiatry.

Given that institutional care for mentally distressed people was in crisis, the conclusion we come to is that the development of the community care policy represents a crisis management strategy. The Ministry of Health undoubtedly achieved some success with this change in policy in reconciling the various problems within mental health service provision; Bennett and Morris go so far as to suggest that '...at the beginning of the 1960s, government policy, psychiatric opinion, and the already established trends were all in harmony.' (1983, p.10). Although as we have seen in our discussion of the process of internal rationalisation a number of tensions did continue to exist between the varied interests and demands that existed. As such the community care policy did not entirely successfully address all aspects of the compatibility problem, but it was adequate to meet the state's needs; at least in the short term.

5 The attempt to consolidate the community care policy, 1964-1974

In our discussion of the 1948-63 period we have attempted to analyse a tangled web of changes in mental health policy and provision. Such change as occurred was rapid and, particularly in terms of policy pronouncements, on a massive scale. By 1963 the new community care policy had been firmly established as the dominant philosophy around which mental health services were to be organised. As such, the state's concern with involving itself in the organisation of services rapidly diminished. Having set the agenda for how services should evolve, the state had little further to achieve. The intention now was to allow the various agencies involved to build up services to provide a comprehensive community care service. The question we need to address here therefore, is to what extent was this goal achieved?

To examine this we will assess how far the various parts of the policy were implemented by the mid-1970s. This can be assessed on five dimensions; the extent to which psychiatric services were integrated with general medicine, trends in the use of mental hospitals, the extent of development of new treatment facilities, the degree of expansion of local authority provision, and the extent to which all these were accepted as an adequate response to the problems of mentally distressed people. In terms of our model, these points provide a basis for assessing how far the cost, control and legitimation criteria of state action in mental health service provision were made compatible by the community care policy.

The 1960s and early 1970s witnessed considerable development towards integration of mental health services with other health and welfare provision. Amongst psychiatrists, there was during the

1960s considerable unease about their status in comparison to other medical specialisms, and a strong movement to address this by forming closer links with the rest of the health service (Jones, 1972, p.333; Martin, 1984, p.126). In 1971 the Royal Medico-Psychological Association changed its name to the Royal College of Psychiatrists in an attempt to bring itself more into line with other medical colleges, and altered its examinations to achieve greater similarity with other medical specialisms (Jones,1972,p.334). Following the 1968 Cogwheel Report, various divisions of clinical specialty in hospitals were created. This included psychiatry, resulting in them losing their own separate organizational framework. The rationale for this was made clear by Keith Joseph in 1971, then Minister of Health and Social Security:

> The treatment of psychosis, neurosis and schizophrenia have been entirely changed by the drug revolution. People go into hospital with mental disorders and they are cured (Quoted in Jones, 1979, p.9).

With the treatment of mental distress being held to be so similar to physical illness - so the argument runs - then the treatment of both should be organised on similar lines. This, the psychiatric profession was glad to embrace.

A similar pattern of integration of mental health services occurred in local authority welfare provision. The Seebohm Report, published in 1968, recommended that new departments should be created, unifying the existing welfare departments in order to provide '...a community based and family orientated service, which will be available to all.' (Quoted in Martin, 1984, p.36). The existing Mental Health Departments had been under medical control as sub-departments of the Health Departments, but with the re-organisation that followed in 1971 they were integrated with other services under local authority control. In the same year the Association of Psychiatric Social Workers was dissolved, and its membership merged with other social workers in the newly created British Association of Social Workers.

By the mid-1970s the administrative structure of mental health services had undergone considerable change. The dominant conceptions of the day of mental distress being a social problem, suited to medical intervention, provided a rationale for the integration of mental health services within general health and welfare provision. Moreover, within this process the separation of health and welfare was further institutionalised, whereby the psychiatric and social work functions were now almost entirely separated.

There were also substantial changes in the provision of in-patient facilities for mentally distressed people during this period. The predictions made in 1961, of halving the numbers held in mental hospitals had initially met a sceptical response from commentators and participants in mental health service provision (Martin, 1984, p.15). Yet between 1964 and 1975 there was significant movement towards this target. The reduction in the mental hospital population which had begun in 1955 continued, and indeed gathered pace.

Table 5.1
English mental hospitals (thousands)

Year	In-patients	% Change over previous year
1964	124.6	
1965	121.7	2.33
1970	107.8	2.53
1975	87.3	3.22

Source: Health and Personal Social Service Statistics for England, 1977.

Moreover, this reduction was achieved despite the admission rate continuing to rise. As Table 5.2 indicates, the increased number of admissions was matched by an increasingly vigorous discharge policy, such that despite the rising numbers of people using the mental hospital service it was through large gains in efficiency able to contract in size.

Table 5.2
English mental hospitals: patient flow (thousands)

Year	Admissions	% change over previous year	Deaths and discharge	% change over previous year
1964	155.5		156.6	
1965	156.2	0.45	159.1	1.52
1970	172.9	0.70	175.7	0.11
1975	180.2	6.44	178.0	1.19

Source: Health and Personal Social Service Statistics for England, 1977.

This reduction in the mental hospital population was not as great as had been hoped for by the Ministry of Health in the early 1960s, but it represented significant movement towards the goal of halving the mental hospital population. So encouraging was it considered to be that by 1971 in the discussion document 'Hospital Services for the Mentally Ill' (DHSS,1971) it is argued that within two decades the old mental hospitals system will no longer be required, and will be replaced by psychiatric units within District General Hospitals. These would provide day patient and out-patient services, together with some 0.5 beds per thousand population. This represented a major step forward in the planning of mental health services, for where Powell's target for 1975 had been to reduce the mental hospital beds to 1.8 per thousand of the population, we were now witnessing an attempt to erode yet further the caring role of the health service for mentally distressed people, and focus almost entirely upon the provision of treatment.

The concentration on providing mental patients with treatment also reflects in the developments in staffing and facilities. Between 1963 and 1970 the numbers of hospital medical staff working with mentally distressed people in England had risen from 1,652 to 1,879 (Martin, 1984, p.20), and by 1975 had reached 2,313 (DHSS, Health and Personal Social Services Statistics for England, 1977). The numbers of nursing staff working in mental hospitals (for both mentally ill and handicapped) in England rose from 45,676 in 1962 to 56,626 in 1970 (Martin, 1984, p.20) and had reached 57,623 by 1974. The change in focus of mental hospital provision that, as we saw in Chapter 4 was being encouraged by the state, also continued. In 1964 there were 2,940 beds in psychiatric units in District General Hospitals (MIND, 1974, p.5) and by 1975 this had risen to 5,400 (Martin, 1984, p.43). Because of the far higher turnover of patients compared to traditional mental hospitals the percentage of admissions made to these units rose from 14.9% in 1964 to 27.5% in 1975 (Mahadevan, 1982). The number of psychiatric out-patients continued to increase until 1969, when some 219,000 new patients were seen and 1.48 million attendances at out-patient clinics recorded. By 1975 the number of new out-patients had dropped slightly to 188,000 although total attendances continued to rise, with some 1.55 million being recorded in 1975 (DHSS, Health and Personal Social services Statistics for England,1977). Equally, the numbers of day patients also rose during this period. In England, there were in 1975 some 36,400 new day patients attending psychiatric day hospitals, and some 2.7 million total attendances (Martin, 1984, p.44).

In addition to these increases in staffing and facilities, new treatments continued to become available. In particular, the pharmaceutical industry put large investments into the search for new drug treatments. Two major new groups were discovered and marketed, monomine oxidase inhibitors and tricyclic anti-depressants, which further increased the battery of physical treatments available to psychiatry.

These changes in the organisation and delivery of treatment services were very much in line with what the Ministry of Health had intended. The trend towards dealing with mental patients on similar lines to the physically ill strengthened, with much less emphasis upon containment and care of patients, and more on treatment. Unfortunately the statistics do not allow us to discover just how many more people were administered to by psychiatric services. But, as Martin concludes, '...there can be no doubt that there was a significant increase in the total number of persons drawn into the ambit of the mental health services.' (Martin, 1984, p.20).

While some progress was made towards the state's goal of a re-organised hospital service that stressed treatment over custody, the related aim of increasing community facilities for the care of mentally distressed people fared much worse. By 1970 local authority social services provided just 1,800 residential places in homes and hostels, and 2,600 places in day centres. By 1975 these figures had only risen to 2,700 and 3,400 respectively (COHSE, 1984, p.18). Voluntary and private provision of places in registered homes provided some 1,100 places in 1970, and 1,600 in 1975 (COHSE, 1984, p.18). By 1975 there were still some 45 English local authorities that spent nothing at all on day centres or clubs for mentally distressed people (Martin, 1984, p.45). Despite the emphasis given to the development of these services by the state, we find that during 1973/4 only some £6.5 million was spent on residential and day care services for mentally distressed people in the community compared to £300 million spent on institutional care (DHSS, 1975).

The legitimacy of the mental health services is more difficult to measure and assess than the more specific changes discussed above; legitimacy is not something that lends itself easily to statistical review. Because of this, we need to be cautious about how quickly we reach any conclusion about the degree of change in the legitimacy of services, and what importance to attach to that change. However, in the 1960s and early 1970s there was an increased level of argument over how mentally distressed people should be provided for.

138

Firstly, the anti-institutional critique became increasingly influential in this period. Goffman's 'Asylums' was widely read and quoted to support an increasingly critical view of the detrimental effects on patients of the old mental hospitals (Martin, 1984, p.31). In addition, several widely publicized instances of cruelty occurred in the late '60s and early '70s, together with a number of studies of poor conditions within mental hospitals, that did much to still further reduce the legitimacy of institutional care (see Jones 1972, pp.327-330; Martin, 1984, pp.30-34). Whereas the developments in after-care that occurred in the 1930s, 1940s and early 1950s had been stimulated by the medicalization of mental health services, we were now seeing increasing emphasis being given to a more social based model of community care. Rather than simply being complementary to institutionally based medical services, the argument being developed was that community care provided a more humane alternative to such services. Thus by early 1970s institutional care was being undermined at two levels. It was argued to be inherently flawed, on top of which its existing organisation was neglectful and at times cruel; 'The 'chintz and cream paint' policy of the fifties had made superficial improvements, but they did not go deep enough to remedy the problems...as the movement gathered force, it brought the attack on all hospitals indiscriminately.' (Jones, 1972, p.330).

While the main force of criticism in the 1960s and early 1970s was against institutional care, there was also some increase in criticism of community care as evidence began to accumulate of the failings of community provision. Attention was focussed upon the excessive burdens being placed upon the families of discharged patients (Hoenig and Hamilton, 1969; Grad and Sainsbury,1968), and claims were made that many discharged patients became destitute or swelled the prison population (Rollin,1969; Tidmarsh and Wood,1972). Furthermore the benefits of locating facilities within the community as an alternative to institutional care proved to be less clear than was initially assumed. A study of local authority and voluntary provision of hostels found that the environments of some were in fact more restrictive than the wards from which the residents had come from (Apte, 1968). Similarly, institutional practices were found to occur within day centre settings; the assumption that large institutions alone had a tendency to create regimented regimes characterised by distance between staff and service users was found to be erroneous (Carter and Edwards,1975).

By the early 1970s some evidence began to accumulate of the neglect of discharged psychiatric patients:

A bare room 6ft by 4ft in a lodging house, paid for by Social Security Benefit, is the home of one (such) man. Fifteen years ago, he would have been a long-stay hospital patient. Today, because of the 1959 Mental Health Act, he lives in 'the community' - except for him, there is no community and very little that could be described as community care (Sunday Times, 20/5/73, quoted in Prins, 1984, pp.188-189).

However this critique never reached the level of intensity as that directed at institutional care; the inference being made was that greater thought had to be given to the process of developing community care, rather than any suggestion that the policy itself was inherently flawed (Bennett and Morris 1983).

A further area of criticism that developed in the 1960s and 1970s concerned the theories and practices of psychiatry; a critique commonly referred to as 'anti-psychiatry'. The arguments and themes developed varied considerably, but all shared the common aim of undermining conventional psychiatric theory, and replacing it with a model of mental distress that emphasised its historical contingency and its social rather than medical nature. Mental distress is not, it was argued, an illness in terms of a disease process, but a response to an oppressive environment (see Sedgwick,1982a;1982b).

Our concern here is not with the correctness or otherwise of these arguments, but with their effect on the legitimacy of dominant conceptions of mental distress. And undoubtedly they tended to undermine the conception of mental distress as an illness to be treated by medical means. As Martin notes:

> 'anti-psychiatry'...harmonized with quite widely prevalent values and aspirations of the time. Models of mental illness which identified the patient (especially the sensitive young schizophrenic) with the radical critic of a dehumanizing society, his family with the oppressive forces of the established order, and defined the collusive psychiatrist as an agent of control and coercion, were dramatically congruent with the sharp questioning of established institutions and the quest for solutions (Martin, 1984, p.33).

Just how significant this critique proved to be is difficult to assess. The psychiatric profession tended to either ignore it, or meet it with hostility. Certainly the model of mental distress as an illness was never seriously under threat, but the climate of opinion, and

140

opinion making, was changed. We saw earlier how the psychiatric theory was never challenged in the 1950s. But now it seemed more reasonable to do so. The pressure group MIND for example slowly became more combative in its approach to mental health policy. By the early 1970s, it was prepared to challenge assumptions made by the state concerning the nature of the problem being addressed:

> The DHSS appears to have shaped its policies on the assumption that chronic mental illness no longer exists. Chemotherapeutic techniques and other therapies are not the panacea of all ills and to assume that chronicity is a thing of the past seems unrealistic in terms of the mentally ill today (MIND, 1974, p.7).

As we saw in our discussion of the 1948-63 period, the community care strategy never enjoyed unanimous support. The state's refusal to provide central funding for local authority community services had always left some sceptical of its real interests and goals. But in this period the degree of legitimacy enjoyed by the policy fell substantially. The failure to develop services in the community in particular was criticised. The pressure group MIND became an increasingly vociferous critic of the failure to adequately fund service development:

> Government policies over the last fifteen years have been unscrupulous in their cheese-paring. They announce a grand programme of transferring the unfortunate chronically mentally ill from institutional care to community care and proceed to implement this by refusing money to improve or extend the hospital services. On the other hand, they defer, on the grounds of economy, requests from local authorities for community services for the chronically mentally ill. In this way they save money at both ends and please the taxpayers, while the chronic psychiatric case is driven into aimless vagrancy or the common lodging house (MIND, 1974, p.9).

The policy of developing psychiatric units within District General Hospitals was also criticised. The Hospital Advisory Service in its 1971 report noted that these units tended to be too selective in their selection of patients. The danger was that by 'creaming off' the patients most likely to respond to treatment, the old mental hospitals were liable to become 'dumping' grounds offering little possibility of therapeutic intervention. In 1963 it had generally been accepted that the community care policy represented an advance in thinking concerning mental health service provision, and whose beneficence to patients was obvious. The goals of the policy went unquestioned; it was only the methods that some doubted because of the state's wavering commitment to funding the service. Yet by 1975 the goals of the policy, the value of psychiatric treatment, and the therapeutic content of care in the community were all being questioned. Moreover the methods of achieving the policy's goals continued to be criticised with increasing vigour.

Conclusion

We noted at the beginning of this section that the aim of the state from the early 1960s onwards was to consolidate the new community care policy. The aim of such consolidation was of course to achieve resolution of the compatibility problem. We might therefore briefly consider the three axis that constitute this, and asses whether or not the tensions within them grew or lessened during this period.

Cost and control

Both the cost and the numbers of people treated by mental health services continued to rise in this period. In one sense, then, this axis became more difficult to reconcile because of the increased tension within it. But if we recall from our discussion in Chapter 4 the aim of the state was not necessarily to reduce expenditure on mental health services (although it might gladly do so if the opportunity arose). Rather, the aim was to concentrate expenditure upon treatment rather than care of mentally distressed people, and this is what tended to occur as the community care policy developed. Thus while the scale of the problem being faced may have grown, the manner in which the state addressed it did become more efficient (in terms of its own interests).

Cost and legitimation

This axis became more difficult to reconcile by the mid-1970s. In particular, there was growing concern about the inadequacy of care facilities for mentally distressed people in the community. Thus, despite the increased cost of the service there was a loss of legitimacy.

In 1963, the medical model of psychiatric intervention was beyond reasonable dispute. The problem was simply how to make treatment more readily available. This was an accepted part of the community care strategy. Yet by 1975 the medical model of mental distress is increasingly questioned, where its asked whether mental and physical illness really are so similar and whether psychiatric intervention really is the most appropriate form of treatment. The issues that follow from this concern questions over just how far mental and general health services should be integrated, and whether patients are really likely to recover when so little attention is paid to the environment in which they live.

By 1975 the attempt to consolidate the community care policy as an adequate solution to the compatibility problem had failed. The policy was still viable, in as much as no threats to its immediate continuation existed. But its success as a policy was declining. Mental health services were increasing in cost, faced a growing problem of control, and were losing legitimacy. Questions were arising, and demands being made, that the state had difficulty in addressing if it was not to lose sight of its own goals for the community care strategy. The policy was losing coherence as each pole of the compatibility problem became more antagonistic to the other two.

6 The socio-economic context of mental health services, 1975-1993

In our analysis of the 1948-63 period we have seen how the environment in which mental health policy making and implementation was conducted did in fact provide some considerable room for manouver by the state. The 'structural space' available was sufficient for it to develop a mental health service policy that adequately addressed the compatibility problem. By the mid-1970s however, with growing tensions within the community care policy that we have examined in Chapter 5, the state was faced with the need to attempt further internal rationalisation in order to avoid losing sight of its own objectives. But of course when coming to do this, the state was faced by a very changed set of circumstances in which it was operating.   To examine just what changes have occurred we will follow the format used in Chapter 3. Our first task, then, is to establish the nature and scale of the 'meta-problem' facing the state.

Economic crisis tendencies

The main theme in our discussion of economic crisis tendencies in Chapter 3 was one of relative decline, hidden by an ostensibly buoyant economy. This continued through the 1960s and early-19-70s; while the British economy continued to grow it was at a slower pace than all its major competitors. In 1961 Britain held ninth place in the league table for GDP per capita. By 1971 it had slipped to fifteenth place and by 1976 eighteenth place. Having held a 25% share in the value of world exports of manufactures in 1950, by

1970 this had fallen to 10.8% and by 1977 to 9.3% (Gamble, 1981, p.21).

Table 6.1
Growth of industrial production: average annual increase (%)
1960-1973

UK	3.0
USA	4.9
Japan	12.6
France	5.9
West Germany	5.5
OECD average	5.7

Source: Prest and Coppock 1986, p.203.

Despite this relatively poor economic performance the British economy continued to appear to prosper. Inflation showed a slight tendency to increase through the 1960s, but not to the extent of threatening economic stability. Unemployment too was largely contained until the mid-1970s, never rising above 3%.

Table 6.2
Changes in retail prices and unemployment 1963-1974

Year	Change in retail prices(%)	Unemployment(%)
1963	2	2.3
1966	4	1.5
1969	5	2.4
1972	7	3.5
1974	16	2.4

Source: Prest and Coppock 1986, p.51.

The mid-1970s however proved to be a turning point in British economic fortunes. Following the quadrupling of oil prices by OPEC member states in 1973 the long boom ended, and with the international economy moving into recession the long term decline of the British economy made it particularly vulnerable to increasing competition for contracting world markets. As Gamble notes, 'Not just relative but absolute impoverishment now threatened Britain.' (Gamble, 1983, p.136).

The effects of this rapidly made themselves apparent on economic conditions within Britain. In the latter half of the 1970s unemployment began to increase. Having stood at half a million in 1970, it reached one and a half million by 1979 and two and a half million by the end of 1980. During the early 1980s unemployment reached over three million, despite numerous changes made to the way in which unemployment figures were calculated and the absorbtion of some of the unemployed on to Government funded training schemes. At the same time, the level of inflation rose far higher than had previously been experienced in the post-war period. Prices had begun to surge in 1974, resulting in an annual inflation rate of 16.1%. By 1975 the annual rate of inflation reached over 24%, giving rise to fears of hyper-inflation overtaking the British economy. Inflation did slowly subside for the remainder of the 1970s, reaching 13.2% in 1979, but then briefly surged again to over 18% in 1980.

Other economic indicators also demonstrate the worsening condition of the UK economy. The rate of growth of industrial production has remained below that of competitors, while the balance of payments was only saved from massive deficit by income from North Sea oil.

Table 6.3
Growth of industrial production: average annual increase (%) 1973-1985

	1973 - 85
UK	0.6
USA	2.3
Japan	3.4
France	1.0
West Germany	1.1
OECD average	1.9

Source: Prest and Coppock 1986, p.203.

Table 6.4
UK balance of payments: annual averages (£m) 1961-1985

Year	Current Balance	Balance on North Sea Oil
1961-64	-8	-
1965-67	-56	-
1968-71	+552	-
1972-78	-739	-2,676
1979-84	+2,779	+3,681
1985	+2,952	+8,163

Source: Prest and Coppock 1986, p.141.

In the mid-1980s there was some evidence of an economic recovery. By 1987 unemployment had fallen below 3 million, to 10.75% of the labour force and inflation had fallen to 3.4%. Between 1980 and 1987 the average output per person employed rose by 20%, helping increase the international competitiveness of British industry. In 1986 Britain experienced a growth rate of 3.3%, which was slightly higher than all its major competitors (OECD, 1987). The relative decline of British industry appeared to some to have been arrested; for some members of the Conservative Party such as Nigel Lawson it appeared as if an economic 'miracle' had been achieved.

The recession of the late 1980s and early 1990s was soon to demonstrate however that the long term decline in Britain's relative position in the world as a trading nation has continued, and with that has gone an increasing vunerability to international recession. By the end of 1992 unemployment was almost 3 million, and the Conservative Government's economic priorities were rapidly shifting from holding down inflation and achieving a stable currency, to achieving economic growth.

This review of economic performace does not perhaps indicate any impending collapse of the British economy, But what it does indicate is that compared to the 1950s and 1960s the British economy is considerably weaker. In the immediate post-war period low inflation, high employment, economic growth and financial stability were promised, and largely delivered. In the more recent period each of these targets has proven more difficult to attain, and together appear to have become impossible to achieve.

Rationality crisis tendencies

In our discussion of the rationale for state action in the immediate post-war period we found that a consensus existed about the scale and scope of state activity. An increased level of management of economic and social affairs by the state was generally accepted to be both feasible and desirable. This situation was to prevail until the mid-1970S, for despite some difficulties in economic management, the twin aims of economic growth and rising expenditure upon the welfare state were basically kept intact. In 1951 total public expenditure accounted for some 36.1% of the Gross National Product at factor cost. By 1964 it had risen to 38.5% and by 1974 to 46.2% (Judge, 1982, p.28). Moreover, within the rising level of public expenditure the share taken by social services increased from 44.9% in 1956 to 48.1% in 1966, and to 55.1% in 1976 (Culyer, 1980, p.66). And yet, as we saw in the last section economic growth was maintained.

Until the mid-1970S therefore, the Keynes/Beveridge combination provided an adequate rationale for state action. By the mid-1970s, however, the economic and social conditions that made such state action viable were rapidly being eroded. Rising public expenditure relied primarily upon continued economic growth yet, as Gamble notes, '...it is precisely growth that can no longer be relied upon or stimulated in the old ways.' (Gamble, 1981, p.11). The result was a rapid reappraisal of the scope for policy making and implementation, as Held notes:

> In the wake of the 'post-war settlement', the attempt to maintain full employment and to meet extensive welfare obligations imposed on the state rapidly escalating costs. In the context of the overall deterioration in Britains's economic performance the problems of meeting these costs through taxations and borrowing became ever more acute. The result has been the mushrooming 'fiscal crisis' of the state (Held, 1984, p.318).

This 'fiscal crisis', where the revenues appropriated by the state appeared insufficient to finance current levels of expenditure, developed rapidly in the mid 1970s. This reflected in the rising public sector borrowing requirement (PSBR), increasing from 6.5% of GDP in 1973 to 11.0% in 1975 (Peden 1985, p.218). In addition, there was a rapid decline in the international value of sterling, as foreign investors lost confidence in the UK economy and the ability of the Labour administration to manage it. By 1976 the consensus,

148

based on keynesianism, about how to manage the economy had been shattered. With rising inflation and unemployment - a condition that came to be termed 'stagflation' - it offered few policy options. The fiscal crisis besetting the state brought this problem to a head, and was only dealt with by the Labour Government applying for a loan from the International Monetary Fund in the autumn of 1976. The conditions laid down for this loan, after protracted negotiations, were that public expenditure would be cut by £1 billion in 1977/8 and by £1.5 billion in 1978/9.

The importance of this monetary crisis lies less in the figures involved than in the changing rationale governing state action. For what it marked was the ascendancy of a new orthodoxy, monetarism, concerning the relationship between economic and social policy, and about the potential of state action in managing the economy. Perhaps most famously this is marked by the speech by Callaghan, then Prime Minister, to the Labour Party conference in September 1976:

> We used to think that you could just spend your way out of a recession and increase employment by cutting taxes and boosting Government spending. I tell you in all candour, that option no longer exists, and that in so far as it ever did exist, it worked by injecting inflation into the economy. And each time that happened the average level of unemployment has risen. Higher inflation followed by higher unemployment. That is the history of the last 20 years (quoted in Peden,1985, p.221).

This is not to suggest that in the space of a year or two the Labour administration was suddenly convinced by monetarist arguments. Rather, the changed economic circumstances appeared to direct its policy more firmly than had previously been the case. The control of inflation and of public expenditure were now paramount, as the fiscal crisis in 1976 had emphatically demonstrated. For the remaining years of the Labour Government this conception of economic reality dominated its overall policy development. Public expenditure cuts were made, although only in terms of reducing intended growth rates, and a wages policy in the public sector was enforced. Increased attention was given to the control of public expenditure by the introduction in 1976 of 'cash limits', which replaced volume planning, and in the same year aggregate monetary targets were announced for the economy in an attempt to control inflation.

With the change of Government in 1979, the newly installed

Conservative administration took the new monetarist rationale for state action a stage further. The control of inflation was further prioritised, to the detriment of economic growth and employment. In the 1980 budget the 'medium term financial strategy' was introduced, which laid down targets for public expenditure and monetary growth for several years ahead. The aim of this was to insulate the Chancellor of the Exchequer from expenditure demands, and to reduce his scope for manouver (Gamble, 1983, p.150). The cash limits established by the Labour administration were extended by the introduction of cash planning, whereby the planning of expenditure in cash terms was extended several years ahead.

This increased concern with controlling public expenditure reflected a major ideological shift in the accepted role of state action. Monetarism was utilised to support two major arguments, that welfare provision is a burden upon the economy that can only be supported when growth has been achieved, and secondly that economic affairs are best conducted within market relations with the state simply regulating rather than directly interfering in the market. As the first White Paper on public expenditure of the Thatcher administration states, the dominant rationale now held that 'Public expenditure is at the heart of Britain's present economic difficulties.' (quoted in Bosanquet, 1983, p.162).

In this discussion of the rationale for state action, we have identified a loss of coherence of the post-war settlement based on the combination of Keynes and Beveridge, and its replacement by monetarism. In this, we can see a change in emphasis from balancing the economy to balancing the budget, and the prioritisation of economic over social policy. This change was largely propelled by the decline in Britain's economic fortunes. However before completing this discussion we should examine just what effect this new rationale has had on the state policy making process in a litle more detail. For despite attempts to curb public expenditure, and welfare expenditure in particular, it has shown some small growth since the mid-1970s (see Table 6.5).

Within these aggregate figures there have been some cuts in welfare expenditure. For example, public expenditure on housing, as a percentage of all welfare expenditure fell from 17.4% in 1974/5 to only 8% in 1987/8 (Le Grand, 1990, p. 341). But in other areas, particularly social security but also health and personal social services, there have been some increases in the expenditure on these services (although possibly not sufficient to keep up with rising need).

:

150

Table 6.5
Public expenditure on the welfare state (1987/8 prices)

Year	Year-on-year change(%)	% of general Government expenditure	% ofGDP
1974/5	13.3	51.0	24.5
1977/8	4.7	55.7	23.7
1980/1	1.0	52.1	24.0
1983/4	4.9	53.3	24.5
1987/8	1.0	55.6	23.2

Source: Le Grand, 1990, p.338.

Yet despite this failure to reduce public expenditure, the state has succeeded in avoiding a repetition of the 1976 monetary crisis. In that year the PSBR had stood at 11% of GDP, by 1979 it had been reduced to 7.5%, and by 1985 to 2.0% of GDP. By the mid-1980s tendencies towards a fiscal crisis of the state, which received such attention in the 1970s, appear less intense. Hill and Bramley note that in fact '...during the 1970s and 1980s...fiscal crisis has been more apparent than real...There has been an atmosphere of crisis at particular times (1976 and 1980-1), fuelled by phenomena such as inflation, the PSBR, and control failures within the public sector, but not really warrented by a broader economic assessment' (Hill and Bramley, 1986, pp.87-88). By 1988 the Chancellor of the Exchequer, Nigel Lawson, was able to announce in his budget statement to the House of Commons an overall aim within Government finances of a 0% overall level of public sector borrowing, and indeed spoke of pursuing public sector debt repayment. The following year this was achieved, with the treasury recording a £15 billion income surplus to requirments.

But such optimism soon proved innappropriate. With the economic recession of the late 1980s and early 1990s we have seen a serious deterioration in Government finances, with annual borrowing requirements approaching £40 billion. Equally, the balance of payments has remained stubbornly within the red at a time, within the economic cycle, when a surplus might be expected. While there has been no repitition of the fiscal crisis of 1976, the Government is nevertheless facing a serious reduction in its policy options. Most dramatically this was demonstrated in the Autumn of 1992 when membership of the European Exchange Rate Mechanism was abruptly terminated. More generally it reflected in the increase emphasis given to the containment of welfare expenditure.

This discussion of the rationale for state action demonstrates the more complicated situation that has existed since the mid-1970s than in the immediate post-war period. Ostensibly at least, with the shattering of the Keynes/Beveridge post-war settlement and its replacement with neo-conservatism as the dominant rationale for state action, scope for state expenditure upon social services has been substantially reduced. Yet, what we have witnessed since the mid-1970s has been a more gradual attempt at paring state expenditure. While relative economic decline has continued, the scope for state expenditure has not been drastically reduced, although this might be put down to temporary favourable circumstances. The decline has however been sufficiently severe to encourage the state to give greater priority to economic over social policy goals (Walker 1982a). The policy of retrenchment of Government expenditure has represented an attempt to arrest long term decline as much, if not more so, than it represents an immediate crisis reaction to existing fiscal conditions. The conclusion we reach therefore is that the rationale for state action has changed, with the scope for state intervention in social and economic affairs reduced. But the reduction in policy options that this implies may only become apparent over the medium to long term.

Legitimation crisis tendencies

We finished our discussion of legitimation crisis tendencies in the immediate post-war period by arguing that consensus existed around the twin goals of economic growth and increased welfare expenditure. But we also noted that the legitimacy this provided was tenuous in that it relied upon continued successful realisation of these goals. And, as we have seen, these goals have become ever more difficult to achieve. We might consider therefore, what this implies for the legitimacy of the social formation since the mid-1970s?

A common theme developed in the 1970s and 1980s has been that with the breakdown of the post-war settlement consensus has been replaced by conflict; Britain is now considered a much harder place to govern. Plant contends that '...a central feature of modern British political life has been the extent of disenchantment - across the political spectrum - with the post-war political settlement and the role of the state within it...Those who proclaimed the end of ideology in the late 1950s and 1960s were profoundly mistaken.' (Plant, 1983, pp.12-13). Similarly, Mishra argues that '...by the mid-1970s the image of post-war society as a smoothly evolving industrial social order, in important and irreversible ways 'post-capitalist', was badly tarnished...The optimistic, evolutionary scenario consisting of affluent industrialism and the welfare state has disappeared leaving the future of the western societies looking uncertain and unpredictable.' (Mishra, 1984, p.20). Kavanagh notes that since the 1950s '...there has been a growing dissatisfaction with the way the system works and with the policies it produces.' (Kavanagh, 1987, p.71.). In short, many social commentators utilising varied perspectives have in recent years argued that a legitimation crisis threatens to overtake British society (Taylor-Gooby,1985). We might, however, consider just how accurate this argument is.

We can guage to some extent the degree of legitimacy of the British social formation in recent years by the results of general elections. The Labour and Conservative parties have attracted a declining share of the vote and number of seats in parliament. In the October 1974 general election, the Conservative's gained 277 seats and 35.8% of the vote, and Labour 319 seats and 39.2% of the vote. Liberals and Nationalists gained some 15.8% of the vote and 27 parliamentary seats. Since then, the Conservative vote has strengthened, receiving between 42% and 44% of the popular vote in 1979, 1983, 1987 and 1992. The Labour vote has tended to fluctuate, from 36.9% in 1979 to a low of 27.6% in 1983, and back to 34.4% in 1992. Of the minor parties, the Nationalist vote has tended to erode and the Liberals increase - particularly after joining forces with the Social Democratic Party in the early 1980s, since when (at least, until their seperation in 1988) they enjoyed approximately a quarter of the popular vote.

These changes in the pattern of voting indicate some reduced legitimacy of the political system. The two parties of Government, Conservative and Labour, have tended to attract a reduced percentage of the vote over the post-war period. Conversely the minor parties have tended to do better. Moreover, within this pattern there has been a tendency towards 'dealignment'; that is, a weakening of party loyalties within the electorate. This has occurred on two dimensions. There has been a tendency towards class dealignment, where '...the association between occupational class and party support has simply faded away.' (Dunleavy, 1983, p.33), and there has been a tendency towards partisan dealignment, where there has been '...a declining association between people's party loyalties and their views on particular issues.' (Dunleavy,1983, p.39).

Overall, this pattern of change indicates a declining legitimacy of the major political parties. The party in power is less and less able to claim to represent a common view of how Britain should be governed, and increasingly relies upon organising a relatively small bloc which only provides the necessary number of seats to rule because of the 'first past the post' electoral system. With growing political instability, the two-party system has been undermined, and with it so too has the authority of the state (Gamble,1981, pp.34-35).

A further problem concerning the legitimacy of the political-administrative system that has in recent years been extensively analysed is that of 'overload'. A number of writers have argued that the increasing scale and scope of Government activity tends to generate two major problems; rising expectations of what Governments can achieve, and increased vunerability of the state to demands from sectional interests (Taylor-Gooby, 1985, p.10). With increasing demands, and without a commeasurate increase in resources, it has been frequently argued that the state will fail to meet expectations. Dahrendorf, in a review of the tendency towards 'overload' affecting the welfare state, suggests that '...there are few today who would doubt that modern Governments have taken on more than they can cope with, and in doing so have partly responded to and partly generated expectations which were bound to be disappointed.' (Dahrendorf,1980, p.399). The result of this process, where Governments fail to meet demands and expectations is, Douglas argues, that the legitimacy of the state tends to be eroded; '...the absence of popular support must undermine the authority of Government and ultimately the authority of Parliament and the whole parliamentary system.' (Douglas, 1976, p.488).

This analysis undoubtedly points to real change within the political-administrative system. Consensus has to a large extent been replaced by conflict and loss of legitimacy of the state. For example a survey in 1973 found that 18% of British people considered breaking the law acceptable 'to combat excessive rent, tax or price increases', while by 1981 in the wake of the inner city riots polls found that 44% of young people considered 'violence to bring about political change can be justified.' (Birch 1984). Our concern, though, is with how far this gives rise to crisis tendencies; and it is this relation between the loss of legitimacy and its presumed association with crisis that we might examine more closely. For in recent years it has become increasingly apparent that the state has been able to avoid the worst prognostications of crisis theorists, and indeed even maintain some semblance of order and direction within

154

its policies.

The electoral success of the Conservative party has brought this issue sharply into focus. With four consecutive general election victories behind them, claims about impending crisis as unemployment rises and social services expenditure suffers retrenchment, now have a somewhat hollow ring about them. Thus in recent years we find that a range of explanations are offered for the popularity of the 'New Right'. Their success in characterising the welfare state as a public burden, that is overly bureaucratic and open to abuse by 'scroungers', is argued to have provided a basis for cutting expenditure (Rose and Rose, 1982, p.18). The political adeptness of the Conservative party to break extra-parlimentary opposition to its policies, to maintain the economic prosperity of large groups within society, and to encourage social trends such as increasing owner occupation of the housing stock has helped maintain their political supremacy (Gamble, 1987, pp.12-17). Bringing these points together, Hall emphasises the importance of the ideological arena for the construction of popular bases of support. In the context of the breakdown of consensus, 'The whole point of Thatcherism as a form of politics has been to construct a new social bloc...In the second term, Thatcherism did not make a single move which was not also carefully calculated in terms of this hegemonic strategy.' (Hall, 1987, p.33).

In addition to this newly found emphasis upon the importance of the ideological arena to explain the absence of crisis developments, attention has also been focussed on a number of other issues. It is suggested for example that while Governments have lost legitimacy, the authority of the state itself remains intact; the greatest demands made simply being for the replacement of one Government with another. Moreover, the 'steering mechanisms' available to the state remain varied and potent. We have in recent years seen a considerable growth in the powers of the police to detect and deal with what is regarded as subversive activity. Additionally, the state has proven adept at appeasing the more powerful groups in society, by displacing problems caused within the economic sub-system onto weaker groups within society (Held, 1987, p.359).

There is today sufficient evidence to demonstrate that the legitimacy of the political system has waned over the post-war period. As Kavanagh notes:

In 1963 Almond and Verba were optimistic about the prospects

155

for the civic culture in Britain...The implicit and benigh scenario was that further socioeconomic development would be associated with a less ideological, more participatory, secular, and pragmatic style of politics. These expectations have not been confirmed....What does seem clear is that the traditional bonds of social class, party, and common nationality are waning, and with them the old restraints of hierachy and deference (Kavanagh, 1987, pp.81-82).

Yet, at the same time, there is limited evidence to suggest any imminent crisis within the political-administrative system. The conflicts and competing demands that appeared so unmanageable in the 1970s have lost their critical appearance. But this is not to suggest that all is well; that the post-war consensus has been replaced by an equally stable new hegemonic bloc, for while a new bloc has been created it rests upon smaller foundations. Continued economic decline has eroded the state's ability to organise majority support for its actions; it rests upon just over 40% electoral support which is only sufficient because of the peculiarities of the British electoral system, and the division that exist amongst opposition parties. As Held notes, '...there is reason to believe that the scepticism and remoteness many people feel in relation to dominant political institutions might be the basis of further political disaffection in the future.' (Held, 1984, p.346).

Motivation crisis tendencies

In finishing our discussion of potential motivation crisis tendencies in the immediate post-war period, we noted an increased level of turbulence at a social and personal level. And of course the point at which we finished our discussion, in 1963, was the start of the 'swinging sixties', a period in which further developments towards a more permissive society occurred, with a far greater variety of personal, political and social expression being made and becoming acceptable within society; 'The 1960s were to see a considerable widening of the frontiers of sexual and fantasy literature, and an acceleration of what came to be called the 'permissive society'...There was a decisive shift to a more secular, permissive, plural society' (Ryder and Silver, 1977, p.262, p.288). Associated with this increased level of questioning of social arrangements, Ryder and Silver argue that people experienced an increased sense of powerlessness and alienation. The authority of the state and unquestioning acceptance of the social organisation of society were no longer to be assumed; 'The confusions, protests, innovations of the 1950s led to the scepticism of the 1960s about the functioning of society itself.' (Ryder and Silver,1977, p.291).

This is not to suggest any unilinear pattern of development towards a breakdown in patterns of motivation and meaning within society. In 1964, under the leadership of Mary Whitehouse, the National Viewers and Listeners Association was formed, intent on reclaiming lost social and moral values. In 1966 a Gallup poll reported that 1 in 3 people still attended church on a regular basis, 1 in 3 attended evening classes, and only 1 in 12 were continually changing jobs. Equally, it is not altogether clear that the social protests and ferment of the 1960s were any great threat to the security of society. On reviewing social protests in the 1960s Bedarida argues that, despite their high profile, they did in fact have little long term impact (Bedarida,1979).

Byrne and Lovenduski argue that the 1970s and 1980s has seen the development of pressure group activity that increasingly seeks to challenge established social attitudes and behaviour, as well as Government policy. In particular they point to the peace and women's movements:

> Both CND and the Women's movement have succeeded in pushing their cause into the realm of public discussion and onto the policy agenda of parties and Governments. Both groups are well known, and there are continual reminders of their existence in all branches of the media. In short, they are popular movements, which have grown as ideas have struck a chord, and as new attitudes have spread. They were helped in this by the radicalisation that overtook much of Britain's youth (and especially middle-class youth) in the late 1960s (Byrne and Lovenduski, 1983, p.235).

In addition to the peace and women's movement, Madgwick argues that a number of social trends are further eroding stable and enduring cultural patterns in society. These include the development of youth culture, the gay movement, the ecology movement, the increased use of contraception and abortion, increased permissiveness in literature and the arts, and the increased use of illegal drugs (Madgwick,1982).

Certainly there is some evidence of increased fragmentation of social life in recent years. In 1975 140,000 petitions for divorce were filed, over four times the number filed in the early 1960s (Home

Office, 1979, p.17). By 1989, the numbers had increased further, reaching a total of 185,000 (CSO, 1991). It is now estimated that 1 in 3 new marriages will end in divorce. In a comparison of family life in the early 1950s and late 1970s Nissel found an increased level of social disruption within domestic settings. In 1978 there were over three-quarters of a million one-parent families, with nearly one and a half million dependant children (Nissel, 1982, p.100). The number of illegitimate births has risen from 5% in 1960, to 11% in 1979 and 27% by 1989 (CSO, 1991).

Changes in people's attitudes towards social and moral values demonstrate some increased permissiveness. In the 1950s, contraception was generally only used by married couples. By the mid-1970s it was commonly used by young single adults. Young people are far more sexually active today than in the 1950s (Nissel, 1982, p.101). Dunnell found that amongst women married in the late 1950s, 35% reported having a sexual relationship with their husband prior to marriage. By the early 1970s this figure had increased to 74%. A survey conducted in 1983 further confirmed this trend, with only 16% of people stating they thought pre-marital sex was always wrong, and 42% reporting it not to be wrong at all (Airey, 1984). Reflecting this, the proportion of all women aged between 18 and 49 who were cohabiting more than doubled between 1981 and 1988 from 3.3% to 7.7%.

At the same time as being able to identify evidence of a tendency towards questioning individual social roles, there is also evidence of considerable stability in some aspects of people lives. While marriage breakdown is increasingly common, the institution of marriage remains popular. Since 1961, the number of marriages each year has remained constant at around 400,000 (CSO, 1987, p.12). Moreover divorced people demonstrate a considerable willingness to marry again, with marriages involving one or both partners having previously been married rising from 9% of all marriages in 1961, to 26% in 1976, and to 32% in 1985 (CSO, 1987, p.12).

Although there has been a rising number of marriage break-ups there is no groundswell of opinion seeking easier divorce. In 1983 31% of a sample questioned thought the process of divorce should be made harder to obtain, 55% that it should stay as it is, and just 11% thought it should be made easier to obtain (Airey, 1984, p.139). Furthermore attitudes towards homosexuality despite (or because of) the gay movement are relatively intolerant. In 1983 nearly two thirds of a sample questioned considered homosexuality to be always or mostly wrong, and only 17% saw it as not wrong at all. Unfortunately there is insufficient data to establish trends on this issue. (Airey, 1984, p.137).

Despite the growth of the feminist movement, the household division of labour reflects little movement toward equality, with women continuing in the early 1980s to take on the bulk of domestic responsibilities (Airey, 1984, p.135). It is difficult to accurately assess just what impact these changing patterns of social action and social attitudes have had on the overall population. Marwick for example acknowledges the importance of varied developments such as feminism, and youth cultures, but nevertheless concludes that:

> from the point of view of the vast majority of the British People, as little interested as ever in major national concerns, the most significant changes in values were probably those related to sexual mores and social relationships: the tight little society of the late forties had expanded much, and the movement begun in the sixties, towards a more humane, more civilized, and more libertarian attitudes and towards a more comprehensive notion of what should be included in the term social welfare, continued on its upward trajectory right to the end of the 1970s (Marwick, 1982, p.272).

With the increasing scale of activities performed by the state, Madgwick argues that new areas of conflict have emerged; 'The state has been a necessary liberating force-liberating in the sense of relieving the common people from the burden of poverty, ill health, deficient education and so on...However, the new liberating movements were directed against the state itself.' (Madgwick, 1982, p.47). Kavanagh, on reviewing the available evidence, suggests that there has been a decline in the extent to which people feel able to influence Government. 'In this context', he notes, '...it is interesting that there has been an upsurge of more direct forms of protest and self-assertiveness in recent years.' (Kavanagh, 1987, p.78).

At a more theorectical level, Offe argues that this process is inherent to capitalism. In its attempts to create the conditions for the successful capital accumulation, a process of 'administrative re-commodification', the state tends only to succeed in further opening up areas of (what was) personal life for social and political questioning:

> By expanding social services and infrastructure investment, the state not only exacerbates the symptoms of the fiscal crisis, it also makes itself the focus of conflict over the mode in

which societal resources should be utilized. The state does not so much, as liberal reformers believe, become a force of social change and social progress, but increasingly it becomes the arena of struggle; it provides the rudimentary model of organisation of social life that is liberated from the commodity form without being able to live up to the promise implicit in that model...this experience must cause specific conflicts and attitudes of frustration over 'false promises' (Offe, 1984, pp.143-144).

The argument developed by Critical Theorists, including Habermas and Offe, concerning the importance of the motivation crisis is dependant upon the assumption that new, equally useful (to capital) motivational patterns will not develop. This has however in recent years been seriously criticised. In a discussion of Offe's work, Keane argues that he fails to give sufficient emphasis to the variety of cultural expression, and personal interpretation that has to be taken into account when assessing potential crisis tendencies:

censoring of this dimension of symbolic interaction, of the human capacity for symbol-making, speech and inter-subjective action, is revealed by his quasi-objectivist theory of crisis. It is as if the late capitalist political economy'sstructural difficulties are translated automatically into widespread consciousness of that breakup, into a disintegration of the identity of this society's constituents...It both underestimates the integrating capacity of new forms of symbolic interaction and...their relative invunerability to disruptions in the political economy (Keane, 1978, p.70).

Equally, attention needs to be focussed upon the varying solutions to the erosion of motivation patterns people will seek and support. As Held argues, not all need be progressive or revolutionary:

Anxiety about directionless change can fuel a call for the re-establishment of tradition and authority. This is the foundation for the appeal for the 'new' conservatives - or the new right - to the people and the nation, to many of those who feel so acutely unrepresented (Held, 1984, p.348).

Perhaps the clearest point that emerges from this discussion is that no single pattern of change and development in patterns of motivation is apparent. Moreover, the importance of any tendencies towards a breakdown in patterns of motivation is open to variable interpretation; whether or not such changes are necessarily related to societal crises is not clear, and certainly cannot be assumed to be the case. The available evidence does however indicate some further movement towards increasing social fragmentation. In some aspects of personal life there is a tendency towards increased questioning of social roles; although as attitudinal surveys suggest, a tendency towards social fragmentation appears to result in some people seeking conformity and social integration.

The compatibility problem.

Following the same format used in Chapter 3, we now need to examine more closely the precise nature of the exigencies affecting mental health policy formulation. This again involves consideration of the three areas of cost, control and legitimation.

Cost

The cost of health services in this period has been a subject of much political controversy. Claims that the service is under-funded, and counter claims that more than ever is being spent, have provided a basis for considerable argument. However our concern here is not so much with the adequacy of the level of expenditure, but rather with how much has been spent and what pressures this exerts upon state finances. There is little doubt that expenditure on social services has risen considerably.

Table 6.6
Patterns of social expenditure: annual changes (%)
1974-1984

	1974-79	1979-84
Totalsocialexpenditure	2.0	1.7
Socialsecurity	5.9	4.9
Education	0.4	0.5
Health and personal socialservices	2.9	2.6
Housing	-7.0	-11.7

Source: Taylor Gooby 1985, p.76.

These increases in expenditure represent an increasing share of overall state spending, under both Labour and Conservative Governments. Between 1951 and 1981 social expenditure accounted for 75% of the growth in public expenditure (Judge, 1982, p.29). This emphasis, as Table 6.8 demonstrates, reflects in the rising levels of expenditure on the National Health Service. Health expenditure has also tended to increase as a proportion of the GNP, between 1975 and 1984 rising from 5.49% to 6.24%. Overall, the amount spent by the state on the NHS since its inception has quadrupled in real terms (Ham, 1992, p.38). While the amounts spent have increased considerably, international comparisons demonstrate that this is from a relatively low base.

Table 6.7
Expenditure on the NHS 1975-1988

Year	Total(£m)	Total at 1949 prices(£m)
1975	5,298	1,229
1978	7,997	1,288
1981	13,720	1,498
1984	17,241	1,581
1988	23,627	1,797

Source: Ham 1992, p.39.

Table 6.8
Total health care expenditure as a percentage of GDP 1975-1983

	1975	1980	1983
Austria	6.4	7.0	6.9
Belgium	5.5	6.3	6.5
France	7.6	8.5	9.3
WGermany	8.1	8.1	---
Italy	6.7	6.8	7.4
Sweden	8.0	9.5	9.6
UK	5.5	5.8	6.2
USA	8.6	9.5	10.8

Source: Office of Health Economics 1986, p.7.

As a proportion of GNP, Britain spends less on health care than most other advanced industrial nations. This at least suggests that the scope for additional health expenditure is considerable, and that while the cost of the NHS has risen this does not necessarily imply that any great constraint exists upon state policy making in this area. International comparisons suggest that if it chose to, the state could spend much more than it currently does on health services. Within the health budget, mental health services have continued to receive a relatively small proportion of the budget.

However, the percentage increase in expenditure on hospital services has been greater for the mentally ill than for acute patients, rising by 7% compared to 4.4% for acute in-patients. This increase has occurred despite the reduction in mental illness beds being greater than for other patient groups. Consequently the increase in the cost of mental patients relative to other groups has risen at a greater rate than all other patient groups. Between 1971-2 and 1981-2 the average cost of a mental illness in-patient rose by 60% in real terms, compared to a rise of 10% for acute in-patients over the same period (DHSS, 1983c, p.7). In 1976-7 the cost per in-patient week for mental hospital patients in England was, at £81, just 24.1% of that spent on acute patients in London teaching hospitals. By 1984-5 these figures had risen to £255 and 30.2% respectively.

Table 6.9
Programme budget for hospital and community health services (gross current expenditure (£m) 1983-84 prices) 1976/77-1983/84

	1976-77	1980-81	1983-84 (Prov.)
Acute IP	2,908.4	2,990.2	3,037.5
Mental Illness IP	793.6	843.7	849.0
Mental Illness OP	37.3	44.6	56.5
Psychiatric DP	36.6	48.9	59.6

Source: House of Commons 1985b.

Despite the emphasis upon developing care in the community, there has been little increase in expenditure on the mentally ill outside of the mental hospital. In 1981-82 local authority personal social services in England spent £27.8 million on community care for the mentally ill, compared with £857 million spent in the same year on hospital services (DHSS, 1983c, pp.19-20). In 1984-85 the situation was little improved, with £60 million spent by personal social services, and £1,090 spent by the National Health Service (Audit Commission, 1986, p.8). Mental health services remain predominantly hospital based, with expenditure being heavily skewed in their favour.

This review of the economics of health care indicates that the cost of mental health service is not a serious burden for the state. In total the expenditure on mental health services in 1984-5 was £1,160 million (Audit Commission, 1986, p.8), constituting less than 1% of total state expenditures. However the cost of provision of health services generally and mental health services in particular has tended to increase rapidly. Whereas in the 1948-63 period we found costs were relatively stable, costs in the latter period have shown a tendency to increase in real terms and as a percentage of the GNP. In terms of pressure brought to bear on the state by the cost of services, then, it is the escalation rather than the scale of costs that is of greatest concern.

Control

With a tendency to increased fragmentation in some aspects of social life, that we have examined in discussion of the 'meta-problem', we might expect to see increasing pressure developing on this criteria of the compatibility problem. To examine this we will, as when discussing the control criterion for the 1948-63 period, examine two areas; concern expressed about a rising problem of control, and the scale of mental health service provision.

Concern about the rising rate of divorce was expressed by the report of a Working Party at the Home Office in 1979. It notes that in the post-war period there has been a considerable reduction in constraints upon, and direction of, personal behaviour:

> The social, economic and legal changes of the last few decades, including the invention of relatively safe artificial means of contraception and the increased availability of labour-saving devices, have created a situation in which men and women can challenge established patterns of partner relationship in home-making and parenting....the future of any marriage no longer depends on the authority of the Church and State, nor in a widespread acceptance of recognised standards and patterns of behaviour, but upon individual choices (Home Office, 1979, pp.22-23).

More specifically it notes that attitudes towards marriage have changed. Whereas in the 1950s expectations of partners were based on fulfilling their role, as either bread-winner or homemaker, there was by the 1970s far greater emphasis upon personal compatibility and the satisfaction of individual and personal desires (Home Office, 1979, p.21). Moreover it is argued that the increasing rate of divorce is associated with disturbed behaviour in children, and increased mental and physical ill health amongst adults (Home Office, 1979, p.17). There is, its argued, a serious problem; 'In sheer numbers alone the present rate of divorce each year affects an alarming number of people.' (Home Office,1979, pp.15-16).

This situation, the Report contends, makes increased levels of state intervention necessary. It is argued that the state has legitimate concern with these problems on two counts. Firstly, the suffering entailed may be alleviated by the provision of services to help maintain family units, and secondly the costs of family breakdown to the public purse are considerable (Home Office,1979, p.17). The report suggests therefore that a range of counselling and supportive services should be made available to help people sustain patterns of behaviour based around maintaining family life.

Groups involved with the care and treatment of the mentally ill have also expressed concern at the rising scale of mental health problems. The Royal College of General Practitioners notes that '...there is some evidence of increase in emotional illness in response to social stress'. (Royal College of General Practitioners,1985). With increasing recognition of the apparent scale of the problem of mental illness, the psychiatric profession has made some attempt to redefine (once again) the nature of the problem being addressed. At a conference in 1984 at the Institute of Psychiatry one of the main problems discussed was that existing taxonomies of mental illness fail to identify many receiving primary care as mentally ill. Anthony Clare argued that a new taxonomy of minor disorders more attuned to the needs of the primary care team was needed, better related to the relatively haphazard combination of symptoms being presented (Lancet, 1984, ii, p.443). By the early 1990s progress on this front appears to have been made with the inclusion of a new mental disorder, termed 'recurrent brief depression', in the International Classification of Diseases (Thomas, 1992).

Miles suggests two reasons for the rising level of identified mental illness. Firstly, she argues that general expectations of the quality of life have tended to increase. As a result '...the threshold at which the problems and discomforts of daily life become unacceptable is, as it were, being progressively lowered.' (Miles, 1981, p.192). Moreover, she contends that there is a generalised expectation within society that over time an increasing range of problems can be solved. This applies as much to mental health problems as any other; 'One result of higher expectations is that people turn to their doctors with a range of minor physical and psychological symptoms which previously seemed to be acceptable parts of daily life.' (Miles, 1981, p.194). This view is certainly supported by the Royal College of General Practitioners; 'Not only are general practitioners bombarded with advertisements for 'quick fix' medication...but the general public hopes for similarly simple 'happiness pill' remedies.' (Royal College of General Practioners, 1985). Secondly, Miles argues that with the development of more humanitarian attitudes within society, and the availability of psychotropic drugs, there has been a tendency to medicalise an increasing range of problem behaviours such as alcoholism and domestic violence. She concludes that some dangers exist in this steady expansion of the concept of mental illness; 'Concern can be more appropriately expressed over the potential dangers of the 'psychitrisation' of problems, until the point is reached when all minor symptoms and misconducts become suitable for some form of treatment.'(Miles, 1981, p.207).

Within the Department of Health there has been a considerable change in the definition of the problem being faced since the mid-1970s. The nature of the problem of mental illness has been expanded, encompassing a range of new social behaviours thought appropriate to psychiatric intervention. The Chief Medical Officer expresses this clearly:

> In considering the problems of mental illness, mental handicap and such psychosocial disorders as drug and alcohol abuse, suicide and marital violence, it is seen as increasingly important to look at wider mental health issues. Social change and technological advance have made it important for the public health and social aspects of mental health to be developed. The aim is to apply mental health principles to social action and to widen the concern for mental illness and psychiatry as a specialised branch of medicine, to enable general health and social services to become more aware and to take part in the promotion of mental health (Chief Medical Officer, 1977).

The definition of the problem of mental illness is being widened to include a range of behaviours, newly defined as 'socio-pyschological' problems that, its argued, mental health services should increasingly be seeking to address (Chief Medical Officer, 1979). With this broadening definition of problems considered suitable for psychiatric intervention, the DHSS argues that increasing numbers of people experiencing both severe and mild mental problems should be catered for. People for whom mental health services should provide for varies between '...people who experience difficulty in performing the roles required in work or family life and who need help to cope with this stress, which may otherwise precipitate mental illness.', through to those '...whose social functioning is so impaired by their disabilities that they require continual care in conditions of restraint.' (DHSS, 1980, Para.4).

This expansion of the nature of the problem provides a rationale for vastly expanding the numbers of people considered mentally ill. In our discussion of the immediate post-war period we noted that the Ministry of Health estimated that some two million people a year consulted their general practitioner with 'psycho-nuerotic' disorders (Chief Medical Officer, 1958,p.126). With developments in psychiatric knowledge and ability, it was argued that more mental illness could be detected and treated (Chief Medical Officer, 1948, p.128). In the 1970s we find the same arguments being presented. For example the White Paper 'Better Services for the Mentally Ill' states:

> It is new advances in scientific knowledge and understanding that have enabled recognition for example of the suffering of the housebound phobic or the young girl starving herself through anorexia nervosa for what they are - namely the manifestation of mental illness for which it is both humane and realistic to offer professional help (DHSS, 1975, Para 1.2).

We are then presented with a new estimate of the scale of mental health problems with, its suggested, some five million people consulting their doctor each year. Furthermore, with some mental illness remaining undiagnosed, its suggested that this figure may itself underestimate the scale of the problem; 'The true need is almost certainly much greater than present demand.' (DHSS, 1975, para.1.6).

By the mid-1980s the estimate made by the DHSS of the scale of mental health problems had grown still further, with it being argued that 25% of people living in the community have a psychiatric illness; '...research findings suggest (crudely summarised) that there are about 250 per 1,000 people in the community with some sort of psychological problem, 230 of whom will go to a GP-who will identify 140 as having some sort of psychological problems, and refer 17 to psychiatric services.' (DHSS, 1985b, p.3). This estimate is based on just one study of an area in Manchester, the authors of which themselves conclude that 'It is now generally conceded that psychopathological symptoms are continuously distributed in populations, so that to ask 'what percentage of the population is mentally ill?' is to pose a question which can only be answered by making arbitary assumptions.' (Goldberg and Huxley, 1980,p.157).   Over the post-war period the state has consistently sought to recognise greater levels of mental illness in the community that it argues requires treatment.   The estimated percentage of the population with a treatable mental illness between the mid-1950s and the mid-1980s has increased five fold, and indeed it appears that this trend looks set to continue:

> Not all those who need help are in fact getting it; some are unwilling to receive it; others have fallen out of the system. It is the behaviour of those people that often worries the community (DHSS, 1985b, p.3).

Since the early 1970s, studies in psychiatric epidemiology have tended to change their emphasis from measuring the level of diagnosed mental illness, to measuring the incidence of psychiatric symptoms within communities (Martin, 1984, p.115).   With this change in research method the net is swung more widely, with attempts being made to assess the mental health of whole communities, irrespective of whether people present themselves to general practitioners and the numbers of those that might then be diagnosed mentally ill.   Furthermore, the wide variation in earlier estimates of the levels of mental illness, which we discussed in Chapter 3, was largely due to the different criteria used to designate mental illness.   But in the last decade greater consistency has been achieved by the use of more uniform methodologies (Goldberg and Huxley, 1980, p.22).

In a review of some of these recent studies, Goldberg and Huxley note '...that the point prevalence of psychiatric disorder is somewhere betwen ninety and 200 per 1,000 at risk, and that the female rates are approximately double the male rates.' (Goldberg and Huxley, 1980, p.24).   The 'point prevalence' refers to the the incidence of mental illness at any one moment in time.   In there own study of South Manchester, Goldberg and Huxley found a 'one year period prevalence' of psychiatric illness at a level of 250 per 1,000 population. 'One year period prevalence' refers to those ill at the beginning of the year (18.4%) combined with those that become ill over that year (6.2%) (Goldberg and Huxley, 1980, p.21). These figures represent a considerable increase in the level of identifiable mental illness within the community, when compared to studies undertaken previously (Sheppard et al.,1966).

The numbers admitted to mental hospitals has continued to increase while, because of the reduction in the average length of stay, the number of in-patients provided for at any one time has decreased. Based on 1975 admission rates, Grimes has estimated that 8.6% of males and 12.6% of females can expect to be admitted to mental hospital at some point in their lives (Grimes,1978). By the late-1970s the rate of increase in admissions to mental hospitals had reduced to zero, and indeed was showing a slight reduction. However the trend upwards has since resumed, with the number of admissions per 100 thousand population rising to over 400 in 1983 for the first time ever.

Table 6.10
Admissions to English mental hospitals (thousands)
1975-1989

Year	In-Patients	Admissions	Admissions (per 100K pop.)
1975	87.3	175.1	377
1978	78.2	170.8	371
1981	73.4	185.5	397
1984	67.0	192.3	409
1987	n/a	203.7	461
1989	n/a	194.5	438

Source: DoH, Health and Personal Social Service Statistics, 1987, 1991.

The number of first admissions has continued to decline, while the number of discharges has increased.

Table 6.11
English mental hospitals: patient flow (thousands) 1975-1989

Year	First admissions	First admissions (per 100k pop)	Deaths and discharges
1975	57.3	124	178.0
1978	51.7	111	173.8
1981	52.6	112	187.6
1984	53.8	115	197.3
1986	51.7	109	203.5
1989	n/a	n/a	214.6

Source: DoH, Health and Social Service Statistics, 1987, 1991.

This decline in the number of first admissions has been concentrated amongst younger adults. While the rate of first admission for the 25-34 age group declined by almost 25% between 1975 and 1985, the rate for the 65-74 age group actually increased by almost 5% in the same period. Thus, for the population in general it does appear as if the likelihood of being admitted as an in-patient to a mental hospital has declined in recent years, though there is clearly an increase in the numbers of aged mentally infirm being catered for.

The number of out-patients has risen slightly in this period. Between 1975 and 1985 the number of new out-patients rose from 187,000 to 201,000, while the total attendances of out-patients rose from 1.55 million to 1.8 million. The number of regular day patients also has risen, with 36,000 new patients in 1975 and 58,000 in 1985. The numbers of people treated by general practitioners for mental illness is unknown, although some evidence exists that it is increasing. National Morbidity Surveys carried out in England and Wales in 1955/6, 1970/1 and 1981/82 found that of total consultations the numbers diagnosed as suffering from a mental disorder has slowly risen, from 5.0% to 6.8% between the first and last surveys. Certainly general practitioners continue to provide the primary source of psychiatric treatment (Sheppard et al.,1966; Royal College of General Practitioners, 1986). The Royal College of General Practitioners estimate that somewhere between 9% and 35% of their time is taken up with dealing with mental illness (Royal College of General Practitioners,1985).

This review of the control criterion suggests that the problems faced, and recognised, by the state are increasing. More areas of social life are thought suitable for psychiatric intervention, and more people are being treated than ever before. With increasing social problems associated with family breakdown, and increasing questioning of social roles and behaviour, its argued that psychiatric services have an increasingly important role to play.

Legitimation

The legitimacy of mental health services has, as we have seen, been maintained in the post-war period by the rhetoric of community care. There has been criticism of the policy since its inception, but generally within the context of accepting its aims (Walker 1982b; Walker 1986). We now need to take this analysis further and consider the support community care has received since the mid 1970s.

Ostensibly, the psychiatric profession has expressed support for the aims and ideals of the community care policy. Their claim is that 'Psychiatrists in the UK have played an active part in the move towards community care over the last 30 years and we welcome further constructive developments in this direction.' (Royal College of Psychiatrists, 1985, p.316). Others however, on reviewing the actions of psychiatrists, have been less convinced by such a claim. Martin argues that the psychiatric profession has never displayed, in practice, any great enthusiasm for community care. With their training continuing to be dominated by an emphasis upon the aquisition of medical skills, psychiatrists tend to be reluctant to engage in work outside of the hospital. They have neither the inclination to consider 'social' factors in the genesis of mental illness, nor the desire to work within collective teams where there own leadership and expertise might be disputed; '...it is difficult for doctors to join teams except in the role of captain.' (Martin, 1984, p.134).

A similar conclusion is reached by Sturt and Waters. In a review of the role of psychiatry within a community based mental health care system, they conclude that 'Many psychiatrists are doubtful about, or even openly hostile to, the developments, and many hospitals continue to function as if nothing is really going to change.' (Sturt and Waters, 1985, p.507). A recent editorial in the Lancet provides a swingeing attack on the role of psychiatry within community care. Its argued that they have failed to take on the leadership role in developing the new service, and instead argue that with community facilities being so little developed hospital facilities are still needed. Thus, little has changed within psychiatric practice; '...nothing was done to develop community psychiatry apart from relabelling some of the activities of hospital psychiatry.' (Lancet, 1985, i, pp.731-732).

General practitioners also have lent support to the community care policy in recent years. They tend to perceive there role as one of providing medical expertise within primary care settings, and taking the leadership role in this field by providing the pivotal role in the organisation of community care services. However, its also argued that hospital services provide a vital part of mental health services, and should not be seen as in anyway antithetical to community services. Moreover the pressures to provide a medical service are acknowledged, and noted to make the implementation of community care difficult (Royal College of General Practitioners, 1985, p.578).

In our discussion of general practitioners in the immediate post-war period we found that they lacked interest in the community care policy. More recently they have shown greater interest, but equally recognised greater problems with the policy. In a survey of general practitioners, Cartwright and Anderson (1981) found that between 1964 and 1977 a significantly greater number considered that personal and family problems should not be within their remit. Overall, Martin concludes that '...one is left with a marked sense of the diminuation in the personal qualities of the doctor/patient relationship, with a growing movement of practitioners into work settings where better organization and greatly increased ancillary help are associatiated with limited availability and a more narrowly 'medical' definition of the physician's role.'(Martin, 1984, p.121). The implication of this is that community care remains a minority interest within general practice. This is not to suggest that as a model for organising mental health services it is criticised, or has lost legitimacy, but rather that it generally remains inappropriate to the everyday activities of general pratitioners.

With the rapid growth in the numbers of social workers since the early 1970s (the figures for which we review later) there has been a change in the style in which they work. Increasing concern about the social conditions of clients and the lack of opportunities available to escape such disadvantage have figured more prominently. The focus of social work has shifted to some extent from individual case-work to political questions concerning the distribution of resources (Martin, 1984, p.89). With this has come an increasingly critical stance to community care. Although the mentally ill do not figure as a high priority within social work, a more general critique of the lack of adequate support for people

172

living in the community has emerged.

Whereas in the 1950s, as we reviewed earlier, psychiatric social workers were generally in favour of community care, there has in recent years been increasing criticism of the lack of facilities. It is noted that 'Restrictions on local Government spending and the spectre of rate-capping do litle to convince BASW that the Government has a real commmitment to developing services within the community.' (BASW, 1985, p.491). While the policy of shutting down mental hospitals is supported, and the advantages of a community based rather than institutional based system of care and treatment is acknowledged, its argued that because of insufficient funding community care has failed to provide an adequate service; 'The result for many mentally ill people is a confusion of unco-ordinated services which cannot be in any sense described as a comprehensive mental health service.' (BASW, 1985, p.492).

Voluntary organisations in the immediate post-war period offered few criticisms of mental health services and supported the community care policy. In the 1950s and 1960s the National Association for Mental Health tended to work in conjunction with service providers and policy makers. It generally maintained a low profile, and made little effort to influence the organisation of services other than by example and by encouragement; 'It was in the very nicest sense something of an Establishment organisation, and if it had a fault it was that it lacked a sharp cutting edge' (Martin, 1984, p.142). However since the early 1970s, under its new name of MIND, it has adopted a more confrontational and active stance in attempting to influence the provision of mental health services. In particular this has involved a campaign to improve the rights of detained patients which, with the passing of the Mental Health (Amendment) Act 1982, met with some considerable success. But it has also involved taking a more critical stance towards the development of community care services. In its submission to the the Royal Commission on the National Health Service in 1979, MIND left little doubt over its assessment of the quality of services available for the mentally ill:

> There is nothing very healthy about the mental health service. Indeed, any searching consideration of their quality and prospects is bound to evoke concern bordering on despair (MIND, 1979, p.2).

In its Report, 'Common Concern' (MIND, 1983), MIND details several criticisms of the community care policy. It notes that while an emphasis on community based services is to be supported, hospitals will retain an important role for the treatment of some people. Moreover, community based provision is only preferable if adequately funded. More recently MIND has argued that this will involve at least another £500 million a year being spent on services, together with improvements in benefit entitlement (MIND,1986).

There is still little evidence collected of the general acceptance or otherwise of the community care policy amongst the public. However some evidence does exist regarding the overall support for the health service, and the favoured manner in which it should be organised. In recent years the claim has frequently been made that public opinion is moving against public provision and in favour of non-statutory welfare services, either privately purchased or personally provided. Golding and Middleton argue that a swing in opinion against public provision of social security and welfare services occurred in the mid-1970s (Golding and Middleton, 1978). They claim that with a more general change in public opinion that existing levels of state taxation and public expenditure were too high, went an increasing level of suspicion that additional expenditure on state welfare services was not providing sufficient benefits to tax-payers.

But while this impression of public opinion has in recent years been strongly promulgated, particularly within the context of Thatcherism, Taylor-Gooby argues that such sweeping claims hides considerable variations. On reviewing survey evidence, he argues that '...a general climate of opinion exists among the public that strongly supports services for the elderly, the sick and disabled, education and the NHS, and is antipathetic to benefits for the unemployed, low paid, lone parents and children, with the other services occupying an intermediate position.' He concludes therefore that it is only by concentrating on certain services within welfare provision that a picture of mounting antagonism can be sustained. The overall level of support for the NHS has tended to remain high throughout the period of the Thatcher administration. A Marplan survey conducted in December 1987 found that a large majority of both Labour and Conservative voters supported increased expenditure upon health services, even if this means tax increases (reported in the Guardian,11/12/85).

In a survey conducted in Medway Taylor-Gooby found that considerable support exists for the NHS. Along with benefits and services for the old and widows, it ranked as the most popular of the welfare services (Taylor-Gooby,1985, pp.30-31). On being asked how much should be spent on the NHS, 11% of the survey population said less should be spent, 36% that expenditure should be kept the same, and 53% that more should be spent (Taylor-Gooby, 1985, p.43). This level of support ranked second in relation to other welfare services. Furthermore, the survey found that while a high level of support existed for private provision of health services, this co-existed with support for the NHS; 'Opinions about private and public provisions are not located at opposite ends of a single dimension, nor do they stand in contradictory relation which obeys a simple law of excluded middle.' (Taylor-Gooby, 1985, p.47).

This survey also provides some evidence of attitudes to providing care in the community. The provision of day care for elderly people was supported, but only for those not living with their families. This, Taylor-Gooby concludes, '...furnishes evidence of substantial minority allegiance to a family ethic despite the level of support for state provision of services.' (Taylor-Gooby, 1985, p.49). In addition, half the respondents considered that the welfare state 'makes people less ready to look after their relatives' (Taylor-Gooby, 1985, p.50). However in other areas, such as social security, it was found that most of those surveyed supported the provision of benefits to people irrespective of available family support. Thus Taylor-Gooby concludes that 'Overall, its seems that the thesis that a powerful family ethic that demands that women remain in the home available to care for children and other dependants and that their social security rights should be related to their position in the family, is not supported.' (Taylor-Gooby, 1985, p.51).

In total, this survey evidence suggests that the general public are in favour of statutory provision of health services, and that only limited devolution of the care of people to the community is acceptable. With particular regard to the mentally ill, the extent of this devolution might be expected to be relatively limited, given the fear and stigma attached to mental illness compared with physical ailments.

Over the last two decades criticism of community care by academics has become more trenchant. Particularly with the growth of the feminist movement in the 1970s, attention has been focussed upon the sexist nature of community care. It has frequently been noted that '...often when the word 'community' is used, and particularly when it is used in relation to welfare provision, it should be read as 'family'. Furthermore, for 'family' we should read 'women'.' (Wilson, 1982, p.40). Increasing attention has been paid to the propogation of sexist assumptions over the assumed roles of men and women within state economic and social policies (Land, 1978; Walker,1982b). This '...has led feminists...to criticize what in Britain are called 'community care' solutions.' (Land and Rose,

1985, p.92), where assumptions about the caring capacities of women results in many cases to little more than 'compulsory altruism'. Similarly, the costs of care have been emphasised. Women, because of responsibilities for dependant relatives, experience opportunity costs, particularly in employment where their predominance in part-time work reflects the other claims made on their time (Finch and Groves, 1980; Ungerson, 1983). Overall, on reviewing the experience of carers, Briggs and Oliver conclude that '...one is left with a feeling that only a Dickens could do justice to the stories they tell... Where there is a cheerfulnesss and a looking forward, it is in the face of adversity, not in the absence of it.' (Briggs and Oliver, 1985, p.105).

Doubts about the desirability of community care, as expressed in Government policy, have also been raised on more general grounds. Its noted that the considerable emphasis upon deinstitutionalisation is being pursued in the context of an already massive amount of unmet need in the community, that people do not necessarily want to be looked after by family and friends, and that services have evolved without reference to the service user (Laurance,1987). Jones, who as we noted earlier was sceptical of the emphasis being placed on care in the community in the early 1960s, has since become far more critical of the way services have developed. She argues that a false dichotomy is posed between institutional and community care (Jones, 1983), with the emphasis on the latter resulting in the loss of a valuable and necessary resource - the mental hospital.

In addition to questioning its desirability, the feasibility of the community policy too is queried. Abrams notes it assumes that care is provided on the basis of locality, whereas in fact '...the effective bases for community care are kinship, religion and race, not community...kinship remains the strongest basis of attachment and the most reliable basis of care that we have.' (Abrams, 1977, p.133). Whereas the policy assumes care is readily available in the community, '...we must start from the finding that in the typical social settings of contemporary British society, community care is typically volatile, spasmodic and unreliable...' (Abrams, 1977, p.130). Research has demonstrated that considerable problems exist with any attempts to greatly increase the pool of available care within the community. With an ageing population the need for care in the community is increasing while the pool of labour to provide this care is decreasing (Walker, 1982b), and with increasing numbers of women working their capacity to provide care is reduced (Wicks, 1982). Similarly, the increasing rate of divorce, a reduction in family size, and a decline in the proportion of single women in the population all suggest that the capacity of the community to provide informal care is limited (Parker, 1985, pp.15-17). Friends and neighbours are less willing to provide support than relatives, while the effectiveness of informal care is in part dependant upon the availability of statutory services, where for example the burden of care is shared such that informal carers have time to attend to their own needs (Walker, 1986, p.11).

Overall, academics have become increasingly critical of the manner in which the community care policy has been implemented; '...when viewed from the perspective of those actually involved in the everyday business of caring, the romantic and cosy perception of community care fostered in some political statements is at best fanciful...services have been confined to a residual system of crisis or casualty intervention.' (Walker, 1982, pp.24-25). Referring to the Mental Health Act,1959 Prins argues that the question that has arisen is that 'Given such admirable provision we must now ask what went wrong...' (Prins, 1984, p.188). Klein suggests there has been a tendency for more groups to want to influence the development of health policy, with less regard being given to 'expert' medical opinion; '...technical questions increasingly became redefined as political issues.' (Klein, 1983, p.105). In its report on services for mentally ill people, the House of Commons Social Services Committee concluded that 'The fact remains that there is a general and growing groundswell of opinion which is questioning the way in which so-called community care policies are operating in practice.' (House of Commons, 1985a, para.28).

The bulk of criticism however concerns the way in which the policy has been operationalised, rather than a critique of the nature of the policy; there is still general acceptance that it represents the most appropriate strategy, with criticism being mainly concerned with the failure to achieve policy goals. As such the Department of Health has been able to maintain the argument that the community care policy, although not yet adequately implemented, remains the best way in which to provide mental health services. It is noted for example in response to the House of Commons Report that, 'The Committee and the overwhelming majority of those giving evidence to it supported community care as a philosophy and as a practical proposition...' (DHSS,1985a, para.2). Thus, as the Government claims, community care tends still to be supported in theory, but as the Social Services Committee recognises considerable criticism has grown about the policy in practice.

Conclusion

This review of the socio-economic context suggests that the problems faced by the state are growing. Continued relative economic decline, a new rationale for state action stressing the limits of potential social expenditures, rising apparent need for mental health services, and a loss of legitimacy of the community care policy, all suggest that the state was facing a more difficult task when addressing the compatibility problem than in the immediate post-war period. Briefly, we can detail this as follows.

Cost and control

With increased emphasis upon constraining social expenditure together with an increased level of need for mental health services, the state must seek to increase the availability of treatment services, but do so more efficiently. The community care policy was, as we argued in Chapter 4, intended to provide this increase in efficiency while maintaining effectiveness. But with tension continuing to rise on this axis of the compatibility problem, the question arises as to whether community care will prove a suitable vehicle for the pursuit of these policy goals.

Cost and legitimation

With expenditure constraints increasing, and rising demands being made for more adequate care facilities for mentally ill people, tension on this axis of the compatibility problem has also risen. On this issue also therefore, the state is faced with increasing obstacles as it attempts to sustain the legitimacy of the policy, while incurring minimum additional expenditure.

Control and legitimation

We have also identified increasing tension on this axis of the compatibility problem. The scale of the problem has risen, with increasing numbers of people considered to be mentally ill. Yet the process of dealing with this by the state, as an illness to be treated by psychiatry, has been subject to growing criticism. In total, the state has been faced over the last twenty or so years with a situation where the community care policy is progressively failing to provide adequate resolution of the compatibility problem. It is this situation that it has been forced to address since the mid-1970s.

7 The policy making process, 1975-1993

There are no easy solutions.

(DHSS, 1975, para. 2.23.)

Having examined the context in which the state has had to develop mental health services, we now need to consider the manner in which it experienced, and responded to those pressures. As with the 1948-63 period we can do this on the three dimensions created by the exigencies of cost, control and legitimation. To recapitulate, these are the dimensions of efficiency and effectiveness, efficiency and acceptability, and effectiveness and acceptability. Whereas in the earlier period we identified four distinct phases in the policy making process there has been greater continuity in this latter period, hence each dimension can be examined without the need for this chronological sub-division.

Until 1975 the state had generally ignored criticism of the community care strategy. Its hope was that as the service evolved criticism would gradually diminish as community resources developed, and as the apparent new curative powers of psychiatry had effect. In this year however the DHSS became sufficiently concerned with problems with the policy that it felt further intervention was necessary, this being reflected in the publication of the White Paper 'Better Services for the Mentally Ill' (DHSS, 1975). In this, the DHSS acknowledges some failings of the policy and accepts that new efforts are required for it to operate successfully. It notes that '...by and large the non-hospital community resources are still minimal...the failure...to develop anything approaching adequate social services is perhaps the greatest disappointment of the last 15 years.' (DHSS, 1975, para.2.6).

At the same time however, the community care policy remains central to the Government's strategy; 'We believe that the failures and problems are at the margins and that the basic concept remains valid.' (DHSS, 1975, para. 2.17). In short, no sea-change in policy for mentally distressed people is required, but further internal rationalisation is needed to address the increasing tensions within the community care strategy; '...we must face up to the problems involved and the need to find satisfactory solutions to them.' (DHSS, 1975, para. 2.17).

In facing up to the problems, however, the White Paper emphasises that resources are limited. It notes that 'In present economic circumstances there is clearly little or no scope for additional expenditure on health and personal social services, at least for the next few years (p.iii)...It is as well to be frank about the difficulties. Financial resource constraints alone, quite apart from the physical and manpower constraints, mean that it will inevitably be a very long time before a broadly comprehensive modern service can be achieved in every district of the country...'(p.84). In presenting this argument the DHSS is prepared to acknowledge the need to improve mental health services, but is attempting to link this acceptance with an equally clear acknowledgement of the primacy of economic over social policy goals. This of course reflects the changing rationale for state action, examined in Chapter 6.

The solution proposed is that a comprehensive, integrated and local district psychiatric service should be established. This has four facets. There needs to be an expansion of local authority personal social services providing a range of facilities to enable mentally distressed people to live in the community. Specialist psychiatric services need to be relocated in local settings to allow greater access to treatment facilities. Greater co-ordination and co-operation is required between the various professions involved in community care. And finally an increased level of staffing is required in order to provide better individual treatment, earlier intervention and preventive work (DHSS, 1975, para. 2.22).

The content of the 'Better Services' White Paper reflects the problems with the community care strategy in the mid-1970s. The attempt to consolidate the policy in the previous 15 years had failed (see Chapter 5), and the state now recognised that its own credibility rested on acknowledging this fact; as Rollin noted soon after its publication, '...the Department of Health and Social Security has performed a nimble somersault.' (1977, p.182). At the same time however, there is no intention to desert the community care policy. It is argued to be the most appropriate strategy for providing mental health services, and that problems that exist can be overcome with greater effort and application; 'The Government hopes that this White Paper will...give the necessary impetus to the general development of community orientated services...' (DHSS, 1975, para. 2.23).

These themes, concerning the acknowledgment of problems with community care policy, and acceptance that further policy initiatives are required, provides the context within which to analyse subsequent events. As we shall demonstrate, the state has over the last two decades been engaged in a constant process of internal rationalisation. This culminated with the major reorganisation of policy in the early 1990s, associated with the National Health Service and Community Care Act, 1990. Whether or not this process has been successful in terms of reconciling the demands of efficiency, effectiveness and acceptability, constitute the central concerns of this Chapter.

Efficiency and effectiveness

In our analysis of this dimension of the compatibility problem so far we have argued that the state's central strategy has been to model mental health services on the structure and organisation of general health services; mental distress is an illness to be treated and cured like any other. This has been central to the community care policy since its inception and, as we shall see, remains so to the present day. However a number of problems have developed with this strategy, resulting in a loss of both efficiency and effectiveness.

Firstly, the considerable stress placed on the rehabilitation of mental hospital patients in the 1950s and 1960s has tended to diminish because of its lack of success. The 'open door', that heralded the new community care strategy, rapidly became a 'revolving door' as patients entered a pattern of intermittent periods in mental hospital characterised by a vigorous discharge policy and rapid relapse by patients once in the community. In a review of studies of the success of rehabilitation Wing found that for many patients it was not effective. He concludes that 'These results suggested that there would be an accumulation of...long-stay patients even when everything was done, within the limits of current knowledge, to avoid this.' (1981, p.144). This has been compounded by demographic changes. With an ageing population demands, as we saw in Chapter 6, have increased for psychogeriatric hospital beds. On reviewing this situation, Freeman concludes that '...the NHS-and particularly its psychiatric services-may well face psychogeriatric demands which jeopardize the whole system.' (1983, p.374).

A further problem derives from the over optimistic view held by the Ministry of Health in the 1950s about the effectiveness of psychiatric treatment. But, as the House of Commons Social Services Committee noted, mental health services have failed to develop in this form:

> Earlier community care policies were embarked on in the apparent belief that...modern medical or psychological techniques would lead to a massive reduction in the need for long-term care. There are now only vestiges of such a blithely over-optimistic attitude (House of Commons, 1985a, para.26).

The limited effectiveness of psychiatric therapies has resulted in a recognition that treatment and care cannot be so easily divorced. The treated patient, rather than leaving hospital and so leaving a vacant bed, all to often is soon being admitted once again. By the mid-1970s, the state was beginning to recognise the implications this had for the organisation of mental health services:

> ...health authorities must appreciate that a general hospital psychiatric unit cannot function efficiently in isolation, it can only function properly as part of a whole network of local services, of which social services residential, day care and domiciliary support are essential elements. Lack of such services might mean, for example, that the day hospital facilities in the psychiatric unit cannot be fully used because patients have not got a sufficiently supportive home environment to return to at night, and as a result patients in the unit might have to remain as in-patients for longer periods than is necessary on medical and nursing grounds (DHSS, 1975, para.11.18).

In 1981 the DHSS estimated that some 5,000 psychiatric patients were in mental hospitals, at a cost of £35 million per annum, who could be moved out if other facilities were available (DHSS, 1981b). In addition to this economic cost there was also an opportunity cost consisting of the lost throughput of mental patients; chronically disabled patients constituted a bottleneck in the system that reduced its efficiency and effectiveness. The community care policy was therefore failing to address this aspect of the compatibility problem adequately; further policy initiatives were required. In an attempt to efficiently treat the maximum number of people at minimum cost, the DHSS sought to place further emphasis upon the specialization and accessibility of treatment services for mentally distressed people:

> This group is frequently provided with services of inadequate standard and services need developing in more accessible facilities... The aim is for people to be able to use the service they need with the minimum of formality and delay, and without losing touch with their normal lives. Services should be readily accessible and, subject to manpower constraints, provide a range of resources to match individual needs (DHSS, 1981c, para. 4.5-5.7).

The strategy that has emerged to deal with this situation has been one of increasing the orbit of what constitutes an effective service. The argument developed has been that effective treatment requires action on four fronts (DHSS, 1983b). Preventive services need to be developed to help reduce the number of people coming forward for hospital treatment. Treatment needs to be available in hospital settings as already provided, but the specific and different needs of psychiatric patients should be more accurately focussed upon in the delivery of services. This has involved a process of specialization in facilities, including new regional secure units, hospital services, together with an increased emphasis upon providing treatment in primary care settings such as general practitioner's clinics, health centres and patient's homes. Rehabilitation services should be further developed, which would help reduce the number of people requiring mental hospital accommodation after treatment had been provided. And finally care, outside of hospital settings, should be given to those who do not respond to treatment. To assess the utility of this strategy we might consider just what progress has been made on each of these four fronts.

Prevention

Since the mid-1970s there has been increased emphasis given to the importance of developing preventive health services. The White Paper 'Better Services for the Mentally Ill' argued for greater emphasis being placed upon '...reducing the exposure of individuals to those circumstances and conditions which are likely to place their mental health at risk.' (DHSS, 1975, para.1.17). The discussion paper 'Prevention and Health' maintained that a preventive strategy would help reduce the cost of hospital services by reducing the numbers admitted (DHSS, 1977d), and the importance of a preventive strategy was confirmed by the 'Priorities for Health and Personal Social Services in England' document (DHSS, 1976). This emphasis within policy statements upon developing a preventive strategy has been maintained since (DHSS, 1985d; DoH, 1989).

Despite this emphasis, little progress has been made. There has since the early 1970s been some growth in the number of community psychiatric nurses. Many authority areas have developed a crisis intervention service, where a multi-disciplinary team is available to patients in their homes at the onset of a psychiatric breakdown (BASW, 1985). Other recent developments include the growth of community mental health centres. These provide supportive services to people, with the intention of helping people live with their disability without the need for mental hospital admission. But overall, the funding of these services remains very small, relative to expenditure upon traditional hospital based psychiatry. Moreover, with limited knowledge of the causes of mental distress a preventive strategy is difficult to pursue; 'It is an unfortunate fact of life that so little is still known of the aetiology of major psychiatric disorders that primary prevention of them is impossible to any significant extent' (Freeman, 1983, p.356).

Nevertheless, the notion of prevention does provide the state some utility in its attempts to reconcile this axis of the compatibility problem. A preventive strategy emphasises the importance of psychiatric practice outside of institutions, and the general management of whole communities, and this has had some effect on the development of psychiatric services. Yet, '...the District Psychiatry policy, as evolved in Britain, has remained fairly closely within the conventional models of medicine, nursing, and social work, but has extended outwards from institutions. Its theoretical basis is an eclectic, but fundamentally biological form of psychiatry.' (Freeman, 1983, p.372). The impact of this is not difficult to predict; prevention comes to consist of the provision of long acting depot neuroleptic drugs to the more seriously disturbed, and minor tranquilizers for the less seriously disturbed. Prevention legitimates 'maintenance therapy', provided by general practitioners, the rapidly increasing numbers of community psychiatric nurses, and psychiatrists who provide clinics at local surgeries.

Since the mid-1970s, we have seen increasing pressure from Government to close down the old mental hospitals, and to relocate treatment services within district general hospitals and within the community. In the consultative paper 'Care in the Community' (DHSS, 1981b) a target of closing 30 hospitals over the next ten years was announced, yet it was not until October 1986 that the first large old mental hospital - Banstead - fully closed down (Reid and Wiseman, 1986). Since then however the pace of closure has quickened. Concurrently, psychiatric units in district general hospitals have become increasingly important centres of treatment. In 1975 they received 25.7% of admissions (Mahadevan, 1982) and by 1983 this had risen to 45% (DHSS, 1985d). For the future, it is anticipated that units in district general hospitals will provide the main centres of psychiatric in-patient admission; 'Most regions are now busy concentrating new general psychiatric services on DGH sites...In general it seems to be accepted that DGH psychiatric units are the face of the future in acute psychiatry.' (House of Commons, 1985a, para.76). By 1987 all but 8 of the 191 District Health Authorities were able to provide psychiatric in-patient facilities (DHSS, 1987). Overall, this emphasis upon the expansion of psychiatric facilities in District General Hospitals, and a reduction in the provision of bed space in the older mental hospitals, reflects in the changing scale of hospital size.

Table 7.1
Distribution of psychiatric hospitals by number of beds (1979-1990)

	1979	1985	1990
Under 50 beds	141	253	224
50-249 beds	114	115	127
250-499 beds	53	69	69
500-999 beds	75	62	41
1,000-1,999 beds	31	12	0
Total	414	511	461

Source: DoH, Health and Personal Social Service Statistics for England, 1991.

Furthermore, out-patient and day patient facilities have been expanded. Between 1979 and 1987 the number of day hospital units for mental patients increased from 315 to 500 (DHSS, 1987). Despite this trend towards day hospital provision rather than full in-patient admission being evident for some thirty years, very little research has been conducted into the efficacy of it (Vaughan, 1983, p.93). The rationale for it is simply that it should prove cheaper to provide treatment to patients in this way, rather than admitting patients to take up expensive hospital beds.

With the anticipated reduction in secure mental hospital facilities as the old asylums closed, the Butler Committee in 1974 recommended the building of regional secure units for mental patients considered too dangerous for containment within general hospitals (Home Office, 1974). The policy has however met considerable regional resistance. In the financial year 1976/77 the DHSS allocated over £5 million to the Regional Health Authorities specifically to develop regional secure units, yet only £0.4 million of this was spent and much of that was used as general revenue (Lancet, 1977, ii, p.618). With continued pressure by the DHSS upon area health authorities it was only by the mid-1980s that this facility has become more generally available, with 11 of the 14 health regions admitting patients to regional secure units by 1985 (DHSS, 1986).

In recognition of the growing scale of the task being faced, with increasing numbers of people being treated for mental illness, the 'Better Services for the Mentally Ill' White paper fully accepted that more psychiatric staff were required (DHSS, 1975, p.ii). Since the mid-1970s the numbers of psychiatric hospital staff has increased substantially, though the increase has only been in line with the general increase in hospital staff.

Table 7.2
Hospital medical staff (whole time equivalent) in England

Year	All specialties	Mental illness	Mental illness: Percentage share of Medical Staff
1975	26,921	2,313	8.59
1980	31,431	2,678	8.52
1989	38,909	3,321	8.95

Source: DHSS, Health and Personal Social Service Statistics for England, 1991.

In addition to this increase in workers providing hospital treatment, there has been a rapid growth in the number of community psychiatric nurses. It is estimated that by 1985 there were a total of 2,701 in England and Wales (Radical Statistics Health Group, 1987, p.87). This group of workers has increasingly straddled the divide between specialist and primary care teams. In 1980 77% operated from hospital based settings and by 1985 this had been reduced to 56%, reflecting an increasing emphasis upon locating community psychiatric nurses in primary care and community settings (Radical Statistics Health Group, 1987, p.86).

Efforts have also been made to develop the availability of psychiatric treatment provided by primary care teams, although with markedly less success than that achieved with specialist services. The number of social workers in England and Wales has steadily increased since the mid-1970s, with 17,848 employed in 1974, and 28,598 in 1989. The number of general practitioners also has increased, by the end of 1989 reaching a total 27,749, although as with social work the pressure of work from other client groups reduces the impact they have had on the treatment of mentally distressed people. The Royal Commission on the National Health Service noted 'It is impossible to do justice to psychiatric problems within the present average consultation time of six minutes.' (Royal Commission, 1979, Para.6.41). Overall however, it continues to be the case that the primary care services are the major suppliers of psychiatric services in terms of numbers attended to (Goldberg and Huxley, 1980).

Rehabilitation

By the mid-1970s it had become apparent that a radical separation between treatment and care services was far more difficult to achieve than had been imagined twenty years earlier. Treatment services rely upon adequate after-care facilities to enable them to maintain their own throughput of patients, yet such facilities had not been developed. Little thought was given in the 1960s to the extent to which community based facilities could provide effective alternatives to mental hospital provision. The latter provided a complete framework of care, control, treatment and custody, while the new facilities provided only shelter and care. The discharged patient, who still demonstrated behavioral difficulties was little catered for in this new community based strategy (Bennett and Morris, 1983).

Furthermore 'The community care facilities that were established

187

were frequently viewed as transitional, a step between acute hospitalization and full reintegration into the community. The notion that some patients might require no less than life-long support in some sort of sheltered, protected setting was either ignored or denied in the hopeful therapeutic climate that prevailed.' (Bennett and Morris, 1983, pp.9-10). The implication of this was substantial for the effectiveness of mental hospitals; if long-stay patients could not be shifted as originally intended the throughput of patients would be greatly reduced.

What we have seen therefore, is an attempt to improve the care available in an attempt to maintain the effectiveness of treatment services. In 1976 a DHSS directive stated that Joint Care Planning Teams should be established, made up of members from the health and local authority social services. The joint planning process has however been dogged with a number of problems. United action by the various agencies involved has proven difficult to organise because of their competing priorities, because of differences in their organizational and management styles, and because of the varying planning time scales to which they operate. A major problem since the reorganisation of the National Health Service in 1982 has been the lack of coterminosity between local authority personal social service areas and district health authority areas. Thus, as the Audit Commission concluded, 'The differences in incentive and style have resulted in an atmosphere where there are hard negotiations and 'horse trading' between separate, self contained and often fiercely independent organisations...' (Audit Commission, 1986, p.60).

In order that Joint Care Planning Teams might have resources to call on, 'joint finance' was introduced to provide money with which to develop new projects. This scheme, introduced by the DHSS in 1976, involved the earmarking of health authority resources for use in conjunction with local authorities to develop schemes beneficial to the National Health Service. Over £600 million was provided in the first eight years of the scheme. The scheme was only intended to provide 'seed money', being given to initiate projects and then after a period of time local authorities would be expected to take over full financial responsibility. This was to include schemes for the development of facilities that would allow patients to be transferred from hospital to community settings, or would provide support to those who would otherwise be likely to be admitted. This would allow mental hospitals to improve their effectiveness by increasing throughput, but because it involved making additional resources available for the care of discharged patients it would tend to reduce efficiency.

Table 7.3
Joint Finance Expenditure (£million at 1984-85 prices)

Year	Capital	Revenue	Total	% Revenue of Total
1976-77	6.6	2.7	9.3	29
1977-78	18.1	17.4	35.5	49
1978-79	29.0	29.2	58.2	50
1979-80	26.0	37.1	63.1	59
1980-81	30.6	48.7	79.3	61
1981-82	27.7	57.8	85.5	68
1982-83	28.9	62.1	91.0	68
1983-84	22.2	68.9	91.1	76
1984-85	22.4	74.2	96.6	77

Source: Audit Commission 1986, p.35.

This tension, between gaining maximum increases in effectiveness at minimum cost, characterises the development of joint finance ever since. When the scheme was introduced joint finance money could be provided for a maximum of five years, the last two of which were provided on a tapering scale. This limit was however criticized as inadequate to tempt local authorities to engage in the scheme, and the tapering arrangements have since been extended. In 1977 the taper was extended to seven years, and in 1983 to 13 years with a maximum of 10 years total financing from health authorities.

Despite these changes to the joint finance scheme it remains the subject of considerable criticism. Firstly the scale of additional resources has been, for mentally distressed people, minimal. By 1985 only 5% of joint finance money been allocated to this group (House of Commons, 1985a, para.105) - an amount totalling a mere £30 million (at 1984/85 prices). Secondly, the scheme has proven difficult to use for its intended purpose of developing new community facilities. Because of local authority wariness about the revenue implications of capital spending, and wariness about the time limits on joint finance, they have proven reluctant to take on new projects funded through this scheme. As a result, joint finance monies have tended to be spent by district health authorities on primary and community health care without collaboration with local authority personal social services (House of Commons, 1985b, para.54). Also schemes developed in the last few years have tended to become smaller, lending weight to the view that the money is increasingly being used to 'plug service deficiencies' rather than promote a major change in direction of service provision (National Audit Office, 1987, para. 4.12).

In the 1980s further steps have been taken to improve the availability of services in the community that can provide alternatives to hospital accommodation. Following on from the consultative paper 'Care in the Community' (DHSS, 1981a), the DHSS eventually produced three proposals for action (DHSS, 1983a). The first of these was the extension of the joint finance arrangements, discussed above. The second was a change in the regulations (implemented by the Health and Social Security Services Adjudications Act, 1983) concerning District Health Authorities, allowing them to use their normal financial allocations to make lump sum or continuous payments to local authorities and voluntary societies for identified patients moving from hospital to community settings (known as 'dowry payments').

This scheme did however prove to be of very limited value. The main source of funds for the scheme has been from cost-savings resulting from the closure of hospital beds. A study by the National Audit Office of four Regional Health Authorities found that they assumed that the money that would be made available to the District Health Authorities from each bed closure would be between 50% and 90% of average in-patient costs. Yet on examining one District Health Authority it found that the closure of one hospital bed provided a saving of only 10% of the average in-patient cost, and even when whole wards were closed these savings only increased to 45% (National Audit Office, 1987, para.4.20). Furthermore, many District Health Authorities based the level of dowry payments upon average in-patient costs but this may not cover the costs of care in the community, particularly for high dependency patients (National Audit Office, 1987, para.4.25). Reflecting these problems, the scheme was wound up in 1990.

The third initiative by the DHSS announced in 1983 was the establishment of funding for a variety of pilot projects. This central initiative was intended to provide resources for specific projects in the community that demonstrated novel and potentially improved practice in community care. The budget for this, at £15 million from central funds, was tiny compared to the scale of resources devoted to treatment services. In itself, such small scale funding clearly will make little difference to resources in the community for mentally distressed people.

These initiatives designed to improve facilities for the rehabilitation of mental patients within community settings have been small in scale, and the regulations concerning the use of monies has hampered the development of projects. Overall, attempts to discharge long-stay patients into the community through greater emphasis upon rehabilitation have demonstrated little success; '...reductions in the number of NHS beds have been possible primarily because of the deaths of old long-stay patients rather than discharges into the community.' (National Audit Office, 1987, para. 6.8).

Care

By 1975 the state was compelled to recognise that mental distress could not simply be treated like any other illness, in that a large number of chronically disabled people continued to exist and unless provision was made for them they would continue to occupy hospital beds (DHSS, 1975, para. 4.52). This the state recognises as a problem; 'An accumulation of...patients...requires the attention of planners because it is undesirable to let patients live in an acute ward, and let the throughput in the DGH progressively decline, and also undesirable to ask the mental illness hospital formerly responsible to take over the care of the DGH's unwanted patients.' (DHSS, 1985b, p.38).

The census of mental hospitals in 1971 revealed that out of 104,638 occupied beds in mental hospitals in England some 75,932 were occupied by patients who had been in hospital for a year or more, and of this latter group 39% had been in hospital for 20 years or more (DHSS, 1975, para.4.51). Thus, in the 'Better Services' White Paper, it is acknowledged that new efforts within the mental health service are required to provide care for mental patients:

> Until local comprehensive services are in being and we are able to monitor their effectiveness planning must nevertheless proceed on the basis that there will continue to be a number of mentally ill people-though smaller than hitherto-who will need long term residential care, and that some of this will need to be in a health service setting (DHSS, 1975, para.4.56).

Since 1975 there has only been limited developments in the provision of such services. The main idea discussed has been the development of 'hospital hostels', which were advocated by the 'Better Services' White Paper and by many subsequent reports and commentaries. These would provide accommodation for long-stay patients in settings that were less therapeutically orientated than other mental hospital wards. In 1977 the first 'ward in a house' was opened at the Maudsley hospital (Wing, 1981, p.144). However there has been no general increase in the availability of such accommodation. By the end of 1985 just two further 'hospital hostels' had opened, giving a total of 3 sites offering just 48 places (DHSS, 1986b).

With this lack of new facilities to solve the problem of chronic patients continuing to take up mental hospital beds a split in function between the old mental hospitals and new psychiatric units has developed; the former have tended to receive patients whose prognosis is poor and the latter patients who are thought more likely to respond quickly to treatment. In this way throughput is maintained in some parts of the hospital system. By 1983 psychiatric units were making some 45% of admissions despite holding less than 10% of in-patient beds for mental patients (DHSS, 1985d, p.24). As a result a two tier system of mental hospital provision has tended to develop; 'The development of psychiatric units in DGHs in itself desirable, has had the effect of leaving to the large specialist mental hospitals the incurable, the behaviourally disturbed, the old and demented.' (Royal Commission, 1979, para.6.44).

The intention of the Government in all the policy changes discussed in this section has been to make psychiatric services more accessible and more flexible in the treatment regimes that can be offered. If we briefly compare these developments to the mental health service that existed prior to the evolution of community care the major trends in service provision become clear. The institutional system had provided a number of services; custody, treatment and care. A comprehensive district psychiatry service tends to divide these functions into specialised services. Custody is provided by regional secure units (as well as in the four special hospitals) and to a lesser degree by mental hospitals and psychiatric units in district general hospitals. Treatment is provided within a range of facilities including hospitals, health centres and the patient's home. Moreover the concept of treatment is extended to include the general surveillance of people seen by the primary care and social services and their referral to specialist services. Care is provided to a limited degree, but primarily in the context of rehabilitation. Care, in the more practical sense of tending, is barely addressed at all.

Overall, there has been an expansion of, and specialization within, the treatment services available to mentally distressed people. The aim has been to make treatment services available to an increased number of people but at the same time minimise the cost of dealing with each patient; an aim of increasing the effectiveness of the service with minimum loss of efficiency.

This logic of development has been taken one stage further in recent years. In 1988 the Royal College of Psychiatrist proposed the introduction of 'community treatment orders'. These would involve the provision of compulsory treatment to people living within the community. Objections to this are many and varied, including civil rights issues and the coherence of the proposals themselves; its noted that if somebody is refusing treatment they should within conventional psychiatric terms be considered too ill to be released into the community. It is proposed that such orders would only be made for relatively small numbers of people, but as Lawson notes, '...what guarantee is there that they would not gradually be seen as useful for wider and wider use.' (Lawson, 1988, p.4). Despite these objections, the Department of Health continues in the early 1990s to consider the introduction of community treatment orders. In terms of reconciling the twin demands of efficiency and effectiveness, there introduction would represent an incremental movement forward within mental health policy. There introduction, however, will depend upon the ability of the state to overcome resistance to the proposal, and how this will resolve itself at the time of writing is not yet clear.

Efficiency and acceptability

The issues we have identified on this axis are threefold; the level of resources available for mental hospitals, the level of resources available for care in the community, and the appropriateness of the community care policy as a means of providing care and support for mentally distressed people. These have all provided grounds for dispute over what the state is, and should be doing. Moreover we have also argued in Chapter 6 that tension between the twin demands for efficiency and acceptability has tended to rise. As Patrick Jenkin when Secretary of State for Social Services made clear in a letter to the chair and members of the District Health Authorities; '...the Government's top priority must be to get the economy right; for that reason, it cannot be assumed that more money will always be available to spend on health care.' (DHSS, 1981c). We might expect therefore to see evidence of this rising tension since the mid-1970s, and additional efforts by the state to resolve the problems that arise.

Because of the continuing importance of the old mental hospitals the state has been faced with pressures to maintain and indeed improve conditions within them (DHSS, 1983, Para. 2.22). This concern became particularly apparent in the early 1970s when a series of scandals about mental hospital conditions greatly increased pressure on the state to improve conditions. The extent of the problem in the mid-1970s, despite all previous progress, was severe. In 79 mental hospitals there were some patients who did not a full range of personal clothing, and many patients did not have their own personal cupboard space. However since then some effort has been put into improving conditions. It is recognised that 'For some years to come, the majority of psychiatric patients will be cared for in the existing mental hospitals. Priorities here are...the achievement of minimum standards for staff ratios, food, accommodation and facilities...(the) improvement of physical standards in hospitals...(and) the improvement of staff levels.' (DHSS, 1976, p.59). Reflecting these concerns, the cost of in-patient care and the number of nursing staff per occupied bed have both risen considerably, both in absolute terms and relative to other patient groups (see Table 7.4). There has also been some improvements made in the level of facilities provided by local authorities for mentally distressed people.

Table 7.4
Mental hospital costs (£million at 1984-85 prices)

Year	In-Patient Costs	Annual Cost per occupied bed
1976-77	£839.6 million	£10,027
1980-81	892.6	11,792
1984-85	900.9	13,315

Source: Audit Commission 1986, p.110.

Table 7.5
Changes in mental illness hospital staff and patient numbers in England 1975-1985

Year	Average daily occupied beds	Nurse numbers (wte's)
1975	86,900	47,259
1980	75,200	52,577
1985	64,800	57,956

Source: Audit Commission 1986, p.111.

Table 7.6
Local authority personal social services homes and hostels for the mentally ill 1975-1989

Year	Staffed		Unstaffed	
	Places	Premises	Places	Premises
1975	1,838	98	707	145
1980	2,333	137	1,391	304
1985	2,563	156	1,800	427
1989	2,703	171	1,994	522

Source: DoH, Health and Personal Social Service Statistics for England, 1981, 1991.

Table 7.7
Local authority day centres for the mentally ill 1975-1990

Year	Places	Premises
1975	3,403	101
1980	4,967	134
1985	5,414	148
1990	6,979	202

Source: DoH, Health and Personal Social Service Statistics for England, 1981, 1991.

Despite these improvements in service provision, conditions in the old mental hospitals has continued to be criticised (MIND, 1986; House of Commons,1985a). Equally, the stark disparity between levels of expenditure within mental hospitals and in the community remains. For the financial year 1987/88, hospital revenue expenditure upon mental illness hospitals was £870 million, compared to Local Authority net current expenditure on the mentally ill of just £74 million; a ratio of over 11 to 1 (Health and Personal Social Service Statistics for England, 1990). A result of the reduction in mental hospital bed space, without a commensurate increase in community care facilities, has been that many people with a mental health problem have simply become homeless (Comptroller & Auditor General, 1990). As the Parliamentary Panel for Personal Social Services recently concluded, 'Budget growth in recent years...has...been insufficient to meet growing need without a deterioration in some services...In particular, more resources are needed to implement the Government's own policy on community care.' (House of Commons, 1986, para.36).

The introduction of the 'block grant' system of distributing resources from central to local Government by the Local Government Planning and Land Act, 1980, that came into operation in 1981/82, has reduced the ability of local authorities to develop care in the community facilities. The allocation of rate support grant intended for social services expenditure is now based upon an assessment of the level of need within each local authority area. The method of assessment of this grant related expenditure has however been subject to a number of criticisms. The size of grant allocated to each area makes inadequate reference to variations in local circumstances, such as levels of poverty and unemployment. No apparent relationship exists between the size of grant allocated and the amounts actually spent by local authorities. Changes in service provision, such as an emphasis on providing domiciliary services for people in their own homes instead of providing residential care, are not taken into account in the assessment of the grant. Insufficient account is taken of a range of pertinent factors, such as the level of informal support available and the numbers of mentally distressed people within local communities, when assessing the size of grant allocations (Walker, 1985, pp.27-29; Audit Commission, 1986, p.35).

Yet despite such criticism central Government strategy remains one of encouraging the development of community care, but limiting the resources it makes available to achieve this. In attempting to balance the twin demands of providing an acceptable service while also constraining the cost implications that that entails, it has been boxed into a position that few are prepared to accept is realistic:

> I believe it is in the capacity of a well-managed local authority to provide care in the community facilities without running into penalties or rate-capping (Kenneth Clarke, in evidence to the House of Commons Social Services Committee, 1985a).

Since the community care policy was formulated the state has emphasised that its success is dependant upon a commitment of effort and resources from non-statutory sources. The importance of this source of care for mentally distressed people living in the community has since the mid-1970s been further emphasised (Brenton, 1985, p.143). Following a change in social security regulations in 1980 there has been a rapid expansion in the provision of privately run accommodation for mentally distressed people, although just how many mentally distressed people are provided for is unknown (House of Commons, 1985a, p.117). Between 1979 and 1990 payments for board and lodging have increased from £ 6 million to £1, 600 million per annum. However, the amounts payable for private accommodation are less than the cost of maintaining patients in mental hospital beds. The voluntary sector also has made some advances in the provision of community care facilities for mentally distressed people.

Table 7.8
Voluntary and private homes and hostels
for the mentally ill 1975–1989

Year	Places	Premises
1975	1,366	67
1980	2,142	122
1985	3,171	250
1989	6,237	481

Source: DoH, Health and Personal Social Service Statistics for England, 1981, 1991.

In total, voluntary and private provision of community care facilities have since the mid-1970s become an increasingly important part of the total services available. The extent of informal care for mentally distressed people is more difficult to measure. Indeed it was only after the policy of decanting mental patients into the community had begun that any research was done to establish the extent of the burden being carried by informal carers (British Journal Of Psychiatry, 1987, p.150; pp.285-292). However, as we saw in Chapter 6, the evidence accumulated since suggests that as a source of care it is limited and not always a willing act of charity. It is suggested that with the growth of the feminist movement women may prove less willing to accept that they should provide the main source of informal care; 'In recent years this assumption has been questioned by women themselves, and this has cast doubt upon the future of community care policies in their present form...' (Walker, 1982, p.13). Few studies have been undertaken to establish the willingness of the community to provide care for dependent groups, but what evidence does exist demonstrates no great desire on the part of the community to accept the major burden of responsibility for the care of mentally distressed people:

> The public, it seems, are not inclined to allocate the major responsibility for the care of dependency groups to the family and close kin preferring instead a continued policy of partnership between informal care systems and the welfare state in which the former does not replicate the latter (West, 1984, p.287).

In the immediate post-war period the Ministry of Health, as we noted in Chapter 4, was keen to stress that the community is becoming more tolerant of mentally distressed people and increasingly prepared to offer them help and support. This provided an important prop to the assertion that the mentally distressed people would receive better care within the community than in institutions. This argument has been maintained, and remains an important prop to the legitimacy of community care. The following quote would not have looked out of place in the Annual Reports of the Ministry of Health in the late 1950s:

> Changes in the type of treatment available, and in social attitudes to people suffering from mental illness, have continued to make the old pattern of health services based on long-term care in large isolated hospitals even more inappropriate.

In fact it is to be found in the Annual Report of the Health Service in England, 1985, and of course the problem that arises for the state from this is whether such a proposition can continue to be justified, that 'During the last 25 years or so there has been a growing recognition that community care would be far better for many such patients than prolonged periods in hospital.' (DHSS, 1983c, para.2.22).

This argument amounts to no more than an unsubstantiated assertion, for still today we have little knowledge about how discharged psychiatric patients fare in the community. As an editorial in the British Medical Journal noted, 'Vast numbers of long term patients have been discharged in the past three decades and it is truly remarkable that we do not know which proportions have settled successfully in the community with family or other support, have struggled on in a lonely abyss, have lived a life of destitution, and have returned to hospital.' (1985, 291, p.1372).

There is however some evidence available from small scale studies about the experience of care in the community. Long-stay patients in mental hospitals rarely state a preference for living in the community; the hospital has become their home. While some criticism might be voiced by patients about inadequate facilities in mental hospitals the response tends to be a desire for an improvement in institutional care rather than a change in service provision towards community care (Peers, 1972). In a recent study Abrahamson found that '...reluctance to leave hospital is in fact common among long-stay patients, and is one of the most frequent problems met by resettlement programmes.' (Abrahamson, 1982, p.95). A study of short-stay patients found that few received adequate support from the community. Of patients admitted over a year to one mental hospital 64.7% were unemployed, 50% were living alone and 40.5% were homeless, while 36.5% had no visitors while in hospital (Ebringer and Christie-Brown, 1980). The extent of preparation and support for discharged patients has also been found to be inadequate. A study of a hospital in London found that patients were not consulted or involved in decisions about their discharge and receive little if any advice about housing, day care, medication, or social security entitlement (Kay and Legg, 1986).

In our discussion of this dimension of the compatibility problem we have established that tension between its two poles is growing. Furthermore, the state has demonstrated an inability to extricate itself from the problems that have arisen. Rather, it has attempted to maintain its stance regarding the adequacy of the quality and quantity of care being offered while attempting to minimise state resources devoted to that care. But it has done so with decreasing success; costs have tended to rise and legitimation decline. However, as we saw in Chapter 6, criticism of the community care policy for mentally distressed people tends to concern the manner in which the policy is implemented rather than upon the principles upon which it is based, hence the policy still meets the state's needs on this dimension of the compatibility problem. But it does so with declining success.

Effectiveness and acceptability

The concerns we have identified on this dimension of the compatibility problem revolve around the state's concern with maintaining a treatment orientated service that effectively deals with mental health problems in terms of an illness model, and at the same time retains legitimacy. As we saw in our analysis of the 1948-63 period this has been undertaken by emphasising the increasing effectiveness of psychiatric treatments, and by maintaining the appropriateness of psychiatric intervention in ever increasing areas of social life.

By 1963 this strategy had been successfully implemented. The medical nature of the problem of mental distress, and the improving abilities of the psychiatric profession to deal with such a condition, were both widely accepted. The success achieved by the state in the 1950s in promulgating a medical conception of the problem was based, in part, upon the perceived effectiveness of the newly available psychotropic drugs. It was genuinely - although without foundation - believed within the Ministry of Health that the new 'wonder drugs' would allow great advances in the treatment of mental distress. In recent years, however, there has been increasing debate and dispute over just how useful these drugs are. Physical treatments, in particular drug therapies, remain the most used method of treating mentally distressed people. In 1965 some 38.5 million prescriptions for psychotropic drugs were made, and by 1975 this had risen to 66.0 million. By the mid-1970s psychotropic drugs constituted a quarter of all medicines taken for a year or more (Lader, 1979, p.41). Since then the numbers of prescriptions for minor tranquilizers has dropped with, for example, some 23 million prescriptions for benzodiazepines being made in 1988 compared to over 30 million in 1979 (CSO, 1991). It is estimated that in 1984 23% of the adult population had used tranquilizers; 3.5 million people for more than 4 months, and 250,000 people for seven years or more

(Rose, 1986, p.69). The number of major tranquilizers dispensed by general practitioners has increased slightly. For this group of drugs in 1980 2.17 million prescriptions were made, and in 1986 2.23 million were made. The quantity of major tranquilizers consumed within mental hospitals is not known (DHSS, 1988).

Yet, while the prescription of drugs remains the dominant form of treatment, there has since the mid-1970s been increased criticism about their efficacy. In a study of patients discharged from hospital after treatment for schizophrenia, it was found that less than 20% were symptom free at follow-up (Johnston et al., 1984). Moreover it has been found that many people who take major tranquilizers over a long period of time tend to develop tardive dyskinesia. This is a condition involving a loss of muscular control. In a review of the literature, Jeste and Wyatt concluded that tardive dyskinesia affects 25.7% of patients on major tranquilizers, and that of this group the drug treatment is directly implicated in the condition of approximately half (Jeste and Wyatt, 1981). Tarsy and Baldessarini estimate that tardive dyskinesia affects between 10% and 15% of those treated with major tranquilizers (Tarsy and Baldessarini, 1984). The use of minor tranquilizers has also become the subject of criticism. Drugs such as valium, librium and ativan have been found to be addictive and of little therapeutic value when prescribed over a long period of time.

The experience of drug treatments, and criticisms of their efficacy that have developed, has resulted in a considerable reduction in the legitimacy of such methods in providing treatment for mentally distressed people. On reviewing changing attitudes towards the efficacy of drug treatments, Sedgwick concludes that 'The pitfalls of an acute and intensive medical-psychiatric technology are already widely canvassed...the current of de-medicalisation is unmistakable.' (Sedgwick, 1982, pp.239-240). Various self help groups, such as 'Survivors Speak Out', and voluntary groups such as 'Tranx' have evolved and taken an active interest in helping people come of drugs. Similarly MIND has displayed an increasingly critical attitude towards drug treatments. It notes that 'The disturbing and expensive increase in the prescription of psychotropic drugs underlines the need to clarify where a medical response is essential and where other forms of help would be more appropriate.' (MIND, 1979, p.2).

These criticisms of the effectiveness and acceptability of drug treatments makes the resolution of this aspect of the compatibility problem more difficult. If it is accepted that treatment is not as effective as once thought the rationale for closing down mental hospitals, and for concentrating resources upon treatment of an illness rather than the more general needs for care of chronically mentally distressed people begins to break down. Scope for argument is created over whether mental health services should indeed be so heavily medically orientated. All these points question the rationale of the community care policy, as envisaged within the Government's conception of the policy.

A further area of criticism that has developed, in part related to the lack of anticipated success in treatment services, concerns increasing questioning of the stark division between health and welfare services; '...the current community-care movement (has) confused the separate aims of social reform and the pursuit of more effective methods of treatment.' (Bennett and Morris, 1983, p.13). With criticism developing over the effectiveness of available treatments and the appropriateness of medically based psychiatric intervention it has tended to be accepted that in fact '...there is always an interaction between clinical and social problems. It is rarely possible to separate the two in a way that would be convenient for the development of independent medical and social services.' (Wing and Olsen, 1979, p.172). Consequently the split that has developed between health and welfare provision has been criticised for failing to meet the needs of mentally distressed people. As Jones notes '...the mentally ill (are) required to carve their needs into neat parcels labelled 'medical' and 'social', and to apply to the appropriate authority for care and treatment.' (Jones, 1979, p.10). As a result standards of care and treatment of mentally distressed people has suffered; 'Patients' needs do not come in packages neatly labelled 'medical' and 'social'. They come in a tangle of emotions and insupportable situations in which physiological, psychological and social factors interact.' (Jones, 1979, p.13). Thus the split between health and welfare services has become less acceptable; '...the assumption that medical and social needs can be dealt with separately, which is built into the present administrative structure, will have to be modified.' (Wing and Olsen, 1979, p.185).

Reflecting this increased level of argument over the appropriate organisation of mental health services, there has developed greater professional rivalry amongst groups who deal with mentally distressed people over how and where they should be provided for. With an emphasis on increased social work and general practitioner involvement in the detection and treatment of mental illness, and on the role of psychiatry outside of institutional settings, there has been a lack of common understanding of the roles that each should play. Psychiatrists, as we discussed in Chapter 6, have tended to remain wedded to an institutional and medical based system, and are wary of attacks on this power base. They fully support the development of community care in principle, but in practice tend to support the need for modern psychiatric treatment facilities based in hospitals (Jones, 1979, p.564). Moreover they display a considerable wariness of sharing power and authority in the treatment of mentally distressed people. In particular social workers are regarded as lacking relevant skills, and of failing to prioritise mentally distressed people in their work (House of Commons, 1985a, p.316). Perhaps as a result, social services and general practitioners are often not informed by hospitals about the discharge of a patient into their area (House of Commons, 1985a, p.573). General practitioners too share this wariness of the role of social workers in the provision of treatment:

> Doctors often feel that social workers do not 'back them up', particularly in obtaining compliance with medication, and are chary of co-operating with people who not only do not have a medical or nursing training, but may have had no formal training at all! (Royal College of General Practitioners, 1985).

Despite the current emphasis in Government policy upon developing an integrated and comprehensive service, the various professional groups involved in the provision of mental health services have demonstrated little inclination to work harmoniously. The Audit Commission noted that there is considerable 'professional fragmentation' amongst groups responsible for the treatment of mentally distressed people (Audit Commission, 1986, p.56), and this undoubtedly reduces the effectiveness of the service provided. As Walker notes, 'So far defensiveness and competition rather than co-operation, have been the more common reactions of medical and other social service professionals.' (Walker, 1982, p.22).

Until the mid-1970s psychiatry occupied the central position of power in the provision of mental health services. The Mental Health Act, 1959 gave the psychiatric profession considerable power to determine appropriate methods of treatment, and to preside over how services should be organised. But with their subsequent reticence to develop services outside of the mental hospital, and the apparent rising scale of need for such services (that we examined in Chapter 6), the relatively harmonious relationship between the state and the psychiatric profession has tended to break down. While the emphasis on the provision of treatment remains a priority to both, disagreement has arisen over the administrative arrangements by which that should be achieved. While the psychiatric profession maintains the importance of hospital provision and their role in it, the Department of Health has sought to 'prise' them out in order to more adequately develop local community psychiatric services (Goldberg, 1986). Equally, hospital psychiatric nurses have displayed considerable wariness about supporting a policy that might lead to their own redundancy as mental hospitals close (COHSE, 1984).

It is in this context that the Department of Health has attempted further internal rationalisation of the community care policy, in an attempt to restore compatibility between the opposing exigencies of effectiveness and acceptability. Since the mid-1970s increasing support has been given to the development of a comprehensive mental health service. As we noted when discussing the 'Better Service' White Paper (DHSS, 1975), this concerns the development of specialist and primary care teams, and their closer co-operation in the provision of a locally based service. It acknowledged that mental health services had failed to meet the needs of mentally distressed people in a variety of ways. Insufficient resources had been made available for 'difficult' and 'chronic' patients, while the needs of many suffering mental distress in the community were not served at all. But with further reorganisation of mental health services, it was argued that the needs of mentally distressed people would be more adequately met.

We discussed earlier the introduction of joint planning of mental health services as a means of improving the throughput of mental hospitals at least additional cost. This innovation also has implications for this dimension of the compatibility problem, as it provides a means of dealing with criticism about the lack of co-ordination between health and welfare services. The result however has been that an increasing number of agencies have become involved in the provision of community care services. The two main agencies, health and local authorities, are funded by two different sources, the Department of Health and the Department of the Environment respectively. With increasing recognition of the complexity of service provision various other bodies have become involved. Local authority housing departments, and voluntary and private sources of accommodation, play a crucial role in providing for discharged psychiatric patients. Other agencies that might be involved include those concerned with education, transport and employment. Indeed the list is potentially endless, simply depending upon how comprehensively it is intended that community care should meet the needs of mentally distressed people.

This emphasis upon joint planning since the mid-1970s has however failed to create a common view over how to provide welfare services, and how these should relate to health services for mentally distressed people. While local authority social service departments are primarily concerned with reducing dependence on residential accommodation by expanding domiciliary and day care, health authorities have shown greatest concern with establishing residential accommodation outside of hospitals in order that the bottleneck of long-stay patients can be removed. The various other agencies involved in providing services also have competing interests and priorities. Private agencies seek a return on investment, local authorities have to meet the needs of various other dependant groups, voluntary groups are torn between acting as pressure groups and service providers. The DOE has demonstrated a greater concern with containing overall costs of local authority expenditure than with attempting to increase the budget available for the development of community care. Overall, there is considerable tension in the joint planning process over just what services should be developed (Webb and Wistow, 1982, p.140).

Overall, there has been a lack of agreement over how to develop care in the community; 'Both the level of expansion of provision and the service structure to be aimed at are...problematic features of the community care policy.' (Webb and Wistow, 1982, p.140). This organizational confusion can be understood in terms of the decreasing success of the policy to organise a consensual view over how to provide services for mentally distressed people. On the one hand, representing the Government's desire for effective services, there is an emphasis upon maintaining the separate provision of health and welfare services. This concerns the emphasis upon medically based treatment orientated services. Welfare needs of patients should only be met in so far as they are necessary to maintain the effectiveness of treatment services; in particular, as we have seen, this concerns measures to improve the throughput of treatment facilities. On the other hand, demands for mental health services to be made more acceptable have resulted in some efforts to recognise the welfare needs of mentally distressed people; that they cannot just be treated and discharged without regard to their wider social needs for housing, domiciliary support and social activity. It is these competing aims that have been fed into the policy making and implementation process, and have resulted in considerable confusion over the purposes and aims of the community care policy.

In our discussion so far of developments within the community care policy since the mid-1970s, we have found a growing number of tensions between the various aims and interests associated with mental health service provision. Despite efforts by the Government to develop further strategies of internal rationalisation, intended to address these various conflicting tendencies, the community care policy has proven progressively less successful at reconciling competing demands. We have found that the legitimacy of the policy has tended to decline. Pressure groups such as MIND and the National Schizophrenia Fellowship are now less supportive of it, and more combative in their approach. The various professional groups involved in service provision display little agreement over how the policy should be implemented, or over their roles in relation to each other. The lack of facilities within the community and accumulating evidence of neglect of discharged patients further erodes support for community care. Yet, the cost of the policy has tended to rise rapidly. The 'Better Services' White Paper, as we noted earlier, emphasised the economic constraints on social policy developments and argued that it would take 20 to 30 years to develop a comprehensive mental health service. In fact, by 1985, the total costs implied by this document had been exceeded by over 10% (Audit Commission, 1986, p.31). Finally, the criterion of control also has tended to be less effectively addressed. The intended roles of hospital and community services, embodying a simple and clear split between health and welfare services, has proven more complex and more difficult to achieve than initially envisaged. The perceived effectiveness of psychiatric treatments has declined, and the numbers of people using mental health services has increased. The scale of the problem that the Department of Health argues requires dealing with has continued to rise, and indeed has done so at an accelerated rate.

Caring for people

It is in this context that the state, in the late 1980s and early 1990s, has once again attempted further internal rationalisation of community care. This process started with the commissioning of a report by Sir Roy Griffiths in 1988, and was followed by the White Paper, 'Caring for People: Community Care in the Next Decade and Beyond' (DoH, 1989), and the National Health Service and Community Care Act in 1990. The Act is to be implemented by April 1993, although many local authorities are not sufficiently well organised to ensure full implementation until some time after this.

The White Paper demonstrates that support for the policy remains undiminished: 'The Government reaffirms its support of the policy as a civilized and humanitarian one.' (DoH, 1989, Para 7.4,). However, it has been forced to accept that substantial problems remain; that the legitimacy of the policy continues to decline. It acknowledges that 'While some areas have made great strides in the development of community services, others are less well advanced' (para. 1.6) and notes '...the justified concern about the availability of community care services for mentally ill people.' (para. 7.2). It accepts that the ambit of community care services needs to be expanded, for example to include extra emphasis on supporting the carers of disabled people and on the development of services with particular reference to the needs of ethnic minorities. Moreover the requirements of an adequate community care policy are acknowledged to be wide, including for example the need for transport, good quality housing, leisure facilities and employment and educational opportunities (para. 2.4). It acknowledges 'legitimate concerns' (para. 7.5) about the failure to develop adequate community facilities prior to the rundown of mental hospitals, and accepts that a package of care must be organised and made available to each patient prior to discharge.

Nevertheless, the White Paper remains optimistic about the future development of community care. It is argued that a series of new measures will help substantially improve services. Local authorities are to be made responsible for organising the care requirements of mentally distressed people. They will receive funds previously allocated through the social security budget for residential care services, and it is intended that this money should be used to place greater emphasis upon the development of domiciliary care than has been the case in recent years. A large part of this money must be spent on services provided by private and voluntary organisations. Also a new 'Specific Grant', to be issued by health authorities after a process of negotiation about what new services should be developed, will be made available to local authorities for the development of community care for mentally distressed people.

Whether or not these attempts at reform of community care will be successful depends in large measure upon how adequately they address long standing tensions within the policy. In our discussion of these, three key issues have arisen; the coordination of service provision, the balance of expenditure between treatment and caring services, and the type of service provision. Consideration of each of these will allow us to assess whether these policy developments are likely to overcome existing problems.

207

The coordination of service provision

Ostensibly, improvement in the coordination of services does in fact appear to be central to the current plans for the development of community care policy. Multi-disciplinary assessment of need, together with the appointment of care-managers holding responsibility for organising the delivery of a 'seamless web' of services to individuals, is intended to overcome problems of coordination between health and welfare services. In total, it is intended that 'Acute hospital care, long-stay care and community care should be complementary and should be planned to provide a co-ordinated range of services' (DoH, 1989, para 4.6). These proposals appear to offer a substantial modification, and perhaps improvement in community care policy. They suggest that the Government is prepared to acknowledge that far greater efforts to coordinate health and welfare services are required.

This apparent committment, however, is contradicted by other aspects of the White Paper. We can illustrate this point by considering the principles of assessment of need as laid down in 'Caring for People'. In the assessment process, the wishes and the choices of service 'consumers' are to be given considerable emphasis (DoH, 1989, para. 3.2.6); '...users and carers will be enabled to exercise the same power as consumers of other services' (Social Services Inspectorate, 1991, p.7). This suggests, for example, that people with mental health problems might choose to be cared for in a variety of settings, including residential, and perhaps hospital settings. This implies the need for the coordination of these various services, in order to enable the service user to choose and then receive the type of care they wish for. This, the Government appears to accept. At the same time however it maintains that:

> The aim should be first to review the possibility of enabling the individual to continue to live at home, even if this means arranging a move to different accommodation within the local community, and if that possibility does not exist, to consider whether residential or nursing home care would be appropriate (DoH, 1989, para. 3.2.3).

The apparent emphasis upon the wishes and choices of service users, together with emphasis upon the enabling functions of service providers, seems to break down here. This is because the policy aim, in terms of expected outcomes, is in effect predetermined; a 'Key Objective' is '...to promote the development of...services to enable people to live in their own homes wherever feasible and sensible'. (DoH, 1989, para. 1.11).

There is a paradox here. On the one hand there is a committment to principles of choice, and meeting need. This, it is accepted, will require the development of a more coordinated set of services. On the other is an assumption, indeed virtually a dictate about where services will be provided; in the user's own home if at all possible. In effect, 'Caring for People' concerns establishing firstly the choices and needs of the state, and only secondarily what users might choose or need.

To develop explanatory understanding of this we need to set it in the context of problems, and criticisms that have arisen because of the lack of coordination of services (reviewed above). The Government has had to accept that a solution to these problems is necessary, in order to maintain the integrity of its own policy aims. The delineation of coordination of services offered in 'Caring for People' is intended to achieve this. Firstly, its hope is that increased emphasis upon the provision of a more coordinated set of services based on keeping service users in their own homes will reduce the need for readmission. This should prove cost-effective (the assumption of the Government here, based on work of the Audit Commission, 1986, is that the unit costs of domiciliary care are less than those associated with residential or hospital care).

Secondly, the emphasis upon coordination is intended to address criticism of community care, but in so doing it also re-defines the problem. We noted earlier that the main criticism made concerning the coordination of services has been the lack of attention given to allowing for the smooth transition of user's from one service to another. But coordination, as far as the Government is concerned, now concerns a process of arranging the variety of services that an individual might need in order to help maintain them in their own home. Rather than allowing the service user choice over where to receive care, they are to be allowed choice (within the limits of available resources) over what services they receive in their own homes.

The balance of service provision

Because of these problems, the Government has once again been put in a position where further fine-tuning of community care policy is required (DoH, 1989). Acknowledging the scale of criticism of the skewed balance of mental health expenditure, the Government has introduced a new 'Specific Grant' for the development of care in the community for people with mental health problems (DoH, 1990). The grant was justified in 'Caring For People' thus:

> In the face of other calls on resources, Local Authorities generally have not been able to give as much priority to providing services to those with a mental illness as other vulnerable groups. It is not possible to give an exact figure but the Department of Health judges that possibly only about 3% of Social Services Authorities expenditure is currently spent on services specifically for those with a mental illness...To increase the social care available for people with a mental illness the Government proposes to make a specific grant to social services authorities from 1991/92 (DoH, 1989, paras. 7.14-7.15).

In the first year, the grant was worth £21 million, with local authorities expected to make an additional 30% contribution, resulting in total new expenditure of £30 million. However, some restrictions on its use exist. It is to be controlled by health authorities and only allocated to local authorities after agreement is reached on what projects to develop, and it is to be available only for 'seriously mentally ill people' (DoH, 1989, para. 1.12). Moreover, the grant will only be available for a three year period, with the expectation that local authorities will then take over projects established through the Specific Grant. Overall, the intention is to focus resources upon those people who are most likely otherwise to be admitted to mental hospital. The primary concern is with avoiding the efficiency of treatment services being reduced by people with chronic mental health problems, although the amounts of money involved suggest that the overall impact of the grant will be minimal.

The importance of contributions to community care by the private, voluntary and informal sectors is further stressed. In particular, concern has developed over the use of social security payments to maintain people in residential accommodation. This budget, in April 1993, is to be transferred to local authorities who will be responsible for need assessment and subsequent allocation of resources. Their leeway in making decisions however will be highly restricted. Firstly, as discussed earlier, the aim is to focus the use of this money upon maintaining people in their own homes. Secondly, the role of local authorities is to be one of an 'enabler', rather than 'provider' of services: 'The Government will expect local authorities to make use wherever possible of services from voluntary, 'not for profit' and private providers insofar as this represents a cost effective care choice' (DoH, 1989, para. 3.4.1).

In all of this the Government is seeking to utilise as far as possible sources of care that are cheaper than those it might fund through directly provided local authority services. Its solution to the problem of the balance of mental health service expenditures, is to attempt to increase the value of care gained within existing budgets (other than the Specific Grant). This is to be achieved by incorporating private, voluntary and informal care within a framework operated by local authorities.

Whether these changes in community care will succeed in reducing criticism of the skewed balance of expenditure is not yet clear. But what information we do have is not encouraging. The pool of available resources within the informal sector is severely limited, while at the same time the scale of need for community care is increasing (Finch, 1989). Health services are under increasing pressure to displace the costs of care onto the community as demands upon them rise. It particular, it is estimated that elderly people account for just over 41% of health expenditure, but that by 2015 this may increase to as high as 58% (International Labour Organisation, 1989).

It is in this context that the Government intends to make some changes to community care, but at the same time largely maintain the existing balance of Government mental health expenditures. In so doing, it hopes to overcome criticism of the skewed allocation of resources. The problems associated with this strategy make it highly unlikely that it will succeed (Goodwin et al, 1991).

The type of service provision

The type of services offered are based, as we have argued, upon an assumption that mental distress is best considered a medical problem open to solution by conventional psychiatric practice. This is despite the fact that 'By the turn of the twenty-first century, Western psychiatry will have endured forty years of sustained criticism' (Pilgrim, 1993). Whereas in relation to the issues of coordination and balance of services some efforts have been made to address problems that have arisen, the Government has proven remarkably intransigent regarding its defence of the type of service to be offered, and the place of community care within that. In 'Caring for People' there is no recognition whatsoever of the lack of success, or any other criticisms of physical treatments:

...research and clinical experience showed that treatment was

211

equally or more effective when less reliance was placed on long term in-patient care...Additionally, more effective drug treatments, such as the major tranquilizers which were introduced in the 1950s, transformed the prognosis of the most serious mental illnesses (DoH, 1989, para. 7.4).

The type of service offered is one concerned with the problem of mental illness; its diagnosis and its cure. Over the last thirty years it has become increasingly apparent that it is the problems these people experience, in terms of housing, employment, loneliness, and so on, that are of equal if not greater importance. But to acknowledge this conflicts with the Government's own aims. It would raise a mine-field of issues concerning the costs and the organisation of service provision that would defeat its own rationale for the community care policy.

Conclusion

The analysis developed here suggests that the community care policy is proving of less value as a means of providing reconciliation of the compatibility problem. Yet, while tending towards crisis, that point has not yet been reached. While costs have risen, expenditure remains focussed upon providing a medically orientated treatment service. While the legitimacy of the policy has fallen, it still retains considerable support in principle at least from a wide range of academics and practitioners. The community care policy still retains some utility.

It is this situation that has prompted the most recent interventions by the Government, and which it hopes will restore community care to a position where it will address adequately the competing pressures and demands that have arisen. The analysis offered here of the proposals within 'Caring for People' suggests however that no such turn around in the fortunes of community care policy is likely. Rather, it is liable to do little more than hold back for some limited period of time the tendency of the policy to fail.

8 Which way forward?

Community care for people with mental health problems can be characterised by reference to two ideas. Firstly, it has failed to live up to expectations. Secondly, problems with the policy are now being recognised, and an improvement in service provision might be expected. The reorganisation of policy, associated with the NHS and Community Care Act 1990, was prompted in part by the first of these, and its rationale relies upon the second. This characterization has come to form the generally accepted view of community care policy; disappointment with the present and past cohabits with optimism for the future.

These two views inevitably tend towards incompatibility as time progresses. As optimism for the future is assimilated into disappointed with the past questions arise: why has the community care policy tended to fail? is there anything new that should support further optimism? should we seek alternative policies? To consider these questions we briefly review current views on these questions. This is followed by a discussion of the necessary components of any move forward, that attempts to allow fully for the constraints, and opportunities present in community care policy as it now stands.

The key concern of feminists in relation to community care has been with gender inequalities. Finch and Groves (1980) were amongst the first to identify the unequal burden placed upon men and women in relation to the caring task. They argued that women's opportunities in employment and other areas were severely limited by assumptions made about their caring role. Since then, a number of feminist writers have sought to analyse and publicise gender inequalities in relation to caring (Ungerson, 1985;

213

Land and Rose 1985; Dalley 1988; Baldwin and Twigg, 1991). For example, its noted that while many men are involved in caring, particularly where it involves the care of a spouse, it is nevertheless still the case that the majority of carers are women. This is particularly so in relation to the direct tending tasks, as opposed to providing other support such as visiting, shopping and so on. In total, the scale of caring and the inequitable distribution of that task has been highlighted by feminist writers.

There is a consensus of opinion amongst feminist writers about the definition of the problem. Understanding the nature of that problem however results in more debate. Key to this discussion is whether community care is inherently gender discriminatory, or whether that is simply its present condition and therefore open to reform. Writing in the early 1980s, Wilson (1982) argued that community care is an inherently gendered concept and therefore by definition exploitative. Finch (1984) maintained a similar position. She argued that social and cultural assumptions about the family, and within the social security system and other welfare institutions, result in few possibilities for developing equal opportunities for women while maintaining the current emphasis upon community care policy. Somewhat contentiously, she has argued that equal opportunities for women necessitates a reversal of policy direction; that community care should in part be replaced by a return to institutional care.

Over the last few years, feminists have been slightly more optimistic about the possibility of reforming community care. Dalley (1988), in a review of the dominant ideologies within which community care occurs, maintains that an ideology of familism is the dominant ideology that structures the experience, perception and lives and women, and an ideology of possessive individualism structures the lives of men. The result is that community care policy tends to result in far greater pressures being placed on women to provide care. However in other societies and at other times this has not always been the case, providing ground for optimism that this gender bifurcation in dominant ideologies is open to alteration. She maintains that there has been an increasing emphasis upon participation and democratisation, providing grounds for optimism about the possibility of developing non-sexist forms of collectivism: '...feminists hold that their belief in the widest possible application of collectivist principles is feasible' (Dalley, 1988, p. 139).

Baldwin and Twigg (1991) also argue that there are some grounds for optimism. They maintain that recent Government policy statements focus more on shared family responsibility than they have done in the past. Equally, the new emphasis upon the rights of the dependant person to exercise choice in use of services, as evident in the Wagner Report and also in the NHS and Community Care Act is regarded as a positive development. In more general terms, they maintain that public awareness of the pressures upon and the needs of carers has grown. Finally, as the economic demand for female labour increases the Government and employers will need to pay greater attention to developing patterns of work and support structures that will enable carers to participate in employment. Although as Lister notes, the Government may prove slow to respond with any concrete proposals: 'I don't think the state should step in to help the working mother unless her life has collapsed' (John Patten, quoted in Lister, 1990, p. 464).

Despite the problems identified with community care policy feminist writers in general continue to offer it support in principle, but argue that a number of reforms should be implemented. At the most general level, Dalley maintains that individual attitudes, and societal norms, need changing; '...it is a question of society's making moral choices about what proportion of its collective resources it wishes to make available for those members of society who are dependent and in need of support' (1988, p.145). The dominant ideologies of familism and possessive individualism need to be challenged, and greater emphasis placed upon the sharing of domestic labour and the collectivization of caring practices. Lister (1991) develops this argument by reference to the concept of citizenship. She argues that women lack full social and political citizenship, and that this can only be overcome through radical changes in the organisation of domestic and personal life, of paid employment, and of state provision. While both acknowledge the scale and difficulty of such a project, both maintain that it is feasible; 'It will require the opportunistic seizing of initiative as and when occasions arise for radically new collectivist - and most importantly - feminist policies to become accepted' (Dalley, 1988 p.150).

Baldwin and Twigg (1991) are less optimistic about the possibil-ities for generating ideological change, but do maintain that change is possible. They argue that feminists have paid insufficient attention to people being cared for, including for example the different needs and wishes of a disabled teenager, and an elderly person. Equally, the relationship between the carer and person being cared for requires further investigation and greater emphasis, concerning for example how different forms of care might be developed that best suit their needs. 'The debate', they argue, 'now centres on the boundaries between individual, 'family' and collective responsibility for meeting needs arising from disability or old age' (1991, p.130). These proposals would rely upon acceptance of collective responsibility, and upon the rights of individuals to choice and self-determination. This would include and emphasis upon minimising dependency via the development of better opportunities in housing, health, employment, and social security, together with the creation of frameworks to enable women to exercise real choice through for example the support for people opting to care. They maintain that such an approach has some chance of success: 'It seems to us quite possible to envisage a tactical approach that would improve the current situation of carers without jeopardizing the longer-term strategic aim of eradicating sexual divisions in caring' (1991, p.131).

Most other accounts of community care policy hold similar sentiments to the feminist analysis; that considerable problems exist but that reform is possible. Tomlinson (1991) argues that insufficient emphasis has been placed upon incorporating the views and aspirations of service users. While he maintains that the policy has resulted in the improvement of service provision for some users, it is necessary to incorporate greater civic participation in the future development of community care.

Bean and Mounser (1993) also maintain that the quality of service provision has not always been adequate. They argue that more information is required on the users experience of care in the community. Improved coordination of service provision and greater regulation of the public and private agencies involved in the provision of care is also considered necessary.

In line with all these accounts Barham (1992) acknowledges that community care is beset by a number of problems, but that this should not lead us to support a return to institutional care (p.143). While images of homelessness and vagrancy sometimes dominate the picture presented of the results of community care, he argues that some examples of good practice do exist and that these should be built upon. What is required, he argues, is a need for greater emphasis on more local, accessible, comprehensive, flexible, culturally and ethnically appropriate, accountable, equitably distributed, based on need services that ensure continuity of treatment and care (p.144). He maintains that there are some encouraging signs, including for example the increasing emphasis upon consumer choice and consumers views being incorporated within service planning.

Equally importantly, Barham argues that greater imagination in the

216

development of community care is required. He notes that the old asylum model allowed for two paths down which people might go; either cure or chronicity. Community care has tended to replicate this, resulting in a lack of attention to the provision of services that might improve the quality of a person's life irrespective of whether there mental condition is improving or worsening. This might for example include the development of employment opportunities, better housing and better transport facilities. It also includes the need for changes in attitude towards people experiencing mental distress:

> we shall want as far as possible to opt for person- and citizen-centred concepts and approaches, rather than patient- and disorder-centred ones...The real dispute is...between those who want to improve the social prospects of people with long-term mental illness, to reclaim them not for mental patienthood but for citizenship, and those who settle for a highly restricted vision of the 'place' of people with mental illness in social life (Barham, 1992, pp.149-151).

This concern with the attitudes of the public to people experiencing mental distress is developed by Rogers and Pilgrim (1989). They argue that greater emphasis is required upon developing their citizenship rights. This should include the full range of civil, political and social rights enjoyed by the rest of the population. With the emphasis placed by Government policy in the early 1990s upon the role of service users as consumers, they maintain that some movement forward on this is possible. Patient groups such as 'Survivors Speak Out' could have role in developing better practice by making demands for greater rights. Overall, Rogers and Pilgrim maintain that empowerment of service users is required. This requires a change in attitudes towards people experiencing mental distress, whereby there ability to participate in the mainstream of society is catered for. As such, they maintain that a return to institutional care would be a retrograde step. Community care should continue to be supported on the basis that desegregation, in the long run at least, is possible.

The voluntary sector remains divided over the question of whether community care should continue to be supported. MIND continues to argue that community care, if adequately developed, can best meet the needs and demands of people experiencing mental distress. It therefore supports the continued rundown of institutional provision, and argues for the development of more comprehensive services within the community. In contrast, the National Schizo-phrenia Fellowship maintains that community care has failed to adequately meet the needs of service users. It supports a suspen-sion of deinstitutionalization until greater resources and a more adequate organisation of services within the community can be created. These two groups also differ radically in their attitude to the citizenship rights of mentally distressed people. MIND supports the movement towards citizenship rights, while the National Schizophrenia Fellowship tends to support traditional psychiatric practice as the means to resolving the problem of mental distress.

These views, derived from variety of political positions, demon-strate the continued success of community care policy to organise a consensus over the future of mental health services. Only amongst some of the more conservative forces, as witnessed by the views of the National Schizophrenia Association, has a clear rejection of the policy taken place. Amongst all other groups, support for the principle of desegregation together will calls for increased resources and improved organisation of services remain largely common ground.

Within the context of the analysis offered in earlier Chapters, the key issue here is one of how adequately the nature and develop-ment of community care policy is incorporated within the views offered. It is this which, to a large extent, determines the possibility for success of the strategies offered. This is fully recognised by Barham:

> The real question, I believe, is about the grounding of hope... grounded that is in an accurate recognition of the type of outcome that is at all likely within the antagonistic processes of a modern society (Barham, p.154)

But while he and perhaps others recognise the importance of this, it fails to reflect in the policy proposals made. Indeed the opposite is the case. Classic social democratic assumptions concerning the essentially neutral role of the state and the idea that evolutionary progress towards a better future is possible and indeed likely, seem to pervade most current analyses almost irrespective of their claimed political position.

What we have attempted to demonstrate in this study is that to understand the community care policy simply in terms of an attempt to reform mental health service provision fails to grasp adequately the complexity of the policy making process. Instead, our argument has been that the community care policy for mentally distressed people was devised by the Ministry of Health in the 1950s in response to the failure of the institutional system to adequately reconcile competing threats, needs and demands. As we argued in Chapter 4, the community care policy is best understood as a crisis management strategy. Yet as we have demonstrated the policy has, particularly in recent years, tended towards failure, in terms of fulfilling the state's objectives. The crisis management strategy is itself tending towards crisis (Offe, 1984).

Nevertheless, the community care policy remains in favour. Although difficulties have arisen, it still represents the least worst solution to the problems the state faces. But while this may be an adequate position for the state to defend, in terms of its own interests, this does not necessarily imply we, as academics, practitioners or users of mental health services, should collude with it. It is, then, at this point that we can return to our original questions; is the policy feasible, and is it desirable?

A major part of the state's rationale for supporting community care, as we have argued in earlier Chapters, is the separation of treatment and care - where the state concentrates on the provision of treatment and leaves, as far as possible, the provision of care to the community. This implies continuing support for medically orientated treatment services, providing increasingly specialised services that are accessible to a growing number of people. It also implies continued pressure to transfer the responsibility of care onto the community. These are central features of the community care policy, intended as far as possible to provide reconciliation of the compatibility problem.

It is only in these limited terms that the policy is likely to be feasible. If for example demands for massively extended caring facilities in the community were successfully pursued, the community care policy would finally fail to reconcile the compatibility problem and it is likely that new policy initiatives would be sought. In short, the very existence of the policy depends upon the objectives of the state being met.

Given this, we might then ask is the community care policy desirable? The analysis presented here suggests no simple answer. The argument developed suggests that the policy represents a tortuous synthesis of conflicting aims and interests; some that might be supported, and some criticized. Perhaps therefore some guarded support might be given to particular aspects of the policy, mostly concerning some of the limited developments made in providing supportive facilities within the community. But if we accept that mental distress is not, as we argued in Chapter 3, best dealt with by medical intervention, then support for the policy is problematic. For as we have argued, part of the rationale for the state's support of community care is that it allows it to concentrate upon expanding the availability of medically based treatment services.

These conclusions, however, do not preclude the development of political strategies. Rather it provides a framework within which to identify potential areas of weakness within the Government's position that might be exploited, and equally allows for some judgement to be made about the possible consequences of particular campaigns. Through the analysis made, we have noted that the state has been concerned with managing the tensions arising upon the axes of efficiency and effectiveness, efficiency and acceptability, and effectiveness and acceptability. On each of these we have argued that the state has enjoyed sufficient success for it to maintain the policy; even if the task is becoming progressively more difficult.

However, while the state has to date had sufficient success in managing these pressures, it has only achieved this through a process of continuous 'fine tuning'. This process, intended to address changing circumstances, has however given rise to a number of competing requirements within the policy itself. The internal rationalisation of one facet of the compatibility problem has tended to make the resolution of the other two more difficult. Some examples of this might illustrate the increasing fragility of community care policy.

Tension between attempts at the reconciliation of efficiency and acceptability, and effectiveness and acceptability

We have argued that reconciliation of the efficiency and acceptability axis of the compatibility problem has involved the state in attempts to transfer, as far as possible, the costs of caring to the community. This has involved an increased emphasis upon the privatization of what has, to a limited extent, been the public provision of care. However, at the same time reconciliation of the effectiveness and acceptability axis has involved the defence of curative services as the primary means of treatment of mental illness. This has involved the state in seeking to further politicise areas of life previously regarded as private (this concerns the massive expansion of the category of mental illness over the last 30 years - see Chapters 3 and 6).

In attempting to address these two dimensions of the compatibility problem, the state faces a major inconsistency within its own policy. Reconciliation of one axis of the compatibility problem requires the withdrawal of services providing care, the other requires an expansion of services providing treatment. When the community care policy was first developed this tension was latent. But with the reduction in hospital beds, the increasing emphasis upon the provision of treatment within the community, the increasing numbers of people deemed to be in need of psychiatric services, and the increasing levels of criticism of both standards of care in the community and of the efficacy of available treatments, the tension between these two policy goals has increased.

It results, for example, in the fissuring of professional workers roles. We are seeing Community Psychiatric Nurses being torn between a medical role of administering drug treatments to people living in the community, and attempting to address some of the more basic needs of mentally distressed people such as housing, companionship and so on. Similarly, General Practitioners are faced with the dilemma of offering repeat prescriptions for drug treatments to people whose mental state is clearly related to social circumstance rather than medical condition. Perhaps the most naked exhibition of this tension lies in the proposal for introducing Compulsory Treatment Orders (see Chapter 7). This idea, which may yet be introduced, makes clear the primary aim of containing the symptoms of mental distress rather than addressing the problems that may create those symptoms. While the Royal College of Psychiatry continues to support the proposal, most of the other mental health professions find it unacceptable.

This debate reflects the increasingly difficulties the state faces in pursuing the implementation of its mental health policy; community care is failing to adequately reconcile competing views and interests. Compulsory Treatment Orders, if introduced, would represent an incremental step in policy development, based on the increasing emphasis given to the provision of treatment in the community. But, as the efficacy of psychiatric treatment increasingly comes into question, and the importance of social support is increasingly recognised, it may yet prove that the legitimacy of the policy has declined to the point where it can not be implemented.

Tension between attempts at the reconciliation of efficiency and effectiveness, and effectiveness and acceptability

This concerns firstly the aim of state policy to concentrate resources on the provision of treatment and to make this available to increasing numbers of people; a process of increased specialization and accessibility of psychiatric services. And secondly it concerns the presentation of this process as an appropriate method of dealing with mental distress. In the early 1960s these policy objectives were, or at least appeared, viable. Confidence about the improving effectiveness of psychiatric treatments led the Ministry of Health to assume that increasing emphasis could and would be given to short-stay patients receiving intensive treatment, and who would be quickly discharged to fully recover within the community. Initially, this proposition was widely accepted (see Chapter 4). Psychiatric treatment was acknowledged to be an appropriate and increasingly effective means of intervention.

This situation allowed for the administrative separation of health and welfare services for mentally distressed people. This split was the major achievement of the Mental Health Act, 1959. For the state this helped achieve an efficient service, by concentrating resources upon addressing the medical problem of mental illness rather than the social problems of the mentally ill. It was assumed that it would be effective, based upon advances in psychiatric technique. And it was held to be acceptable, based upon the proposition that cure was now possible and that mentally distressed people are best helped to recover within the community.

These policy aims have however proven less realistic than initially imagined. This reflects in the failure to 'cure' people, as witnessed by the increasing number of readmissions to mental hospitals and the failure to reduce the long-stay population as quickly as intended. Equally the medicalization of mental health problems has, to some extent, been rejected as therapeutic intervention with new treatments failed to have the curative effects once hoped for. It has been increasing argued that the quality of the social environment is an important factor influencing mental health (see Chapter 6).

These changes in the policy making environment create a dilemma. To address the efficiency and effectiveness axis of the compatibility problem, the state has sought to separate the provision of treatment and care. To address the efficiency and acceptability axis it has been forced to accept that greater coordination of service provision is necessary, whereby the social needs of mental patients discharged from hospital are acknowledged and provided for.

Developments made since the mid-1970s in coordinating health and welfare provision reflect this increasingly complicated set of problems facing the Government (see Chapter 7). The main efforts to address these concerns have been the creation in 1975 of Joint

Planning between health and social services, and the development of Case Management in the early 1990s. Through these initiatives, the state's concern has been to address criticism of the failures of policy while at the same time maintaining its own policy goals.

These efforts however, as we argued in Chapter 7, are limited in scope. With severe resource constraints upon social service departments, considerable difficulty is being experienced in adapting to the new role established for it. Equally, with continuing pressure within the NHS to run down mental hospital beds and to focus expenditure upon the treatment rather than care of mentally distressed people, the ability of case managers to develop a coordinated set of services will become increasingly constrained. The likely, and emerging result, is that the comprehensive needs of only the most severely affected users of services are likely to be addressed.

A further issue where this tension in policy aims has become increasingly apparent is the balance of expenditure between treatment and care services. Despite the strong support offered community care policy by Government, it has proven reluctant to fund it. As we noted in Chapter 4, the Mental Health Act, 1959, made no financial provision at all for the development of services in the community. The assumption made was that local authorities, and the community, would make adequate provision. Thus, notwithstanding the emphasis placed upon the development of caring facilities in the community by the Government, its own pattern of expenditure has failed to reflect this, with hospital treatment services continuing to receive by far the largest proportion of funds (see Chapter 7).

The extent of this skewing of resource allocation has resulted in much criticism of the lack of facilities to support people with mental health problems in the community. This situation has resulted in some further attempts by Government to increase the availability of social care. The encouragement of the voluntary, private and informal sectors, together with small amounts of money such as the 'Specific Grant' (see Chapter 7) have been intended to redress the balance of service provision. The overall impact of these efforts however have been minimal, and criticism of the lack of state funded supportive services within the community continues to grow.

Conclusion

We started this Chapter by contrasting the generally pessimistic views of the history of community care, with the generally optimistic views expressed for its future. The state remains the greatest advocate of this position:

> We believe that the proposals in the White Paper provide a coherent framework to meet present and future challenges. They will give people a much better opportunity to secure the services they need (DOH, 1989, Foreword).

The argument presented here does not support such a view. The current changes associated with 'Caring for People' either maintain, or alter only marginally, long-standing assumptions of Government thinking regarding policy towards people with mental health problems. In many ways the Report of the Percy Commission in 1957 provides greater insight upon present problems and more useful suggestions for the way forward than does the 1989 White Paper, 'Caring for People'.

The analysis developed here suggests two points relevant to the development of a more adequate mental health strategy. Firstly, that continued optimism is inappropriate. Community care policy objectives are designed to meet the needs of the state first, and those of mentally distressed people second. If nothing else, we have over 30 years of experience to demonstrate this. Secondly, the policy is approaching a crisis. This crisis is not based upon normative concerns such as the quality of service provision, but rather lies in the tendency to stultification it is now demonstrating. Irrespective of the efficacy of community care it is, more importantly, proving to be of declining value to the state.

In terms of the development of strategy the implications of this are varied. Firstly, and of greatest immediate importance, the points of tension within community care policy provide scope for the organisation of resistance to the state's own policy goals. In part this is already occurring. It concerns the demands of carers for better support and the demands of users for greater participation in service planning and delivery. It concerns the increasing ambiguities and tensions within professional roles, and it concerns the critique of psychiatric intervention and more generally of assumptions within the policy. Where this will lead however, is not as most hope towards a reform of policy; rather, it will lead to a situation where community care no longer addresses the state's own needs.

In the same manner in which a 'crisis of crisis management' beset the system of institutional care in the 1950s, community care appears to be moving - perhaps slowly - towards a similar condition.

Pressure for reform, together with other constraints upon the state's room for manoeuver, has resulted in a tendency to stultification and is likely to result in an eventual destruction of the policy. This suggests that the dominant assumptions that guide the present debate are to some extent inadequate. Rather than seeking a reform of policy that is not open to substantial change, we should look towards the construction of alternative models that might be realistically sought within the current turmoil. In part, this is already in place. It concerns the development of theoretical work such as that by Dalley (1988) on the notion of collectivisation, and of Gough and Doyal (1991) on the concept of need. It concerns the development of theoretical models of the nature and development of policy, as hopefully this study has contributed towards. It concerns the development of a coherent account of mental distress that perhaps incorporates some aspects of the medical model, but more importantly allows for the diverse nature of the condition and grounds this within the social, political and economic relationships pertaining (Ingleby, 1982; Elliot, 1993). It concerns greater importance being attached to the voice and accounts of mentally distressed people when developing services (Campbell, 1990). It concerns the incorporation of citizenship rights, and the whole arena of human need such as for employment, housing ,income and choice into mental health policy (Pilgrim, 1991).

But what is not in place is a vision of how these varied parts should coalesce. This reflects in the debate, noted earlier amongst feminists and voluntary groups, over the relative merits of community and institutional care. An assumption implicit in this debate is that the only policy options available are those already in existence. Thus, more imaginative thinking is required. A move forward should allow for the criticism of community care policy, without implication that this necessarily implies a negative view of the value of care in non-institutional settings. It is the medicalization of social problems, together with the expansion of treatment and contraction of caring services, that constitute central themes of community care policy and which should be criticised. At the same time a vision of a policy that allows for the various concerns listed above needs to be propagated.

Finally, any such vision must of course itself be grounded within the existing social formation. To understate the case, this implies difficulties. The relative strength of the advanced capitalist countries is far greater than the Left imagined would be the case in the late 1970s. At the same time, some tendencies towards fiscal, legitimation and perhaps other crises is certainly evident, both in general terms and specifically in relation to mental health policy. Possibilities for change may therefore arise, concerning the development of a more progressive set of services within and beyond the faltering framework of existing provision. What will be required however within this process is full recognition of the aims and objectives, and the considerable power, of the state. The space that might be generated for progress is therefore very uncertain, but are there any alternatives?

References

Abel-Smith,B. and Titmuss,R. (1956), *The Cost of the National Health Service in England and Wales*, Cambridge, Cambridge University Press.

Abrahamson,D. et al. (1982), *'Do long-stay patients want to leave hospital?'*, Health Trends, vol.14, no.14.

Abrams,P. (1977), *'Community Care: Some Research Problems and Priorities'*, Policy and Politics, no.6.

Airey,C.(1984), *'Social and Moral Values'*,in Jowell,R. and Airey,C (eds), British Social Attitudes: the 1984 Report, Aldershot, Gower.

Almond, A and Verba, S. (1963), *The Civic Culture: Political Attitudes and Democracy in Five Nations*, Princeton USA, Princeton University Press.

American Behavioral Scientist (1981), *'Special issue on new forms of social control: The Myth of Deinstitutionalisation'*, vol 24, no. 6.

Anderson,D.and Anderson,I. (1982), *'The development of the voluntary movement in mental health'*, The Mental Health Year Book 1981/82, London, MIND Publications.

Anton-Stephens,D. (1954), *'Preliminary Observations On The Psychiatric Uses Of Chlorpromazine (Largactil)'*, Journal of Mental Science, vol. 100.

Arnhoff,F. (1975), *'Social Consequences of Policy Toward Mental Illness'*, Science, no. 188.

Audit Commission. (1986), *Making a Reality out of Community Care*, London, HMSO.

Baker,J. (1979), *'Social Conscience and Social Policy'*, Journal of Social Policy, vol.8, no 2.

Baldwin, S. and Twigg, (1991), *Women and Community Care - Reflections on a debate*, in M. Maclean and D. Groves (eds.) Women's Issues in Social Policy, London, Routledge.

Bamford,T. (1984), *'The mirage of Community Care'*, Community Care, 15th Nov.

Banting,K. (1979), *Poverty, Politics and Policy: Britain in the 1960s*, London, Macmillan Press.

Banton,R. et. al. (1985), *The Politics of Mental Health*, Oxford, Macmillan.

Barham, P. (1992) *Closing the Asylum*, London, Penguin.

Barrett,M.(1980), *Women's Oppression Today*, London, Verso.

Barton,R.(1959), *Institutional Neurosis*, Bristol, Wright.

Baruch,G. and Treacher,A.(1980), *Towards a Critical History of the Psychiatric Profession*, in Ingleby, D. (ed.), Critical Psychiatry, New York, Pantheon Books.

Baruch,G. and Treacher,A.(1978), *Psychiatry Observed*, London, RKP.

Basaglia,F.(1980), *'Breaking the Circuit of Control'*, in Ingleby,D. (ed.), Critical Psychiatry, New York,Pantheon Books.

B.A.S.W. (1985), *Memorandum submitted to the House of Commons Social Services Committee.*

Bean, P. (ed.)(1983), *Mental Illness: Changes and Trends*, London, J. Wiley.

Bean, P. & Mounser, P (1993) *Discharged from Mental Hospitals*, Basingstoke, Macmillan.

Beck, B. (1979), *'The Limits of Deinstitutionalisation'*, in Lewis, M. (ed.),Research in Social Problems and Public Policy, Greenwhich USA, JAI Press.

Bedarida, F.(1979), *A Social History of England 1851-1975*, London, Methuen.

Bennett,D.(1978),*'Community Psychiatry'*, British Journal of Psychiatry, vol. 132.

Bennett,D. and Morris,I. (1983), *'Deinstitutionalization in the UK'*, International Journal of Mental Health, no. ii.

Berry,D. (1985), *'The Clients Who Demand Reasonable Treatment'*, Guardian, 18/9/85.

Beveridge,W.(1942), *Social Insurance and Allied Services*, Cmnd 6404, London, HMSO.

Bewley,T.H. (1981), *'New Chronic Patients'*, British Medical Journal, no. 283.

Birch (1984), *'Overload, ungovernability and deligitimation: the theories and the British case.'* British Journal of Political Science, Vol. 14, No. 2.

Blacker,C.P.(1946), *Neurosis and the Mental Health Service*, London,Oxford University Press.

Board of Control, *Annual Reports*, London, HMSO.

Bott, E. (1976), *'Hospital and Society'*, British Journal of Medical Psychology, vol. 49.

Bowen,A. (1979), *'Some Mental Health Premises'*, Milbank Memorial Fund Quarterly, vol. 57, no. 4.

Braff,J. and Lefkowitz,M.M.(1979), *'Community Mental Health: What Works For Whom'*,Psychiatric Quarterly, vol. 51, no. 2.

Brenner, M.H. (1973), *Mental Illness and the Economy*, Cambridge USA, Harvard University Press.

Brenton,M.(1985), *The Voluntary Sector In British Social Services*, London, Longman.

Briggs,A. and Oliver,J. (1985), *Caring: Experiences of looking after disabled relatives*, London, RKP.

Brill,E. (1980), *'Notes on the history of social psychiatry'*, Comprehensive Psychiatry, vol. 21.

British Medical Journal (1976), editorial, *'Asylums are still needed'*, no. 1.

Brooke,E.M. (1963), *A Cohort Study of Patients first admitted to Mental Hospitals in 1954 and 1955*, London, HMSO.

Brown,C.V. and Jackson,P.M.(1978), *Public Sector Economics*, Oxford, Martin Robertson.

Brown,G.W. and Harris,T. (1978), *Social Origins of Depression*, Tavistock Publications.

Brown,G.W. et.al. (1985), *Depression: Distress or Disease? Some Epidemiological Considerations*, British Journal of Psychiatry, vol. 147.

Brown, M (1985), *Introduction to Social Administration*, (6th edition), London, Hutchinson.

Brown,P. (1984), *Marxism, Social Psychology, and the Sociology of Mental Health*, International Journal of Health Studies, vol. 14, no. 2.

Brown,P. (1984), *'Psychiatric Reform And Transformation'*, International Journal of Health Services, vol. 14, no. 2.

Brown,P. (1985), *The Transfer of Care: Psychiatric Deinstitutionalisation and its Aftermath*, London, RKP.

Brown, R.G.S. (1977), *'Accountability and Control in the NHS'*, Health and Social Services Journal, 28th October.

Burchill, J. (1987), *New Society*, 24th July.

Burton, M. (1983), *'Understanding Mental Health Services:Theory and Practice'*, Critical Social Policy, Summer.

Busfield, J.(1986), *Managing Madness: changing ideas and practice*,

London, Hutchinson.

Butler, D. and Stokes, D. (1974), *Political Change in Britain*, London, Macmillan.

Byrne,P. and Lovenduski,J.(1983), 'Two New Protest Groups;The Peace and Women's Movements', in Drucker, H. (ed.), Developments in British Politics, London, Macmillan.

Campbell (1990) 'Mental health self-advocacy', in Winn, L. ed. Power to the People, London, Kings Fund College.

Carstairs,G.M. and Wing,J.K.(1958), *Attitudes of the General Public to Mental Illness*, British Medical Journal, no. ii.

Cartwright,A and Anderson,R.(1981), *General Practice Revisited*, Tavistock Publications.

Castell,F.Castel,R. and Lovell,A.(1982),*The Psychiatric Society*, Columbia University Press, New York.

Charatan,F. (1954), *An Evaluation of Chlorpromazine (Largactil), in Psychiatry*, Journal of Mental Science, vol. 100.

Chief Medical Officer, *Annual Reports*, London, HMSO.

Clare,A. (1980), *Psychiatry in Dissent* (Second edition), Tavistock Publications.

Clare,A. and Lader,M. (eds.)(1982), *Psychiatry and General Practice*, London, Academic Press.

Clarke,G. (1979), *In Defence of Deinstitutionalisation*, Milbank Memorial Fund Quarterly, vol. 57, no. 4.

Coates,D.(1984), *The Context of British Politics*, London, Hutchinson.

Cochrane,R. (1983), *The Social Creation of Mental Illness*, Harlow, Longman Group Ltd.

Cockburn,C.(1977), *The Local State-management of cities and people*, London, Pluto Press.

Cohen,G.A. (1984), *Karl Marx's Theory of History; a defence*, Oxford, Clarendon Press.

Cohen,S. (1984), *The Future of Social Control*, Oxford, Martin Robertson.

COHSE (1984), *The Future of Psychiatric Services*, Centurion Press, London.

Coleman,J. and Patrick,D. (1976), *Integrating mental health services into primary medical care*, Medical Care, vol. 14, no. 8.

Conrad,P. (1981), *On the Medicalization of Deviance and Social Control*, in Ingleby,D. (ed.),Critical Psychiatry, New York, Pantheon Books.

Conrad,P. and Schneider,J.(1980), *Deviance and Medicalization:from badness to sickness*, St. Louis, Mosby.

Cooper,D. (ed.)(1968), *The Dialectics of Liberation*, London, Penguin.

Corser,C.M. and Ryce,S.W.(1977), *'Community Mental Health Care: a model on the primary health care team'*, British Medical Journal, no. ii.

Coulter,J. (1973), *Approaches to Insanity*, London, Martin Robertson.

Craib,I. (1984), *Modern Social Theory: From Parsons to Habermas*, Brighton, Wheatsheaf Books Ltd.

Crossland,A.(1956), *The Future of Socialism*, London, Cape.

CSO (1984), *Social Trends No.14*, London, HMSO.

CSO, *Economic Trends*, HMSO, London.

CSO (1987), *Key Data 1987*, HMSO, London

CSO (1991), *Social Trends No. 21*, London, HMSO.

Culver,C. and Gert,B.(1982), *Philosophy in Medicine: Conceptual and Ethical Issues in Medicine and Psychiatry*, Oxford, Oxford University Press.

Culyer, A. J. (1980), *The Political Economy of the Welfare State*, Oxford, Martin Robertson.

Dahrendorf,R.(1980), *'Efficiency and Effectiveness'*, Political Quarterly, vol. 51, no. 4.

Dalley,G. (1983), *'Ideologies of care: a feminist contribution to the debate'*, Critical Social Policy, no. 8.

Dalley,G.(1988), *Ideologies of Caring*, London, Macmillan.

Davis, A. (1988), *'User's Perspectives'*, in Ramon, S. (ed), Psychiatry In Transition: The British and Italian Experiences, London, Pluto Press.

Dear, M. et.al. (1979), *'Economic Cycles and mental health care: an examination of the macro-context for social service planning'*, Social Science and Medicine, vol. 13C.

DoH et al (1989), *Caring for People: Community Care in the Next Decade and Beyond*, London, HMSO.

DHSS, *Health and Personal Social Service Statistics for England*, London, HMSO.

DHSS, *Health and Personal Social Service Statistics for Wales*, London, HMSO.

DHSS (1974), *Collaboration between health and local authorities: reports of a working party: establishment of Joint Consultative Committees*, London, DHSS.

DHSS (1975), *Better Services for the Mentally Ill*, Cmnd 6233, London, HMSO.

DHSS (1976), *Priorities for Health and Personal Social Services in England*, London, HMSO.

DHSS (1977a), *Priorities for Health and Personal Social Services: The Way Forward*, London, HMSO.

231

DHSS (1977b), *Standing Mental Health Advisory Committee: The Role of Psychiatrists in the Health Services,* London, HMSO.

DHSS (1977c), *Joint Care Planning: Health and Local Authorities,* circular HC(77),17/LAC (77), 10, London, DHSS.

DHSS (1977d), *Prevention and Health,* London, HMSO.

DHSS (1978), *A Review of the Mental Health Act 1959,* Cmnd.7320, London, HMSO.

DHSS (1979), *Mental Health Policy Formulation,* London, HMSO.

DHSS (1980), *Day Care For The Mentally Ill-A Discussion Paper,* London, DHSS.

DHSS (1981a), *Care In The Community: A Consultative Document On Moving Resources For Care In England,* London, DHSS.

DHSS (1981c), *Care In Action: A handbook of Priorities for the Health and Personal Social Services in England,* London, HMSO.

DHSS (1983a), *Health Service Development: Care in the Community and Social Finance,* London, DHSS.

DHSS (1983b), *Mental Illness: Policies for Prevention, Treatment, Rehabilitation and Care,* London, HMSO.

DHSS (1983c), *Health Care and its Costs,* London, HMSO.

DHSS (1984), *The Report Of The Mental Illness Services Working Group Of The Joint Group On Performance indicators,* London, DHSS.

DHSS (1985a), *Memorandum Submitted to the House of Commons Social Services Committee.*

DHSS (1985b), *Government Response to the Second Report from the Social Services Committee,* 1984-85 Session. London, HMSO.

DHSS (1985c), *The Facilities and Services of Mental Illness and Mental Handicap Hospitals in England, 1982.* HMSO, London.

DHSS (1985d), *Annual Report of the Health Service in England 1985,* London, HMSO.

DHSS (1986a),*General Managers: arrangements for renumeration and conditions of service,* personnel memorandum PM(86),7, London, DHSS.

DHSS (1986b), *Annual Report of the Health Service in England 1985-6,* London, HMSO.

DHSS (1986c), *Memorandum on Hospital Hostels,* London, DHSS.

DHSS (1987), *Annual Report of the Health Service in England 1986-7,* London, HMSO.

DHSS (1988), *House of Commons Written Answers,* Vol 125, Col 566.

Douglas,J.(1976), 'The Overloaded Crown', British Journal of Political Science, vol. 6, no. 4.

Dowdall,G. (1982), 'Alternative Conceptions of Class and Status and Symptoms of Psychological Distress', International Journal of

Health Services, vol. 12, no. 1.

Doyal,L. (1979), *The Political Economy of Health*, London, Pluto Press.

Drucker,H. et.al.(1983), *Developments in British Politics*, Macmillan, London.

Dunnell,K.(1979), *Family Information*, London, HMSO.

Edelman,M. (1971), *Politics of Symbolic Action*, London, Markham.

Elliot, A. (1993), *Social Theory and Psychoanalysis in Transition*, Oxford, Blackwell.

Ennals,D. (1973), *Out of Mind*, London, Arrow.

Estroff,S.(1981), *'Psychiatric Deinstitutionalisation: A Cross Cultural Analysis'*, Journal of Social Issues, vol. 37, no. 3.

Eyerman,R. and Shipway,D.(1981), *'Habermas on Work and Culture'*, Theory and Society, vol. 10.

Fenton,F.R. et.al. (1982), *Home and Hospital Psychiatric Treatment*, London, Croom Helm.

Figlio,K. (1979), *'Review of A. Scull's 'Decarceration''*, Radical Science Journal, no. 8.

Finch,J. (1984), *'Community Care: Developing non-sexist alternatives*, Critical Social Policy, no. 9.

Finch,J (1987), *'The Family; Unreal expectations'*, New Society, 24/7/87.

Finch, J. (1989), *Family Obligations and Social Change*, Polity, London.

Finch,J.and Groves,D. (1980), *'Community care and the family: a case for equal opportunities?'*, Journal of Social Policy, vol. 9, no. 4.

Foucault,M. (1971), *Madness and Civilization*, London, Tavistock Publications.

Frank,R. (1981), *'Cost Benefit Analysis For Mental Health Services: a review of the literature'*, Administration In Mental Health 8,3,161-176.

Frankel,B. (1982), *'On the State of the State: Marxist theories of the state after Leninism'*, in D.Held (ed.), Classes Power and Conflict, Oxford, Martin Robertson.

Freeman,H (ed.) (1963), *Trends in the Mental Health Services*, London, Pergamon Press.

Freeman,H. (1983),*'District Psychiatric Services: Psychiatry for defined populations'*, in Bean. P, (ed.), op. cit.

Gamble,A. (1981), *Britain In Decline*, London, Macmillan.

George,V. and Wilding,P.(1984), *The Impact of Social policy*, London, RKP.

Ginsburg,N. (1979), *Class, Capital and Social Policy*, London,

Macmillan.

Glendinning, C. (1990) *Dependency and Interdependency: the Incomes of Informal Carers and the Impact of Social Security'*, Journal of Social Policy, Vol. 19, No. 4, pp. 469-497.

Gloag,D. (1985), *'Rehabilitation in Psychiatric Conditions'*, British Medical Journal, no. 290.

Goffman,E.(1961), *Asylums: Essays on the social situation of mental patients and other inmates*, London, Penguin.

Gold,D.A. (1975), *'Recent Developments In Marxist Theories of The Capitalist State'*, Monthly Review, Oct/Nov.

Goldberg, D. (1986), *'The Assault on Psychiatry'*, Lancet, no.1.

Goldberg,D. and Huxley,P. (1980), *Mental Illness in the Community: The Pathway to Psychiatric Care.* London, Tavistock Publications.

Golding,P. and Middleton,S.(1978), *Images of Welfare* (mimeo), London, research report to the Nuffield Foundation.

Goldstein,M (1982), *'Review of Andrew Scull's 'Decarceration'*, Contemporary Sociology, vol. 11.

Goldstein,M. (1979), *'The Sociology of Mental Health and Illness'*, Annual Review of Sociology, vol. 5.

Goodwin, S. (1989) *'Community Care for the Mentally Ill in England and Wales: Myths, Assumptions and Reality.'* Journal of Social Policy, Vol. 18, No. 1.

Goodwin, S. et al (1991) *'A New Deal for the Mentally Ill: Progress or Propaganda'*, Critical Social Policy, Autumn, Vol. 32.

Gough,I. (1978), *'Theories of the Welfare State'*, International Journal of Health Services, vol. 8, no. 1.

Gough,I. (1979), *The Political Economy of the Welfare State*, London, Macmillan. Gough,I. (1983), *'The Crisis of the British Welfare State'*, International Journal of Health Services, vol. 13, no. 3.

Gough, I. & Doyal, L. (1991) *A Theory of Human Need,* London, Macmillan.

Gove,W. (ed.)(1982), *Deviance and Mental Illness*, London, Sage Publications.

Grad,J. and Sainsbury,P.(1968), *'The effects patients have on their families in a community care and a control psychiatric service-A two year follow-up.'*, British Journal of Psychiatry, vol. 114.

Griffiths,R. (1988), *Community Care: An Agenda for Action,* London, HMSO.

Guillebaud (1956), *Report of the Committee of Enquiry into the Cost of the National Health service*, Cmnd. 9663, London, HMSO.

Habermas,J.(1970), *'On Systematically Distorted Communication'*, Inquiry, vol. 13.

Habermas,J. (1973), 'What does a Crisis Mean Today? Legitimation Problems in Late Capitalism', Social Research, no. 40.

Habermas,J. (1976), Legitimation Crisis, London, Heinemann.

Habermas,J. (1979), 'Conservatism and Capitalist Crisis', New Left Review, no. 115. Habermas,J (1982), 'A Reply to My Critics', In Held, D. and Thompson, J.B. (eds.), Habermas: Critical Debates, Basingstoke, Macmillan.

Hafner,H. (1985), 'Changing Patterns of Mental Health Care', Acta Psychiatrica Scandinavica, vol. 71, no. 19.

Hall,P. et.al. (1975), Change, Choice and Conflict in Social Policy, London, Heinemann.

Hall,S (1987), 'Blue Election,Election Blues', Marxism Today, July 1987.

Ham,C. (1981), Policy-Making in the National Health Service, London, Macmillan.

Ham, C. (1992), Health Policy in Britain, 3rd edition, Basingstoke, Macmillan.

Ham,C. and Hill,M. (1984), The Policy Process in the Modern Capitalist State, Brighton, Wheatsheaf Books Ltd.

Hamilton,J.(1986), 'The Mental Health Act Commission', British Medical Journal, no. 292.

Harris,N.(1955), 'The Contribution of Psychological Medicine to General Medicine', Journal of Mental Science, vol. 101.

Hearns, F.(1979), 'Adaptive Narcissism and the Crisis of Legitimacy', Contemporary Crisis, vol. 4.

Held,D. (1980), Introduction to Critical Theory: Horkheimer to Habermas, London, Hutchinson.

Held, D. (1983), 'Beyond Liberalism and Marxism?', in McLennan, G. et. al. (eds.), The Idea of the Modern State, Milton Keynes, Open University Press.

Held, D. (1984), 'Power and Legitimacy in Contemporary Britain', in Hall, S. et. al. (eds.), State and Society in Contemporary Britain: A Critical Introduction, Cambridge, Polity.

Held,D. and Kreiger,J.(1983),'Accumulation,Legitimation and the State: the ideas of Claus Offe and Jurgen Habermas', in Held, D.(ed.), States and Societies, Oxford, Robertson.

Hennelly, R. (1988), 'Mental Health Resource Centres', in Ramon, S. (ed.), Psychiatry In Transition: The British and Italian Experiences, London, Pluto Press.

Hepstinall,D. (1980), 'Mentally Ill: Can We Make The Community Care?', Community Care, no. 306.

Hill,D.(1980), 'Progress but in Slow Tempo', Health and Social Services Journal, vol. LXXXX.

235

Hill,M. and Bramley,G. (1986), *Analysing Social Policy*, Oxford, Basil Blackwell.

Hoch,P. (1958), *'The Use of Tranquilizers in Psychiatry'*, Journal of Mental Science, vol. 104.

Hoenig,J. and Hamilton,M.(1969), *The De-Segregation of the Mentally Ill*, London, RKP.

Hoggart,R.(1958), *The Uses of Literacy*, London, Pelican.

Home Office (1949), *Report of the Departmental Committee on Grants for the Development of Marriage Guidance*, Cmnd. 7566, London, HMSO.

Home Office; DHSS (1974), *Committee on Mentally Abnormal Offenders, Interim Report (Butler Report)*, London, HMSO.

Home Office (1979), *Marriage Matters; Report of a Working Party*, HMSO, London.

House of Commons (1985a), *Second Report from the Social Services Committee: Community Care with special reference to adult mentally ill and mentally handicapped people*, London, HMSO.

House of Commons (1985b), *Sixth Report from the House of Commons Social Services Committee: Public Expenditure on the Social Services*, London, HMSO.

House of Commons (1986), *Fourth Report from the House of Commons Social Services Committee: Public Expenditure on the Social Services*, London, HMSO.

Howat,J. and Kotney,E.(1982), *'The outcome for discharged Nottinghamshire long-stay in-patients'*, British Journal of Psychiatry, vol. 141.

Hudson,B. (1984), *'The rising use of imprisonment: the impact of 'decarceration' policies'*,Critical Social Policy, Winter.

Illich,I, (1975), *Medical Nemesis*, London, Calder and Boyars.

Illife,S. (1985), *'The Politics of Health Care: The NHS under Thatcher'*, Critical Social Policy, vol. 14.

Ingle,S. and Tether,P.(1981), *Parliament and Health Policy: The Role of MPs 1970-75*, Farnborough, Gower.

Ingleby,D. (1981), *Critical Psychiatry*, New York, Pantheon Books.

Ingleby,D (1982), *'The social Construction of Mental Illness'*, in Wright, P. and Treacher, A. (eds.), The Problem of Medical Knowledge: Examining the social construction of medicine, Edinburgh, Edinburgh University Press.

Ingleby,D. (1983), *'Mental Health and Social Order'*, in Cohen, S. and Scull, A. (eds.), op. cit.

International Labour Organisation (1989), *From Pyramid to Pillar - Population Change and Social Security in Europe*, London, ILO.

Ives,G. (1979), *'Psychological Treatment in General Practice'*, Journal of the Royal College of General Practitioners, vol. 29.

Jeffereys,P. (1979), *'Joint Approaches to Community Care'*, in Meacher, M. (ed.), New Methods of Mental Health Care, Oxford, Pergamon Press.

Jenkins,R. and Shepherd (1983), *'Mental Illness and General Practice'*, in Bean, P. (ed.), op.cit.

Jeste,D and Wyatt,R.(1981), *'Changing epidemiology of Tardive Dyskinesia: An Overview'*, American Journal of Psychiatry, vol. 138, no. 3.

Johnson, N. (1987), *The Welfare State In Transition: The Theory and Practice of Welfare Pluralism*, Brighton, Wheatsheaf Books.

Johnston,A. et.al. (1984), *'Schizophrenic patients discharged from hospital: A follow-up study'*, British Journal of Psychiatry vol. 145.

Jones,C. and Novak,T.(1980), *'The State and Social Policy'*,in Corrigan, P. (ed), Capitalism, State Formation and Marxist Theory, London, Quartet Books.

Jones,K. (1964), *'Revolution or Reform in the Mental Health Services'*, in Farndale, J. (ed.), Trends in the National Health Service, London, Pergamon Press.

Jones, K.(1972), *A history of the mental health services*, London, RKP.

Jones,K. (1977), *'The Wrong Target In Mental Health'*, New Society, vol. 39.

Jones,K. (1979a), *'Integration or Disintegration of the Mental Health Service'*, Journal of the Royal Society of Medicine, vol. 72.

Jones,K. (1979b), *'Deinstitutionalisation in Context'*, Milbank Memorial Fund Quarterly, vol. 57.

Jones, K.(1981), *'Re-Inventing The Wheel'*, in MIND, The Future of the Mental Hospitals: a report of MIND's 1980 annual conference, Brighton, Marshallarts Print Services.

Jones,K. (1982), *'Scull's Dilemma'*, British Journal of Psychiatry, vol. 141.

Jones,K. (1983a), *'Services for the Mentally Ill: the death of a concept'*, in Bean, P. and Macpherson, S. (eds.), Approaches to Welfare, London, RKP.

Jones, K.(1983b), *'Community Care'*, in K.Jones et.al. (rev. ed), Issues in Social Policy, London, RKP.

Jones,K. and Sidebotham,R.(1962), *Mental Hospitals at Work*, London, RKP.

Jones,K. and Fowles,A.(1982), *'People in Institutions: rhetoric and reality*, Yearbook of Social Policy.

Judge,K.(1982), *'The Growth and Decline of Social Expenditure'*, in

Walker, A. (ed), Public Expenditure and Social Policy, London, Heinemann.

Kaplan,L.(1978), 'State Control of Deviant Behaviour: A Critical Essay On Scull's Critique Of Community Treatment And Deinstitutionalisation', Arizona Law Review, vol. 20.

Kavanagh, D. (1987), 'The decline of the 'Civic Culture'?', in Burch, M. and Moran, M. (eds.), British Politics: A Reader, Manchester, Manchester University Press.

Kay,A. and Legg,C. (1986), 'Discharged to the Community': A review of housing and support for people leaving psychiatric care', London Housing Research Group, City University.

Keane,J. (1978), 'The Legacy of Political Economy: Thinking with and against Claus Offe', Canadian Journal of Political and Social Theory, vol. 2, no. 3.

Keat,R. (1981), The Politics of Social Theory: Habermas, Freud and the Critique of Positivism, Oxford, Basil Blackwell.

Kennedy,I. (1983), The unmasking of Medicine, London, George Allen and Unwin.

Keynes,J.(1936), The general theory of employment, interest and money, London, Macmillan.

Klein,R. (1983), The Politics of the National Health Service, London, Longman.

Klein,R. (1984), 'Who makes the decisions in the NHS', British Medical Journal, vol. 288.

Klerman,G. (1982), 'The Psychiatric Revolution Of The Past Twenty-Five Years', in Gove, W. (ed.), op. cit.

Klerman,G and Weissman,M (1980), 'Depression Among Women: Their Nature and Causes, in Guttentag, M. (ed.), The Mental Health of Women, London, Academic Press.

Knight,L.(1977), 'Still the Cinderella', Community Care, no.156.

Knight,L. and Murray,J. (1976), 'Ready to Leave? A survey of rehabilitation and aftercare for mentally ill patients', Community Care, vol. 116.

Kovel,J. (1976), 'Therapy in Late Capitalism', Telos, no. 30, pp. 73-92.

Lader, M.(1979), 'Drug Research and Mental Health Services', in, Meacher, M. (ed.), New Methods of Mental Health Care, Oxford, Pergamon Press.

Land,H.(1978),'Who cares for the family?', Journal of Social Policy, vol. 7, no. 3.

Land,H. and Rose,R. (1985), 'Compulsory altruism for some or an altruistic society for all?', in Bean, P. et.al. (eds.), In Defence of Welfare, London, Tavistock Publications.

Lasch,C.(1979), The Culture of Narcissism, New York, Warner Books.

Laurance,J. (1987), 'The Crisis in Community Care', New Society, 24/7/87.

Lawson,D.(1988), 'Community Treatment Orders', Asylum, vol. 2, no. 3.

Le Grand, J. (1990) The State of Welfare, in J. Hills (ed) The State of Welfare: The Welfare State in Britain since 1974, Oxford, Clarendon.

Lee,P. and Raban,C.(1988), Welfare Theory and Social Policy: Reform or Revolution, London, Sage Publications Ltd.

Lemert,E.(1972), Human Deviance, Social Problems, and Social Control (2nd edition), Englewood Cliffs, Prentice Hall.

Leonard,P. (1984), Personality and Ideology-Toward a materialistic understanding of the individual, London, Macmillan.

Levene,L. et.al. (1985), 'How Likely is it that a District Health Authority can Close its Large Mental Hospitals?', British Journal of Psychiatry, vol. 147.

Lipsett, S. (1963), Political Man, NY USA, Doubleday.

Lister, R. (1990) 'Women, Economic Dependency and Citizenship', Journal of Social Policy, Vol. 19, No. 4, pp. 445-467.

Lloyd,T.O.(1970), Empire to Welfare State: English History 1906-1967, London, Oxford University Press.

Lockwood,D.(1981), 'The Weakest Link in the Chain? Some comments on the Marxist theory of action', Research in the Sociology of Work, no. 1.

McCarthy,T. (1978), The Critical Theory of Jurgen Habermas, London, Hutchinson.

McLennan,G. et.al. (1983), The idea of the Modern State, Milton Keynes, Open University Press.

Macmillan Commission,(1926), Report of the Royal Commission on Lunacy and Mental Disorder, London, HMSO.

Madgwick,P. et.al. (1982), Britain Since 1945, London, Hutchinson.

Mahadevan,S. and Forster,D.(1982), 'Psychiatric units in general hospitals: some recent evidence', British Journal of Psychiatry, vol. 140.

Malin,N. (ed.) (1987), Reassessing Community Care, London, Croom Helm.

Mangen,S. (1982), Sociology and Mental Health, New York, Churchill Livingstone.

Mangen,S.P.(ed.) (1985), Mental Health Care in the European Community, London, Croom Helm.

Mann, M. (1970), 'The Social Cohesion of Liberal Democracies', American Sociological Review, vol. 35.

Mann, M. (1973), Consciousness and Action among the Western

Working Class, London, Macmillan.

Marcuse,H. (1964), *One Dimensional Man,* London, RKP.

Marsh,D.(1965), *The Changing Social Structure of England and Wales,* (rev.ed.), London, RKP.

Marshall,T.H. (1967), *Social Policy,* (2nd edition), London, Hutchinson.

Martin, F.M.(1984), *Between The Acts: Community Mental Health Services 1959-1983,* London, Nuffield Provincial Hospitals Trust.

Masefield,W. (1948), *'Report of the Presidential Address',* Journal of Mental Science, vol. 94.

Matthews,R. (1979), *"Decarceration' and the fiscal crisis',* in Fine, B. et.al. (eds.), Capitalism and the Rule of Law, London, Hutchinson.

Matthews,R (1987), *'Decarceration and social control: fantasies and realities',* in Lowman, J. Menzies, R. and Palys, T. (eds.), Transcarceration: Essays in the sociology of social control. Gower, Aldershot

Maynard,A.(1985), *'The Economic Evaluation of Mental Health Policies',* in Mangen, S. op.cit.

Mechanic,D. (1969), *Mental Health And Social Policy,* Englewood Cliffe, Prentice Hall.

Melossi,D. (1979), *'Institutions of Social Control and Capitalist Organisation of Work',* in Fine, B. (ed.) Capitalism and the Rule of Law, London, Hutchinson.

Melville,J. (1988), *'Troubles behind the calm',* The Guardian, 17/8/88.

Miles,A. (1981), *The Mentally Ill in Contemporary Society,* Oxford, Martin Robertson.

Miliband,R (1972), *'Reply to Nicos Poulantzas',* in Blackburn, R. (ed.), Ideology in Social Science, London, Fontana.

Miliband,R.(1977), *Marxism and Politics,* Oxford University Press, Oxford.

Miller,P. and Rose,N.(eds.) (1986), *The Power of Psychiatry,* London, Polity Press.

Miller,P. (1986), *'Critiques of Psychiatry and Critical Sociologies of Madness',* in Miller, P. and Rose N. ibid.

MIND (1974), *Co-ordination or Chaos? The run-down of the psychiatric hospitals,* MIND Report No.13, London, Mind Publications.

MIND (1979), *Services for Mentally Ill People: MIND's evidence to the Royal Commission on the NHS,* London, MIND Publications.

MIND (1981), *The Future of the Mental Hospitals: a report of MIND's 1980 annual conference,* Brighton, Marshall Arts Print Services.

MIND (1983), *Common Concern: MIND's Manifesto for a New*

Mental Health Service, London, MIND Publications.

MIND (1985), *Memorandum submitted to the House of Commons Social Services Committee*.

MIND (1986), *'A Better Life'*, Campaign conducted by MIND, 1986-7.

Ministry of Health, *Annual Reports*, London, HMSO.

Ministry of Health (1962), *A Hospital Plan for England and Wales*, Cmnd 1604, London, HMSO.

Ministry of Health (1963), *Health and Welfare: the Development of Community Care*, Cmnd 1973, London, HMSO.

Mishra,R. (1977), *Society and Social Policy*, London, Macmillan.

Mishra,R. (1982), *'System integration, social action and change: some problems in sociological analysis'*, Sociological Review, vol. 30, no. 1.

Mishra,R. (1983), *'Sociology and Social Welfare: The analytic Connection'*, American Behavioral Scientist, vol 26, no. 6.

Mishra,R. (1984), *The Welfare State in Crisis: Social Thought and Social Change*, Brighton, Wheatsheaf Books Ltd.

Morrissey,J. (1982), *'Deinstitutionalising the Mentally Ill: Process,outcomes, and new directions'*, in Gove, W. op.cit.

National Association Of Health Authorities (1985), *Memorandum Submitted to the House of Commons Social Services Committee*.

National Audit Office (1987), *Community Care Developments*, London, HMSO.

National Schizophrenia Fellowship (1988), *Mental Hospital Closures: what the run-down means to people with schizophrenia*, National Schizophrenia Fellowship.

Navarro,V. (1978), *'The Crisis Of The Western System Of Medicine In Contemporary Capitalism'*, International Journal of Health Services, vol. 8, no. 2.

Navarro,V. (1982), *'The Crisis Of The International Capitalist Order And Its Implications For The Welfare State'*, International Journal Of Health Services, vol. 12, no. 2.

Nissel,M.(1982) *'Families and Social Change Since The Second World War'*, in Rapoport, R. et.al. (eds.), Families in Britain, London, RKP.

Nocon,A.(1988), *Ph.D. thesis*, University of Sheffield.

Nodder (1980), *Report on the organisational and management problems of mental illness hospitals*, London, HMSO.

O'Connor,J. (1973a), *'Summary of the Theory of the Fiscal Crisis'*, Kapitalistate, no. 1.

O'Connor,J. (1973b), *The Fiscal Crisis of The State*, NY USA, St. Martins Press.

O'Connor,J. (1981), *'The Fiscal Crisis of the State Re-visited'*,

Kapitalistate, no. 9.

O'Connor,J. (1984), *Accumulation Crisis*, Blackwell, Oxford.

OECD (1987), *Economic Outlook no.42*.

Offe,C. (1972), *'Advanced Capitalism and the Welfare State'*, Politics and Society, vol. 2, no. 4.

Offe,C.(1984), *Contradictions of The Welfare State*, (Keane,ed.), London, Hutchinson.

Offe,C. (1985), *Disorganised Capitalism*, London, Polity Press.

Office of Health Economics (1986), *The Cost of the National Health Service*.

Ollman,B. (1971), *Alienation: Marx's conception of man in capitalist society*, London, Cambridge University Press.

Parker,G. (1985), *With due care and attention; a review of research on informal care*, London, Family Policy Studies Centre.

Parker,L. (1981), *'Neopositivism and dialectics'*, Psychology and Social Theory, no. 1.

Paykel,E.(1982), *'Community psychiatric nursing for neurotic patients: a controlled trial'*, British Journal of Psychiatry, vol. 140.

Peacock,A. and Wiseman,D. (1966), *The Growth of Public Expenditure in the UK*, (2nd edition), London, Allen and Unwin.

Peden,G.C. (1985), *British Economic and Social Policy: Lloyd George to Margaret Thatcher*, Oxford, Philip Allan Publishers Ltd.

Peers, V.(1972), *Psychiatric Hospitals Viewed By Their Patients*, London, King Edwards Hospital Fund.

Percy Commission (1957), *Report of the Royal Commission on Mental Illness and Mental Deficiency*, Cmnd 169, London, HMSO.

Pilgrim, D. (1993) *Mental Health Services in the Twenty-first Century: the User-Professional Divide?* in J. Bornat et al (eds) Community Care: A Reader, Milton Keynes, OUP.

Pilling,S. (1983), *'The Mental Health (Amendment), Act 1982: reform or cosmetics'*, Critical Social Policy, no. 7.

Plant,R. (1974), *Community and Ideology*, London, RKP.

Plant,R.(1983), *'The end of Consensus'*, In Drucker, H. et.al., Developments in British Politics, London, Macmillan.

Poulantzas,N (1972), *'The Problem of the Capitalist State'*, in Blackburn, R.(ed.), Ideology in Social Science, London, Fontana.

Prins,H. (1984), *'Attitudes towards the mentally disordered'*, Medicine, Science and the Law, vol. 24.

Pritlove,J. (1978), *'What Future For The Mentally Ill'*, Community Care, no. 208.

Radical Statistics Health Group (1987), *Facing The Figures: What really is happening to the National Health Service?*, London,

Radical Statistics.

Ramon,S. (1982), 'The Logic of Pragmatism in Mental Health Policy: The implications of the government position in the 1959 debate for the 1980s', Critical Social Policy, vol 2, no.2.

Ramon,S. (1985), Psychiatry In Britain: Meaning and policy, London, Croom Helm.

Ramon,S. (1986), 'The Category of Psychopathy: its professional and social context in Britain', in Miller, P. and Rose, N.,op.cit.

Ramon, S. (ed.) (1988), Psychiatry In Transition: The British and Italian Experiences, London, Pluto Press.

Rees,J.R.(1949), 'The Tasks of Psychiatry', Journal of Mental Science, vol. 95.

Rehin,G.F. and Martin, F.M. (1968), Patterns of Performance in Community Care, Oxford, Oxford University Press.

Reid,H. and Wiseman,A (1986), When The Talking Has To Stop, London, MIND Publications.

Richmond Fellowship (1983), Mental Health and the Community, London, Richmond Fellowship Press.

Roderick,R. (1986), Habermas and the Foundations of Critical Theory, London, Heinemann.

Rogers, A & Pilgrim, D. (1989) Mental health and citizenship, Critical Social Policy, Autumn, Vol. 26, pp. 44 -54.

Rogers, A. & Pilgrim, D. (1991) 'Pulling Down the Churches': Accounting for the British Mental Health Users' Movement', Sociology of Health and Illness, Vol 13, No. 2, pp.129-148.

Rollin, H. R. (1969), The mentally abnormal offender and the law, Oxford, Pergamon Press.

Rollin,A. (1976), 'Are Mental Hospitals Really Necessary?', Public Health, vol. 90, no. 2.

Rollin,H. (1977), 'Deinstitutionalisation and the Community: fact and theory', Psychological Medicine, no. 7.

Room,G. (1979), The Sociology of Welfare, Oxford, Basil Blackwell and Mott Ltd.

Rose,H. and Rose,S. (1982), 'Moving right out of welfare-and the way back', Critical Social Policy, vol: 2, no. 1.

Rose, N.(1986), 'Psychiatry: the discipline of mental health', in Millar, P. and Rose, N. (eds.),The Power of Psychiatry, Cambridge, Polity Press.

Roth,A. (1970), Enoch Powell: Tory Tribune, London, Macdonald.

Royal College of Psychiatrists (1980), Psychiatric Rehabilitation in the 1980s.

Royal College of General Practitioners (1958), 'Psychological Medicine in General Practice', British Journal of Medicine, no. i

Royal College of General Practitioners (1985), *Memorandum submitted to the House of Commons Social Services Committee.*
Royal College of General Practitioners (1986), *Morbidity Statistics from General Practice,* 1981/1982.
Royal College of Psychiatrists(1985), *Memorandum submitted to the House of Commons Social Services Committee.*
Ryder,J. and Silver,H. (1977), *Modern English History,* (rev.ed.), London, Methuen.
Sands,D.(1948), *'Psychiatric treatment outside Mental Hospitals',* Journal of Mental Science, vol. 94.
Scheff,T. (1984), *Being Mentally Ill: A sociological theory,* (2nd edition), Aldine, NY USA.
Scull,A. (1976), *'The Decarceration of the Mentally Ill: A critical view',* Politics and Society.
Scull,A. (1981a), *'Review of 'Decarceration', and the economy of penal reform',* Canadian Journal of Sociology, vol. 6, no. 4.
Scull,A. (1981b), *'Progressive Dreams, Progressive Nightmares: Social Control in Twentieth Century America',* Stanford Law Review, no. 33.
Scull,A (1981c), *'A New Trade In Lunacy: The Recommodification of the Mental Patient',* American Behavioral Scientist, vol. 24, no. 6.
Scull,A. (1982), *Museums of Madness: The Social Organisation of Insanity in Nineteenth-Century England,* London, Penguin.
Scull,A. (1983a), *'Humanitarianism or Control? Some Observations on the Historiography of Anglo-American Psychiatry',* in Scull, A.and Cohen, S., op. cit.
Scull,A. (1983b), *'Whose Dilemma? The Crisis of the Mental Health Services',* British Journal of Psychiatry, vol. 142.
Scull,A. (1983c), *'Community Corrections: Panacea, Progress or Pretence',* in Garland,D. and Young,P. (eds.),The Power to Punish, London, Heinemann.
Scull, A. (1984a), *Decarceration: Community Treatment and the Deviant-A Radical View,* (2nd edition), Cambridge, Polity Press.
Scull,A. (1984b), *'Competing Perspectives On Deviance',* Deviant Behaviour, vol.5. Scull,A. (1985), *'Deinstitutionalisation and Public Policy',* Social Science and Medicine.
Sedgwick,P.(1973), *'Mental Illness is Illness',* Salmagundi, vol. 20.
Sedgwick,P.(1982a), *PsychoPolitics,* London, Pluto Press.
Sedgwick,P. (1982b), *'Anti-Psychiatry From the Sixties to the Eighties',* in Gove, W., op.cit.
Seebohm Report (1968), *Report of the Committee on local authority and allied personal social services,* Cmnd 3703, London, HMSO.

Seve,L.(1978), *Man in Marxist Theory*, Sussex, Harvester.

Shepherd,M. et.al.(1966), *Psychiatric Illness in General Practice*, Oxford, Oxford University Press.

Siegler,M. and Osmond,H.(1966), *'Models of Madness'*, British Journal of Psychiatry, vol. 112.

Silverman, M.(1955), *'The Clinical Response of PsychoNeurotics To Chlorpromazine'*, Journal of Mental Science, vol. 101.

Skultans, V.(1979), *English Madness: Idea on Insanity 1580-1890*, London, RKP.

Strong,P. (1979), *'Sociological Imperialism and the Profession of Medicine'*, Social Science and Medicine, vol. 13A.

Sturt,J. and Waters,H.(1985), *'The Role of the Psychiatrist in Community-based Mental Health Care'*, Lancet, no 1.

Szasz,T.(1974), *Law,Liberty and Psychiatry: An Inquiry into the Social Uses of Mental Health Practices*, London, RKP.

Tarsy,D. and Baldessarini,R.(1984),*'Tardive Dyskinesia'*, Annual Review of Medicine, vol. 35.

Taussig,M (1980), *'Reification and the Consciousness of the Patient'*, Social Science and Medicine, vol. 14B.

Taylor-Gooby,P. (1985), *Public Opinion, Ideology and State Welfare*, London, RKP.

Taylor-Gooby,P and Dale,J. (1981), *Social Theory and Social Welfare*, London, Edward Arnold.

Thane,P (1982), *The Foundations of the Welfare State*, Harlow, Longman Group.

Thomas,K. (1981), *'Attitudes to Psychological Illness in General Practice: a historical cycle complete'*, British Medical Journal, vol. 283.

Thomas, T. (1992) *'When a disease is welcome news'*, The Guardian, 2nd October.

Tidmarsh,D and Wood,S (1972), *'Psychiatric aspects of destitution; A study of the Camberwell Reception Centre'*, in Wing, J.K. and Hailey, A.H. (eds.), Evaluating a community psychiatric service, London, Oxford University Press.

Titmuss, R.(1963), *'Community Care-Fact or Fiction?'*in Freeman, H.(ed.), Trends in the Mental Health Services, London, Pergamon Press.

Tomlinson, D. (1991) *Utopia, Community Care and the Retreat from the Asylums*, Milton Keynes, OUP.

Tooth,G.C.and Brooke,E.(1961), *'Trends in the mental hospital and their effect on future planning'*, Lancet, no. i.

Twigg, J. (1989) *'Models of Carers: How Do Social Care Agencies Conceptualise Their Relationship With Informal Carers'*, Journal of

Social Policy, Vol 18, 1, pp. 53-66.

Ungerson,C. (1983), *'Why do women care?'*, in Finch, J. and Groves, D. (eds.), A Labour of Love; Women, Work and Caring, London, RKP.

Ungerson, C. (1985) *Women and Social Policy: A Reader*, Basingstoke, Macmillan.

Unsworth,C. (1979), *'The balance of medicine, law and social work in mental health legislation,1889-1959'*, in Parry, N. et.al. (eds.), Social Work, Welfare and the State.

Urry,J. (1981), *The Anatomy of Capitalist Societies*, London, Macmillan.

Vaughan,P. (1983), *'The disordered development of day care in psychiatry'*, Health Trends, vol. 15, no. 4.

Walker,A. (ed.)(1982a), *Public Expenditure and Social Policy: An Examination of social spending and social priorities*, London, Heinemann.

Walker, A.(ed.)(1982b), *Community Care: The Family, The State and Social Policy*, Oxford, Basil Blackwell and Martin Robertson and Co. Ltd.

Walker,A. (1983), *'A Caring Community'*, in Glennester, H. (ed.), The Future Of The Welfare State: Remaking Social Policy, London, Heinemann.

Walker,A. (1984), *'The Political Economy of Privatisation'*, in LeGrand, J. and Robinson, R. (eds.), Privatisation and the Welfare State, London, George Allen and Unwin.

Walker,A. (1985), *The Care Gap; How can local authorities meet the needs of the elderly*, London, Local Government Information Unit.

Walker,A. (1986), *'Community Care: Rhetoric and Reality in Policy Towards People with Mental Disabilities'*, Edited text of a lecture given at the Conference 'A Better Deal for the Mentally Ill and Mentally Handicapped: the co-ordination of effort', Humberside College of Further Education, 11 April 1986.

Walker,A. (1988), *'Paradoxes and possibilities'*, Community Care, 28th April.

Walkley,F. et.al. (1981), *'Community Attitudes to Mental Health: A Comparative Study'*, Social Science and Medicine, vol. 15E.

Warren,C. (1981),*'New Forms of Social Control: The Myth of Deinstitutionalisation'*, American Behavioral Scientist, vol. 24.

Watson,J. and Barber,J.(1981),*'Depressive Illness in General Practice: A pilot study'*, Health Bulletin, vol. 39, no. 2.

Watts,C. (1962), *'Psychiatric Disorders'*, in Morbidity Statistics from General Practice: Studies on Medical and Population subjects

No.14, General Register Office,   London, HMSO.

Webb,A and Wistow,G. (1982), *'The Personal Social Services: Incrementalism, Expediency or Systematic Social Planning?'*, in Walker, A. (ed.), Public Expenditure and   Social Policy; An Examination of Social Spending and Social Priorities, London, Heinemann.

Webster,F.(1948), *'Modern trends in the planning of mental hospitals and other psychiatric units in England'*,   Journal of Mental Science, vol. 94.

Whitehead,T. (1982), *Mental Illness and the Law*, Oxford, Basil Blackwell.

Whitfield,M. and Winter,R.(1980), *'Psychiatry and General Practice: Results of a survey of Avon general   practitioners'*, Journal of the Royal College of General Practitioners, vol. 30.

Wilding,P. (1982), *Professional Power and Social Welfare*, London, RKP.

Williams,P and Clare,A.(1984), *'Changing Patterns of Psychiatric Care'*, British Medical Journal, no. 282.

Willmot,P. (1986), *Social Networks,Informal Care and Public Policy*, London, Policy Studies Institute.

Wilson,E (1982), *'Women, the 'Community' and the 'Family''*, in Walker, A., op. cit.

Wing,J.K. (1978), *Reasoning About Madness*, Oxford, Oxford University Press.

Wing,J.K. (1979), *'Trends in the care of the chronically mentally disabled'*,in Wing, J.K. and Olsen, R. (eds.), Community Care for the Mentally Disabled, Oxford, Oxford University Press.

Wing,J.K. and Olsen,R.(1979), *'Principles of the New Community Care'*, in Wing, J.K. and Olsen, R. (eds.), Community Care for the Mentally Disabled, Oxford, Oxford University Press.

Wing,J.K. (1981), *'From Institutional To Community Care'*, Psychiatric Quarterly, vol. 53, no.2.

Wolfe,A. (1977), *The Limits of Legitimacy*, NY USA, Free Press.

Woodiwiss,T. (1978), *'Critical Theory and the Capitalist State'*, Economy and Society, vol. 7, no. 2.

Wright,E.O. (1975), *'Alternative Perspectives In Marxist Theory of Accumulation and Crisis'*, The Insurgent   Socialist, vol. 6, no. 1.

Zola,I.K.(1975), *'In the Name of Health and Illness: On some Socio-political Consequences of Medical Influence'*, Social Science and Medicine, vol. 9.